Xmas '02
From: Pete
Beth
Mike
& Sara

W.H.
KOer

THE Wild West

Bill O' Neal

James A. Crutchfield

Dale L. Walker

Publications International, Ltd.

Bill O'Neal's 22 book credits include *Legends of the Wild West, Ghost Towns of the American West, Best of the West, Encyclopedia of Western Gunfighters,* and *Fighting Men of the Indian Wars.* He is a member of Western Writers of America, Inc., a past president of the East Texas Historical Association, and a board member of the National Association for Outlaw and Lawman History. He has been a member of the history department of Panola Junior College in Carthage, Texas, since 1970.

James A. Crutchfield has written more than a dozen books, including *It Happened in Colorado, Tenneseeans at War, The Natchez Trace: A Pictorial History,* and *Footprints Across the Pages of Tennessee History.* His articles have appeared in many magazines, including *Old West, True West, Early American Life,* and *Nashville.* He was a contributing writer to *Encyclopedia of the American West* and is secretary-treasurer of Western Writers of America, Inc.

Dale L. Walker is a freelance writer, historian, and editor. He has written more than a dozen books, including *Mavericks: Ten Uncorralled Westerners, Will Henry's West,* and *Buckey O'Neill: The Story of a Rough Rider.* His contributing writer credits include *The Reader's Encyclopedia of the American West, Encyclopedia of the Old West, Wild West Show!,* and *The West That Was.* He is a member of the Texas Institute of Letters and is a former president of Western Writers of America, Inc.

Editorial Assistants: John P. Herron, M. David Key, Brett J. Olsen, Jeff Roche

Louis Weber, CEO
Publications International, Ltd.
7373 North Cicero Avenue
Lincolnwood, Illinois 60712

Permission is never granted for commercial purposes.

Manufactured in China.

8 7 6 5 4 3 2 1

ISBN: 0-7853-4935-9

Library of Congress Control Number: 2001116330

Photo Credits

LEGENDS
OF THE
WILD WEST

Vast and beautiful, filled with the promise of riches and adventure, the West attracted men and women of heroic qualities. Mountain men such as Kit Carson and Jim Bridger were fearless and utterly self-reliant. Wyatt Earp and Pat Garrett pinned on badges and risked their lives to impose law upon a lawless land. General Sam Houston and Chief Crazy Horse led brave men into battle for control of the West.

On a smaller scale, deadly shootists such as Doc Holliday and Tom Horn battled other gunfighters. The West produced a fascinating roster of outlaws: Jesse James, Billy the Kid, Butch Cassidy, Killin' Jim Miller, and Belle Starr. Other notable women of the West included Calamity Jane and Annie Oakley. Good and bad, they each were colorful, captivating legends of the Wild West.

Buffalo Bill Cody poses with Red Cloud (*left*) and American Horse (*right*), both Dakota chiefs. The legends appeared together at a Wild West show in New York in the late 1890s.

MOUNTAIN MEN

Mountain men! The words ring with high adventure. Mountain men led the American westward movement, ranging far in advance of other pioneers, restlessly exploring mountain ranges, river valleys, and deserts. Fiercely independent, they were solitary fur trappers who braved war parties and grizzly bears and hazardous weather. Instead of fighting against Native Americans, mountain men often found it profitable to trade with them— and agreeable to marry their women. The annual gatherings of mountain men were legendary orgies of ribald celebration.

Their boisterous braggadocio served to advertise the West. Mountain men were hired to lead pioneer wagon trains, rendering the trade routes of fur trappers into the highways of the West. The army employed mountain men as scouts and interpreters. By introducing whiskey and other trade goods, as well as such diseases as smallpox, mountain men broke down the self-sufficiency of the Native Americans. In these ways, mountain men were indirectly "civilizing" influences upon the very wilderness that they loved.

Inspired by profit but driven by a taste for adventure, the legendary mountain men explored the untamed land west of the Mississippi.

JIM BRIDGER

1804—1881

Born two months before Meriwether Lewis and William Clark began their epic journey from the Mississippi to the Pacific, Jim Bridger was a legend by the age of 20. His exploits are recounted in any number of

Called Old Gabe by his friends, Jim Bridger was known as much for his tall tales as he was for his skills as a mountain man.

biographies and memoirs of those who lived west of the Mississippi before the Civil War.

The son of a surveyor and innkeeper, Bridger was born in Richmond, Virginia, on March 17, 1804. He moved west with his family and in 1818 was apprenticed to a St. Louis blacksmith. Living along the Mississippi, he learned to handle boats, guns, and horses, making him an ideal recruit when he joined the Ashley-Henry fur-trading expedition to the Upper Missouri River in 1822.

With such comrades as Jedediah Smith, Tom Fitzpatrick, and James Clyman, Bridger learned the ways of the wilderness and the trapper's life as the band made its way by keelboat up the Missouri. At the mouth of the Yellowstone, he assisted in building the log outpost named Fort Henry and waded miles of icy streams to find beaver and lure them into his traps.

Unschooled and illiterate, Bridger had an instinct, perhaps the keenest of all the mountain men, for surviving in the wilderness. He knew he must understand the ways and languages of the Native Americans and learn the lay of the land. Within a few years, he had honed these rare skills to a phenomenal degree. General Grenville M. Dodge, who sought Bridger's advice while surveying a portion of the route of the Central Pacific Railroad, remarked about his trail-wise friend, "The whole West was mapped out in his mind."

Bridger, at the the ripe old age of 21, may have been the first white man to see the Great Salt Lake. At least, he liked to boast that he had discovered it. To settle a wager about the ultimate course of the Bear River, he traveled down river by boat until he came upon a large body of water. When he discovered that the water tasted salty, he assumed he had reached the Pacific Ocean. The following year, four other trappers made their way down the Bear River and established that it emptied into the famed saltwater lake.

In 1830, Bridger and four others bought out their employers to gain control of the Rocky Mountain Fur Company, coming into rivalry with the powerful American Fur operation owned by John Jacob Astor. With his partners, he continued to trap and engage in numerous skirmishes with Native Americans. Bridger was never much of a businessman and was relieved when the Rocky Mountain Fur Company sold out in 1834. That year he married Cora, daughter of the Flathead chief Insala, and visited St. Louis briefly before returning to the mountains.

Bridger attended the rendezvous at Green River in 1839, which turned out to be the last rendezvous, a sign that the beaver trade was playing out. Bridger decided he could make a living as a trader to the increasing emigrant traffic heading west along the Oregon Trail. For his post, he chose a grassy valley at Black's Fork on the Green River. In 1843, in partnership with veteran fur trader Louis Vasquez, he built cabins, corrals, and a blacksmith shop, and he bought supplies and stock from St. Louis. Fort Bridger became the only emigrant way station on the 620-mile stretch between Fort Laramie, at the junction of the Laramie and North Platte rivers, and Fort Hall on the Snake.

At his fort, Bridger settled down with his wife and three children. He sent his daughter Mary Ann to Marcus Whitman's mission school in Washington. Between 1846 and 1848, Bridger suffered three great personal tragedies: His wife Cora died, his daughter was killed by Cayuse Indians at the Whitman

Could this graffiti along the Oregon Trail be the work of the virtually illiterate Jim Bridger? Or did some would-be mountain man want to steal the mighty Bridger's considerable thunder?

mission school in Walla Walla, and his second wife, a Ute woman, died in childbirth. After each personal calamity, he escaped to the mountains to trap and hunt.

In June 1847, Bridger met Mormon leader Brigham Young on the trail to Fort Laramie. Young was leading his party of Mormon emigrants in search of a place to build a settlement. Bridger, in his customary forthright fashion, warned Young and his followers not to travel to the barren Utah country on faith alone. The old mountain man was skeptical

THE RENDEZVOUS

William Ashley, loaded down with supplies, left Fort Atkinson on a cold day in November 1824 for Henry's Fork on the Green River in the distant Rocky Mountains, a journey of some six months. His intention was to make a profit, not to begin one of the most colorful and raucous traditions associated with the early West. He did both, grossing $50,000 and having arranged the first of the annual gatherings known as the rendezvous.

The purpose of the rendezvous was to provide traps, weapons, liquor, trade goods, and supplies to the mountain men and Native Americans in exchange for the rich furs they had trapped during

At the rendezvous, the poor mountain men were often at the mercy of greedy suppliers: Whiskey selling at 30 cents a gallon in St. Louis was sold for three dollars a pint to the trappers.

the previous fall and spring. The benefits of such a system were meant to be mutual. Operating a rendezvous allowed Ashley to obtain the best pelts at the point of origin, rather than forcing him to compete with other fur companies in the busy markets of St. Louis. It also allowed the trappers to acquire badly needed supplies

and equipment in their home territory, thus saving them hundreds of miles of travel to and from St. Louis. From a social standpoint, the rendezvous was an opportunity for trappers to leave their lonely vigil in the remote Rocky Mountains to relax, drink, gamble, and womanize for several weeks in high summer.

Often the pricing structure at the rendezvous was weighted heavily in Ashley's favor. He paid the trappers as little as half the going rate in St. Louis for their pelts and marked up his goods tenfold or more.

The rendezvous became a fixture of the fur-trading industry during its peak years. Trappers, traders, and Indians met for the event each year between 1825 and 1840, except for 1831 when there was no gathering. The majority of the 15 rendezvous took place at various sites in the western part of present-day Wyoming, although two of them occurred in eastern Idaho and four were held in northern Utah.

that the Salt Lake region could support any farming enterprise no matter how assiduously pursued. The encounter apparently offended Young and his followers and began a period of enmity between Bridger and the Mormon church. In the decade that followed, the Mormons moved into the Green River Valley, opened rival trading posts, and accused Bridger of selling arms to Native Americans and inciting them to war. The church headquarters in Salt Lake City also resisted the attempt to convert Fort Bridger into an army post, claiming that the fort and the entire Green River Valley belonged to the Mormon-controlled Utah Territory.

In the meantime, Bridger had left his fort in the care of others and had returned to the wilderness. He lived for a time with the Shoshonis and courted Little Fawn, daughter of Shoshoni chief Washakie. Bridger and Little Fawn were married in 1850 at a Christian ceremony performed by his friend, the Jesuit missionary Father Pierre De Smet.

Bridger spent his summers at the fort and his winters with Little Fawn's people, but this tranquil period was marred when the Bridger-Mormon rivalry flared anew in 1853. A band of Mormons tried to arrest Bridger as an outlaw. He escaped with his wife and children into the mountains. When he returned to his fort, he found it burned and gutted, his trade goods and livestock stolen. His response to the depredation was to have a professional survey made of his 3,900-acre tract of land and to file

the paper with the General Land Office in Washington to establish his ownership. In the meantime, he bought a farm south of Westport, Missouri, where he took Little Fawn, now called Mary, and his children.

In the fall of 1854, Bridger met Sir George Gore, who was an Irish nobleman with a huge inherited fortune, and hired on as Gore's hunting guide in the Yellowstone and Powder River country. The hunting trek took two years, during which time Sir George read to Bridger and taught his rough-edged guide to love Shakespeare. By the time the long odyssey ended, the illiterate mountain man was able to recite long passages from the Bard's works.

After being paid by Gore, Bridger took a boat down the Missouri to visit his wife and

Old Gabe established Fort Bridger as a trading post and way station along the Oregon Trail in southwest Wyoming.

family and began thinking of his rebuilt fort on the Green River. He traveled to Washington to plead his case for ownership of the Fort Bridger lands at a time when anti-Mormon sentiment was being heard in the halls of Congress. He found sympathy for his case, and the Buchanan administration declared Utah Territory to be in a state of insurrection. The government ordered an infantry regiment under Colonel Albert Sidney Johnston to march from Fort Laramie into the Green River country. Bridger was selected as the guide.

In the ensuing Utah War of 1857–58, in which the Mormons under Young's leadership waged war against federal troops, Bridger leased his fort as a supply base. He led the infantrymen through winter blizzards with such skill that Johnston appointed him to his personal staff with the rank of major. When the war ended with a peaceful settlement, Bridger led Johnston's force in a parade through the streets of Salt Lake City. While he could take some satisfaction in having evened the score with the Saints, Bridger found little peace on returning home to Westport. During his absence or soon after his return, Mary Washakie Bridger died. He placed his children in the care of a tenant farmer and returned to the West.

So great was Bridger's fame that his name is attached to a city, a lake, a fort, a pass, a mountain, and a national forest.

After he sold Fort Bridger in 1858, he served as a guide along the Yellowstone and the Missouri throughout the Civil War years. He was employed as an army scout in the early Indian campaigns of 1865–66, including the Powder River Expedition against Cheyenne, Sioux, and Arapaho raiders, and he witnessed the establishment of Fort Phil Kearny on the Bozeman Trail. But, with failing eyesight and rheumatism, he was discharged from further duties in 1868.

He retired in Westport to a life of cultivating apple trees and telling tales of his adventures, true and tall, to his grandchildren. His mastery of the tall tale was recorded by many who knew him. One of his most oft-repeated stories involved his favorite camping spot, opposite a bald mountain so far distant that any sound made in his camp would take six hours to echo back. He said that just before he retired for the night he would shout, "Time to get up!" and the call would echo back to his camp at the precise hour he needed to awaken the next morning. "They said I was the damndest liar ever lived," he liked to say. "That's what a man gets for tellin' the truth."

Jim Bridger died on his farm near Westport on July 17, 1881.

TRADING
POSTS

Trading posts played an extremely important role in the North American fur trade. From the earliest days of fur exploitation in the Great Lakes region, the British and French built trading posts for dual reasons. First, the posts served as secure and tenable bases of operation for the traders. They also acted as storehouses for furs brought in by American Indians and for the numerous trade goods that were to be swapped with the natives for their furs. In later years, such posts became equally important in the Rocky Mountain fur industry. They were synonymous

Trading posts, such as the Hubbell Trading Post in Arizona, fulfilled many functions in the West, from serving as bases of operation for commercial enterprises to providing havens for weary travelers.

with forts until the American military arrived, and they were frequently a haven for the trappers during the most brutal months of the Rocky Mountain winters.

Fort Laramie, located in present-day eastern Wyoming, was a trading post built in 1834 on the bank of the Laramie River near its confluence with the North Platte. Its builder was William Sublette, a well-known and experi-

enced mountain man. The Fort went on to become one of the anchor points of the famous Oregon Trail traveled by countless emigrants to the West. Sublette became one of the primary partners in the Rocky Mountain Fur Company and a wealthy man.

Another notable trading post of the period was Bent's Fort, located on the Arkansas River in present-day southeastern Col-

orado. Completed in 1833 by Charles and William Bent and their partner Ceran St. Vrain, the fort was built of adobe, making it the only such structure in that part of the country. The building style may have been the contribution of St. Vrain, a naturalized Mexican citizen of French ancestry who had spent considerable time in the Southwest. With its two circular towers guarding opposite corners, Bent's Fort rose above the prairie grass like a castle in the wilderness and ruled the southern Great Plains for many years as the center of a far-reaching fur empire run by the Bents and St. Vrain.

JEDEDIAH
SMITH

1799–1831

Tall, lean, tireless, and intrepid, Jedediah Strong Smith has been called the perfect model of the mountain man. His restless eyes were forever turned westward, with his Bible always at hand and his Hawken rifle cradled and ready.

He was born on January 6, 1799, in Bainbridge, New York, and grew up in Erie County, Pennsylvania, and the Western Reserve of Ohio. He received only a rudimentary frontier education and was raised in a staunchly Methodist family. While a teenager and working as a clerk on a Lake Erie freighter, Smith supposedly read the journals of the Lewis and Clark Expedition. He soon made his way west, lured by the adventurous life of the trailblazer. By 1822, he reached St. Louis, where he answered an advertisement in the *Missouri Gazette* in which "enterprizing young men" were sought to ascend the Missouri River to locate fur-trapping grounds. The notice had been placed by Missouri Lieutenant Governor William H. Ashley and fur trader Andrew Henry of the Rocky Mountain Fur Company. From the time he threw in with Ashley and Henry until he died, Smith's life was one of relentless exploration through the trackless wilderness of the Northwest.

In the fall of 1823, he crossed the plains south of the Yellowstone River in search of new beaver grounds with a party that included Jim Clyman and Tom Fitzpatrick. He was mauled so badly by a grizzly bear that his scalp and ear were torn loose from his head. Clyman gingerly sewed them back on, and Smith survived to experience other adventures.

Smith's greatest venture began in August 1826 when he led a party of trappers on an overland journey from Utah to the Colorado River, then across the Mojave Desert, and into Southern California. Despite being ordered by Spanish authorities to leave the territory of California, Smith wintered in the San Joaquin Valley. He trapped along the Stanislaus River, and then with only a few of his men, he began the journey back, leading the first Anglo-American party to cross the Sierra Nevada and the Great Salt Lake Desert. The latter was an arduous trip as described by Smith. "We frequently travelled without water sometimes for two days across sandy deserts, where there was no sign of vegetation. . . . When we arrived at the Salt Lake, we had but one horse and one mule remaining, which were so feeble and poor that they could scarce carry the little camp equipment which I had along; the balance of my horses I was compelled to eat as they gave out."

Retracing his trail to California, Smith set out the following year with 18 men to relieve his hunting party and to explore the Oregon coast. At a Mojave Indian village at the Colorado River crossing, half of his group

Jed Smith lived a brief but furiously active life. He left his mark from the Great Salt Lake to the Pacific Coast, from the Columbia River to the Mojave Desert.

were massacred in a surprise attack. Smith led the remnant of his band into California. After being jailed briefly at the San Jose Mission, he journeyed on northward along the California coast. When he reached the Klamath River in Oregon, his party faced another attack by Indians, this time the Kalawatsets near the Umpqua River. Finally, in July 1828, Smith and the three surviving men reached Fort Vancouver.

Two years later, he sold out his interest in his beaver trapping enterprise to the Rocky Mountain Fur Company. He traveled down to St. Louis, moderately wealthy and semiretired. More devout and viceless than most of the hard-living mountain men, he had, in his own words, "missed the care of the Christian church."

Smith grew restless, however, because as one anonymous writer described, "His altar was the mountaintop . . . his sacraments were mountain skills." In 1831, he organized a trading caravan of 74 men, including his old friend Tom Fitzpatrick, and 22 wagons. They left St. Louis, bound for Santa Fe, New Mexico, in April. After several days of searching for water in the arid country between the Arkansas and Cimarron Rivers, Smith and Fitzpatrick rode ahead to find a stream bed to dig for water. The two men split up, and Smith soon found a small water pocket in a buffalo wallow in the Cimarron. Unfortu-

nately, he also found a Comanche war party. He managed to get one shot off with his Hawken rifle, which supposedly killed the leader of the Comanche band, before dying at their hands. The body of the legendary mountain man was never found.

Bible-toting Jedediah Strong Smith led the first group of Anglo-Americans across the daunting Sierra Nevada.

Jedediah Smith's achievements as a post-Lewis and Clark explorer are unparalleled. He was the first Anglo-American to discover and travel the length and breadth of the Great Basin. He pioneered the overland trail to California and was the first Anglo-American man to cross the Sierra Nevada and the Great Salt Lake Desert. He was the first to travel overland from California to the Columbia River in Oregon. Many of his trails were later followed by California-bound pioneers, making him one of the West's first and great pathfinders.

JAMES P. BECKWOURTH

1798—1866

Jim Beckwourth was what mountain men called a yarner, an adventurer who was never satisfied with the plain truth of his travels and exploits. Unlike Jim Bridger, another celebrated teller of tall tales, Beckwourth's yarns never had Bridger's elbow-in-the-ribs quality of obvious fun and ruse. Because he came to believe his own mythmaking, the real story of Jim Beckwourth—an eventful and tempestuous tale that required no embroidery—is cloudy and confused.

He was born James Pierson Beckwith in Fredericksburg, Virginia, on April 26, 1798, the son of plantation overseer Sir Jennings Beckwith (the title apparently inherited from a British baronet ancestor) and a black woman, probably a slave.

In 1810, Beckwith and his family moved to St. Charles, Missouri, then a part of the Louisiana Territory. At age 14, Jim, like his contemporary Jim Bridger, was apprenticed to a blacksmith in St. Louis. He may have also worked as a lead miner and hunter throughout his teens and early youth.

In 1824, Beckwourth (who changed the spelling of his surname for unknown reasons) became one of 25 men—including the redoubtable fur traders Tom Fitzpatrick and Jim Clyman—to join William H. Ashley's third trapping expedition to the Rocky Moun-

James P. Beckwourth's familiarity with several Native American nations lured him away from Anglo-American society.

tains. The venture proved to be a dangerous and eventful debut to the life of a mountain man: The party trudged through snowdrifts in subzero temperatures; survived near-starvation in the Platte River Valley; tramped across northern Colorado and southern Wyoming in search of new beaver streams; lost several horses to a band of Crow raiders; and survived an Indian attack, which resulted in the death of one of Ashley's party.

Over the next few years, Beckwourth operated as a free trapper, meaning he was not associated with any fur-trade company. He trapped along the Upper Missouri, Platte, Snake, Green, Bear, and Yellowstone rivers, and he traded with Blackfeet, Snakes (Shoshonis), Cheyenne, and Crows.

Some time between 1826 and 1828, after trapping along the Powder River in Wyoming, Beckwourth abandoned his native society to live with the Crows. The Crows were generally friendly to the trappers, and he was welcomed among them. In his dictated memoirs, titled *Life and Adventures of James P. Beckwourth*, he stated that, with the Crows, he knew he could trap in their streams unmolested. He felt better protected with the Crows than with his fellow trappers. "I therefore resolved," he told his scribe, "to abide with them, to do my best in their company, and in assisting them to subdue their enemies."

Beckwourth claimed, and it may be true, that he became a chief among the Crows within a year. He learned their language, customs, and daily living habits, and he married at least two Crow women and fathered several children. He called one of his spouses Little Wife and the other Pine Leaf.

By his own account, he raided with and fought alongside Crow war parties, though it is not clear how often he participated. He supposedly learned how to steal horses while living with his adopted people.

He took advantage of his Crow connection to serve as a fur trader and agent among the tribe for the American Fur Company, John Jacob Astor's powerful enterprise. The American Fur Company had established the trading post of Fort Union on the Yellowstone River in 1828.

In the summer of 1835, Beckwourth made the first of several ventures to southern California to trade furs for cash and horses. Accompanying him on the expedition were trapper Thomas "Pegleg" Smith, a renegade

This likeness of Pine Leaf, one of Beckwourth's Native American brides, accompanied the mountain man's memoirs in *Harper's New Monthly Magazine*.

Ute chief and slave dealer named Walkara, and about 60 of Walkara's band. In the vicinity of Los Angeles, Walkara and his Utes stole 600 horses from a rancher and drove them off into the desert while Beckwourth and Smith were dickering with Spanish officials. Beckwourth and Smith followed after their companions, becoming horse thieves in the process. Neither man seems to have been guilt-ridden over the escapade since they sold their share of the stolen animals at Bent's Fort for a tidy profit.

Beckwourth grew weary of life with the Crows and joined the Missouri Volunteers as an army scout. He traveled to Florida and

THE ASHLEY-HENRY EXPEDITION

Americans had been trapping beaver on the Missouri River for more than a decade when General William H. Ashley and his partner, Major Andrew Henry, decided to give it a try. Henry had already been to the headwaters of the Missouri River in 1809, when he built a fur post at the Three Forks. Ashley, the lieutenant governor of Missouri, was new to the business. Following in the steps of Manuel Lisa and John Jacob Astor, they intended to establish a trading base in the wilderness so that they could offer freelance trappers transportation and supplies and get a share of the profits from shipping the pelts back to St. Louis.

Fur trade luminary William H. Ashley established a fort along the Yellowstone River in 1822 with the help of a party of trappers.

In April 1822, Henry led a party up the Missouri from St. Louis and established a fort for winter quarters at the mouth of the Yellowstone River. The following spring, Ashley and some 70 adventurers started back upriver to begin trapping. They happened upon an encampment of Arikara Indians along the west bank of the Missouri River in present-day South Dakota. The timing was bad; the Arikara had never been sympathetic to encroaching easterners, and in a recent skirmish between the Arikara and their longtime enemies the Sioux, a group of white trappers had intervened on the side of the Sioux. The Arikara forced Ashley and his vastly outnumbered party back downriver. Ashley returned shortly with the U.S. 6th Infantry in tow, under the command of Colonel Henry Leavenworth. Leavenworth's forces were far greater, but the Arikara had little trouble fending them off long enough to escape relatively unscathed.

This first battle west of the Mississippi between Native Americans and U.S. forces had significant ramifications. The natives of the area were left unimpressed by the performance of the army and so adopted a bolder attitude, making Ashley and Henry's plans for the area no longer tenable. As a result, the entrepreneurs took their Rocky Mountain Fur Company in a new direction—west. In later expeditions, they pushed overland into the very heart of the Rockies, opening up the secluded valleys and snakelike river systems that would, over the next two decades, produce the legendary mountain men.

took part in the Seminole War, serving as a dispatch rider under General Zachary Taylor at the Battle of Lake Okeechobee in December 1837. Beckwourth's life seems a mixture of brave deeds and unscrupulous acts: After serving with Taylor, he returned to horse stealing. In 1840, he went back to California with Smith and Walkara for an unabashed horse rustling raid in the Santa Ana Valley.

Beckwourth hunted along the Green River while operating as a free trapper. As "beaver waters" go, the Green proved to be lucrative.

After the beaver trade declined, Beckwourth—like most of the mountain men—worked a number of jobs. He settled in Taos, New Mexico Territory, married a girl from Santa Fe, assisted in erecting a fort on the Arkansas River in Colorado called Pueblo, and entered a partnership in a hotel and saloon in Santa Fe. During the Mexican War of 1846–1848, he served as a dispatch rider for General Stephen Watts Kearny during the New Mexico campaign and for Colonel Sterling Price in the Taos area.

After the hostilities ended, Beckwourth made his final journey to California, selling trade goods to '49ers in the Sonoma area. He discovered a pass through the Sierra Nevada that became part of a major pathway for settlers en route to California. He searched for gold in the Sierra Nevada, guided wagon trains over the passes to the supply base north of Sacramento, and operated a hotel and store in the vicinity.

Beckwourth settled near Denver in the early 1860s, married again, managed a store, and took occasional trips into the mountains

to mine, hunt, and trap. He also found work as a guide for military parties. In this latter employment, he had a role, perhaps unwittingly, in one of the most reprehensible acts in the history of the American West. Beckwourth was a guide for the 3rd Colorado Volunteer Cavalry, under Colonel J. M. Chivington, in the massacre at Sand Creek on November 29, 1864, in which a camp of 500 Cheyenne and Arapaho were slaughtered.

After the Sand Creek atrocity, Beckwourth settled near Fort Laramie, where he worked occasionally as a scout, guide, and messenger. Not long after, he turned his back on Anglo-American society once again and returned to his Crow people.

Beckwourth died in 1866, though the precise date and circumstances are unknown. He probably died in a Crow village near Fort C. F. Smith on the Bozeman Trail near the Bighorn River in Montana Territory. He was laid to rest in Crow fashion on a tree platform.

KIT
CARSON

1809—1868

Christopher Houston Carson was born in Richmond, Madison County, Kentucky, on Christmas Eve, 1809, the sixth of ten children of Lindsey and Rebecca Carson. Kit's father served in the Revolutionary War before settling along the Kentucky River to farm. According to Carson's autobiography, Lindsey Carson pushed westward with his family about a year later, settling in Howard County, Missouri.

For a future frontiersman, Kit Carson seemed to have landed in a perfect spot: In 1821, the Virginian William Becknell and his partners left the settlement of Franklin, Missouri, to take their first pack train of trade goods to the town of Santa Fe in the Mexican province of New Mexico. That venture marked the opening of one of the most significant roads in western history—the Santa Fe Trail. But, at first, young Christopher—called Kit since childhood—was not in a position to blaze

Kit Carson's feats as a guide, scout, and Indian fighter are comparable to those of earlier mountain man Daniel Boone.

trails, forge pathways, or open territories, because in 1823, he became apprenticed to a saddle maker in Franklin.

After three years of watching from his saddle-shop window as the wagons wound westward to New Mexico, the teenaged Kit ran away from home and work. He joined a trade caravan heading first to Kansas, Colorado, and the Raton Pass, and then southward to the Sangre de Cristo Mountains of New Mexico and the fabled town of Santa Fe.

Over the next five years, while based in Taos, New Mexico, Carson learned the trades, crafts, and ways of the Southwestern mountain man. He worked as a teamster for a dollar a day on trade wagons. He rode with merchants into Chihuahua, Mexico, where he quickly learned Spanish, enabling him to serve as an interpreter. And he undertook his first California expedition, traveling with a brigade of 40 men led by veteran trapper Ewing Young. Though illiterate, Carson gained skills and experiences during this period that would save his life and those of his companions many times over.

Around 1831, Kit met the celebrated Irish mountain man Thomas Fitzpatrick in Santa Fe. Fitzpatrick was called Broken Hand by Native Americans because his hand had been mangled when his musket exploded. He offered Kit a billet among the free trappers he was leading north to the Rockies. Kit readily signed on for the adventure.

He also gained his experience as an Indian fighter. In January 1833, while Carson was trapping with 50 men on the Arkansas River in Colorado, nine of his party's horses were stolen by a band of Crows. Kit led a dozen men, including two Cheyenne Indians, 40 miles through the snow in pursuit of the thieves. He found the Crow camp, retrieved the horses, and attacked the band of Crows.

The Green River rendezvous in the summer of 1835 turned out to be an auspicious occasion for Kit Carson. There he fought his storied duel with a French-Canadian trapper named Shunar (probably Chouinard). Shunar took delight in insulting and bullying the Americans, aiming his sharpest insults at Carson. Kit quickly grew weary of it. "I did not like such talk from any man," he stated

in his memoirs, "so I told him I was the worst American in camp. . . . and that if he made use of any more such expressions, I would rip his guts." The rivalry culminated dramatically, with the two men riding toward each other on horseback with pistols drawn. Kit not only won the fight but also a young Arapaho woman named Waanibe—who may have been the cause of the rivalry with Shunar. Waanibe became Kit's wife and bore him a child named Adaline. Carson does not mention Waanibe in his memoirs. All that is known of her is that she died of some unexplained illness around 1841.

With the fur trade in decline, Carson returned to Missouri in the

Carson led a life of such adventure that his exploits became the stuff of romance. Painter Charles Russell idealized Carson as a western legend in "Carson's Men" (left), while a print from a popular magazine sensationalized his celebrated fight with Shunar (above).

PORTRAIT OF A
MOUNTAIN MAN

The men who roamed the uncharted wilderness of the Rocky Mountains in the 1830s and 1840s made a remarkably diverse group—black and white, old and young, Irish, French, Scottish, and German, businessmen and backwoodsmen. Deeper than all that, though, they shared a characteristic resilience, self-reliance, and fierce individualism that served them well in their rugged environment. On the surface, the demands and rigors of their lifestyle also gave them a characteristic and unmistakable appearance, as described here by veteran trapper Rufus Sage.

"His skin, from constant exposure, assumes a hue almost as dark as that of the Aborigine, and his fea-tures and physical struc-ture attain a rough and hardy cast. His hair, through inattention, becomes long, coarse, and bushy, and loosely dangles upon his shoulders. His head is sur-mounted by a low crowned wool-hat, or a rude substi-tute of his own manufac-ture. His clothes are of buckskin, gaily fringed at the seams with strings of the same material, cut and made in a fashion peculiar to himself and associates.

The mountain men outfitted themselves for survival, not for appearances. In a harsh, demanding wilderness, their lives and their livelihoods depended on what they carried on their backs.

The deer and buffalo fur-nish him the required cov-ering for his feet which he fabricates at the impulse of want. His waist is encircled with a belt of leather, hold-ing encased his butcher-knife and pistols—while from his neck is suspended a bullet-pouch securely fastened to the belt in front, and beneath the right arm hangs a powder-horn tra-versely from his shoulder, behind which, upon the strap attached to it, are af-fixed his bullet-mould, ball-screw, wiper, awl, &c. With a gun-stick made of some hard wood and a good rifle placed in his hands, carrying from thir-ty-five balls to the pound, the reader will have before him a correct likeness of a genuine mountaineer when fully equipped."

spring of 1842 to visit friends and relatives and to put his daughter Adaline in school. On a steamer on the Missouri, he met John C. Frémont of the U.S. Army's Corps of Topographical Engineers, who was beginning a series of expeditions into the Rocky Mountains and the areas beyond for the government. Frémont hired Carson, at $100 a month, to serve as a guide for the expedition.

In Carson, Frémont found the perfect guide for his expeditions, and together, the pair helped fulfill the goals of the western expansionists, who believed it was America's destiny to conquer and settle the West. In the three-month 1842 expedition, in which Frémont was to map the Oregon Trail, Kit led

Carson fends off a couple of grizzly bears, as depicted in one of the many fictionalized accounts of his life.

the group through the South Pass (in today's Frémont County, Wyoming) and into the Wind River Range.

Between the end of his first expedition with Frémont and the start of the second, Carson spent some time at Fort Laramie and at Bent's Fort, then returned to Taos. There, in February 1843, he married Josepha Jaramillo, the 15-year-old sister-in-law of his friend, the trader Charles Bent. Josepha proved to be the love of his life as well as his partner in a 25-year marriage that produced seven children.

In the spring of 1843, Carson rejoined Frémont. The second expedition explored the Great Salt Lake, made a dangerous winter crossing of the Sierra Nevada, and followed the Oregon Trail to Fort Vancouver. The party arrived at Sutter's Fort in March of the following year. Carson then led Frémont and his party south to the Mojave Desert, where the celebrated mountain man Joseph Reddeford Walker joined them for the return trip to the Rockies in Colorado. Frémont's reports of these first two expeditions made both Carson and Frémont famous and earned the ambitious surveyor his nickname, the Pathfinder.

Carson took time to build a cabin for Josepha on the Little Cimarron River near Taos and start up a small farming operation before he rejoined Frémont at Bent's Fort in the summer of 1845 for a new expedition to California. By the time the 62-man party reached Sutter's Fort, California, that November, the United States was poised for a war with Mexico. On May 13, 1846, war was declared, and Frémont's men were ordered to combat duty. Carson served daringly and

Josepha Jaramillo Carson was 18 years old when this photo was taken— three years after she married Kit.

THE LONG WALK

In 1864, thousands of Navajo men, women, and children left their last refuge in Canyon de Chelly and marched under duress 300 miles to the Bosque Redondo reservation along the Pecos River in New Mexico. The Navajo were allowed to bring with them 3,000 sheep, a few hundred horses, and a mere 30 army wagons loaded with personal belongings. The leader of this final effort to subjugate the Navajo Nation was Colonel Christopher "Kit" Carson.

The barren Bosque Redondo was already a forced home to the Mescalero Apache, who could barely scratch out a miserable existence from the arid countryside. With the Navajo presence, life on the reservation became nearly impossible. An 1868 treaty granted the Navajo a reprieve, returning 3.5 million acres of their homeland near the New Mexico-Arizona border in exchange for their vow never to go to war with the United States.

The Navajo made their last stand against Carson's men around the rim of the red sandstone walls of the Canyon de Chelly. Their efforts failed, and they were forced to move from the Canyon to the Bosque Redondo.

earned a personal appointment from President James K. Polk as Lieutenant of Rifles.

Between the Mexican War and the outbreak of the Civil War, Carson and his friend Lucien Maxwell, who had served with Kit in the Mexican War, began a ranching and farming operation on Maxwell's enormous land grant at Rayado, New Mexico. Kit was never quite satisfied with the life of a gentleman rancher, however, and periodically took other, less mundane work. Late in 1849, he joined in the pursuit of a band of Jicarilla Apache who had kidnapped Mrs. J. M. White and her child after attacking the White caravan along the Cimarron River. Carson and a company of Taos dragoons found the Apache camp and routed it, but they proved too late to save the captives. Mrs. White's body was located, still warm, with an arrow in her heart. Her baby was never found. Though Kit was a seasoned mountain man who had participated in skirmishes with Native Americans from the Canadian border to the Rio Grande, he never forgot this incident. In the rubble of the Jicarilla camp, he found a dime novel recounting the hair-raising adventures of Kit Carson. He wondered if Mrs. White, in her last hours, was waiting for the daring Kit Carson of the dime novel to rescue her.

In 1854, he was appointed Indian Agent at Taos with responsibilities among the Ute, Jicarilla Apache, and Pueblo nations. He served credibly in that capacity despite his near-illiteracy. During his tenure as agent, he dictated his memoirs to his secretary, John Mostin.

During the Civil War, Carson was named colonel of the 1st New Mexico Volunteer Infantry Regiment. He fought his single engagement against the Confederates at the

Battle of Valverde, on the Rio Grande above Fort Craig, on February 22, 1862.

More significant than his Civil War service was his return to fighting Indians, this time under the auspices of the U.S. military. In the winter of 1862, under the direction of Brigadier General James H. Carleton, commander of the Department of New Mexico, Carson began the long campaign against the Navajo, who had been rustling cattle from the New Mexican settlers. Carson and 400 men starved the Indians into submission by burning their crops and stores and killing their livestock.

Carson's last battle with Native Americans occurred late in 1864 when Carleton decided to put an end to depredations by the Kiowa and Comanche along the Santa Fe Trail. On Carleton's orders, Carson assembled a force at a fort along the Canadian River in the Texas Panhandle and marched against the Kiowa in their winter camps on the river. He led over 300 officers and troops, supply wagons, mountain howitzers, and an ambulance wagon across the Canadian in November to a large Kiowa village near an abandoned trading post called Adobe Walls. The Kiowa and Comanche, reinforced by other camps, made their stand there. They outnumbered Carson's force, but the odds were evened out by the military's deadly cannon fire. The Kiowa and Comanche bands, who suffered a combined loss of 60 men, retreated to their camps. Carson returned with only two men dead and 21 wounded.

After a brief command at Fort Garland in the Colorado Territory, Kit was mustered out of the army in November 1867. He settled with Josepha and his family at Boggsville, Colorado, where he was appointed Superintendent of Indian Affairs for the Colorado Territory. Unfortunately, by now he was growing increasingly ill.

His failing health notwithstanding, he made a final trip to Washington in February 1868, accompanying a delegation of the Ute to negotiate a treaty concerning their tribal lands. He returned to Boggsville in April, just in time to see Josepha give birth to their seventh child, a daughter. Ten days later, Josepha Jaramillo Carson died. Kit survived his wife by only a month.

KIT CARSON

Whether he was the simple, noble mountain man of Frémont's memoirs or the daredevil Indian fighter of the cheap dime novels, Kit Carson was painted in heroic tones with the broad strokes of hyperbole. His adventures and exploits helped construct the popular image of the self-reliant trailblazer who conquered the forces of nature for the good of the country. Yet, even without the exaggeration, his accomplishments— from leading Frémont's surveying expeditions to participating in the Mexican and Indian wars—helped settle the West for future generations.

Truly a legend in his own time, Carson lived long enough to see his life story interpreted and reinvented in the sensationalized dime novels.

LAWMEN
AND
SHOOTISTS

Nothing is more dramatic than a life-and-death battle between armed men facing each other at close range. In the saloons and on the dusty streets, Westerners blazed away at each other with Colt revolvers, Winchester carbines, and double-barreled shotguns.

Gunfighters . . . shootists . . . pistoleers . . . leather slappers. Men of the West used their guns in defense of the law, themselves, or their property. Displaying a marked tendency toward violence, western gunfighters exposed themselves to peril by wearing badges, robbing people, or associating with dangerous men in dangerous places.

Wyatt Earp took part in the West's most famous shootout at the O.K. Corral. Wyatt's deadly friend, gambler/dentist Doc Holliday, participated at the O.K. Corral and in numerous other lethal encounters.

Bill Tilghman, the most distinguished lawman in the West, was gunned down while still wearing a badge at the age of 70.

Isaac Parker, the "Hanging Judge," sent scores of deputy U.S. marshals into lawless Indian Territory. And the most famous gunfighter of all was Wild Bill Hickok, the "Prince of Pistoleers."

A deputy U.S. marshal and his staff reveal that they are armed and ready for duty as they pose in front of the jailhouse at Fort Smith, Arkansas.

WYATT EARP

1848–1929

No more controversial shootist exists in western history than Wyatt Berry Stapp Earp. During his long life, Wyatt restlessly traveled throughout the West: He served as a peace officer in a succession of raw frontier communities; he worked as a buffalo hunter, saloon keeper, professional gambler, and prizefight referee; he joined in the rush to Alaska at the turn of the century; and he served as a technical adviser in Hollywood for such western movie stars as William S. Hart and Tom Mix. Wyatt was a principal in the most famous of all gunfights, then led a violent vendetta after the bloody ambushes of two of his brothers.

Born on March 19, 1848, in Monmouth, Illinois, Wyatt was named Wyatt Berry Stapp Earp after a captain under whom his father had served during the Mexican War. When he was two, the Earps moved to Pella, Iowa, where Wyatt spent most of his boyhood toiling on the family farm under the stern eye of his father, Nicholas.

During the war, Nick Earp was town marshal of Pella, and Wyatt watched his two-fisted father batter troublemakers into submission, thus preventing more lethal incidents. This is a lesson that Wyatt would repeatedly apply while wearing a badge in Kansas cow towns. The hard-bitten Nick once said, "I taught all my boys to fight and I'm damned proud of it!" The youngest Earp offspring, Adelia, later told her daughter, "All of your uncles—especially Wyatt—would rather fight than eat. They must have got it from Pa."

In 1864, Nick uprooted the family again, joining a wagon train for California. A couple of years later, Wyatt began chafing under his father's heavy hand at the Earp ranch in San Bernardino. One day, he lost his temper and hit Nick. Nick reacted with a kick to the groin, then wrestled Wyatt into a horse trough. Both understood that it was time for Wyatt to leave home, so he joined his brother Virgil in driving a freight wagon to Salt Lake City.

Wyatt and Virgil then worked as construction laborers on the westbound Union Pacific Railroad, before rejoining their father as he relocated the family to Lamar, Missouri. Wyatt became the town constable and in 1870 married Urilla Sutherland, with his father presiding as justice of the peace.

Less than a year after their marriage, Urilla Earp died in childbirth, along with her baby daughter. Despondent, Wyatt left Lamar and roamed the West. He was arrested in Indian Territory for horse stealing and then

Few western lawmen can surpass Wyatt Earp in legend and fame. Though dauntless, he was also cold and steely.

THE EARP FAMILY

While Wyatt remains the most famous Earp, there were five other brothers and four sisters in the family. The patriarch of the family was Nicholas Porter Earp, born in North Carolina in 1813. Nick's first wife was Abigal Storm, who bore him a son and a daughter, but he later married Virginia Cooksey and sired eight more children. A veteran of the Black Hawk and Mexican wars, the hot-tempered and bellicose Nick spent time living in Kentucky, Illinois, Iowa, Missouri, and finally California, where he died in 1907.

Newton, Wyatt's half-brother, was the oldest of the Earp brothers. He was born in Kentucky in 1837 and died in California in 1928. Like most of the younger Earps, Newton followed a career in law en-forcement, serving as town marshal of Garden City, Kansas, for a while. He was the only one of the six brothers to father children.

James was born in Kentucky in 1841 and died in 1926 in Los Angeles. James preferred running a saloon to law enforcement duties, and although he may have been in Tombstone during the gunfight at the O.K. Corral, he did not actively participate in the fracas. James also differed in stature from most of his other brothers, standing only five feet eight inches tall, while the others stood around six feet.

Left: Passive James Earp was never interested in being a lawman. **Middle:** Like Wyatt, Virgil was fearless and good with firearms. **Right:** Morgan, generally a pleasant man, became hot-tempered under duress.

Virgil was born in Kentucky in 1843. He worked as a stage driver and as a deputy marshal before joining his brothers in Tombstone as the city marshal. Later he would serve as the marshal of Colton, California. In 1905, Virgil died of pneumonia in Nevada.

Morgan, the only Earp brother not to live into the 20th century, was born in Iowa in 1851. He recovered from wounds he received at the O.K. Corral only to be murdered in 1882, most likely as retribution for his role in the famed shoot-out.

The youngest Earp brother, Warren, was born in Iowa in 1855. He was probably living in Tombstone in 1881 but did not join his brothers in the shoot-out. He died in Arizona in 1900 when he was shot in a run-in with John Boyett.

spent the next couple of years farming in Kansas, where he took on Cecila Ann "Mattie" Blaylock as a common-law wife. In 1873, he left farm work and joined his older brother James in Wichita, Kansas, the rowdy terminus of the Chisholm Trail. Wyatt again pinned on a badge, apparently as a member of a private force paid by subscription to keep law and order in the saloons and business houses. Later, he became a city policeman.

Wyatt frequently engaged in target practice with the Remington cap and ball revolver that he had used in Lamar. Unlike the famous Navy Colt, the Remington had a backstrap that reinforced the weapon as a club. Wyatt found it so

Wyatt's parents, Virginia and Nicholas Earp, moved their considerable brood around a great deal. Rugged Nick Earp—a cooper, bootlegger, and lawman—was married twice and sired ten children.

handy in knocking out drunks and other revelers that he later had it converted to cartridges. He also avoided shooting his opponents by using his fists. "There were few men in the West who could whip Earp in a rough-and-tumble fight 30 years ago," wrote his friend Bat Masterson in 1907. Wyatt was lean and tall and quick. "In his prime Wyatt was greased lightning," related James Earp. "I saw a couple of fights where guys swung at him and only hit thin air. And, he had a punch like a mule, with those long arms. Virge and I used to call him the Earp Ape."

On April 2, 1876, a candidate for city marshal named William Smith made remarks against opponent Mike Meagher, who was a friend of Wyatt's, and some of the Earp brothers. Angered by the remarks, Wyatt whipped Smith, causing Earp's dismissal from the force. "It is but justice to Erp [sic] to say he has made an excellent officer," observed the *Wichita Beacon*.

Wyatt promptly moved to Dodge City, an even wilder Kansas cow town. A man of his experience, rough skills, and courage was appreciated by the city fathers of Dodge, who appointed him to the police force. While Wyatt helped keep the peace in Dodge City, several other western legends lived there, including Doc Holliday and Bat, Jim, and Ed Masterson. During his four seasons as a Dodge lawman, Wyatt continued to buffalo troublemakers with his fists and gun barrel, resorting to gunfire only on July 26, 1878. At three o'clock in the morning, a small group of drunken cowboys began firing their guns into the air, bringing Wyatt and Jim Masterson on the run. The two parties traded shots, and as the cowhands tried to ride off, one young Texan, George Hoy, fell out of the saddle with a bullet in the arm. Infection set in and Hoy, who was under a $1,500 bond in Texas, died four weeks later.

Following the 1879 cattle season, Earp resigned as assistant marshal of Dodge and traveled to Las Vegas, New Mexico, where he joined other members of his family and Doc Holliday. Within a few months, Wyatt, Virgil, and James Earp moved to the Arizona boomtown of Tombstone and settled their families in three houses at the intersection of First and Fremont. Soon after, Morgan and Warren Earp, Doc Holliday, and Bat Masterson turned up in Tombstone.

Wyatt became a shotgun guard for Wells Fargo. He also gambled professionally and speculated in mining claims, and he acquired an interest in the flourishing Oriental Saloon. Twice Wyatt tried unsuccessfully to obtain an appointment as county sheriff. In July 1880, he did become deputy sheriff, stationed in Tombstone. His brother Virgil held a deputy U.S. marshal's commission.

Within a year, Virgil and Wyatt began tangling with rustlers Tom and Frank McLaury, who were involved in criminal activities with the Clanton clan. Earp detractors would later emphasize unsubstantiated rumors that the Earps had been involved with the Clanton-McLaury ring, and that the animosity between them was the result of a falling-out among thieves. They would also claim that James Earp's teenaged stepdaughter had been involved with a McLaury brother. When the McLaury brothers testified against Doc Holliday in connection with a March 1881 stagecoach robbery in which two men were killed, they earned the vengeful enmity of the Earps in general and Doc in particular.

The feud came to a head on October 26, 1881, erupting into a 30-second shoot-out that has generated more investigation than any other gunfight in frontier history. When the smoke cleared, Virgil had mortally wounded Billy Clanton; Doc Holliday had blasted to death Tom McLaury; and Wyatt and Morgan had shot and killed Frank McLaury, because according to Wyatt, "He had a reputation of being a good shot and a dangerous man." Meanwhile, Ike Clanton and Billy Claiborne had fled the scene. On the lawmen's side, Virgil had been shot through the calf, while Morgan had taken a bullet in the left shoulder. Doc had received a flesh wound. Only Wyatt remained unhurt.

The O.K. Corral incident climaxed but did not end the bitter, violent feud between the Earps and the Clantons. Two months after the shoot-out, on December 28, 1881, Virgil Earp left the Oriental Saloon half an hour before midnight. As he crossed the street, he was cut down by several shotgun blasts, throwing buckshot into his left side, back, and left arm. Virgil survived, but he lost the use of his arm. "Never mind," he comforted his wife, "I've still got one arm left to hug you with."

On March 18, 1882, Morgan was playing billiards as Wyatt and a number of other men watched. Suddenly two shots were fired into the room. The first slug entered the right side of Morgan's stomach, shattered his spinal column, and emerged to inflict a flesh wound on one of the onlookers. Morgan was carried into an adjacent card room and placed on a sofa, where he died surrounded by Wyatt, Virgil, James, Warren, and their wives. Friends of the Clantons were supposedly seen running away from the scene.

WYATT EARP AND THE MOVIES

Wyatt Earp spent the latter years of his life in Los Angeles. The old lawman met western movie stars William S. Hart and Tom Mix, along with director John Ford, and he hoped that his western adventures might be filmed.

The first film version was *Law and Order*, released in 1932, just three years after Wyatt's death. Starring Walter Huston, Harry Carey, and Walter Brennan, *Law and Order* is a stark and entertaining film, even though the characters were given fictional names. An uninspired remake of *Law and Order* was filmed in 1953, with Ronald Reagan in the Wyatt Earp role.

Wyatt met with a biographer, Stuart N. Lake, shortly before his death. Lake's book, *Frontier Marshal*, was published in 1931. A 1934 film adaptation, *Frontier Marshal*,

Kurt Russell as Wyatt (*left*) and Val Kilmer as Doc (*right*) starred in 1993's *Tombstone*.

starred George O'Brien. A better version, also with the same title, was released in 1939, with tall Randolph Scott as Wyatt and handsome Cesar Romero as Doc. Richard Dix played Wyatt in 1942 in the mediocre *Tombstone*.

In 1946, John Ford turned his enormous talents to the story Wyatt had told him. *My Darling Clementine* starred Henry Fonda as Wyatt, muscular Victor Mature as a robust Doc, and Walter Brennan as a wicked Old

Man Clanton. Despite inaccuracies, *My Darling Clementine* is a classic motion picture. Fonda and Anthony Quinn played Wyatt and Doc under different names in *Warlock*, a 1959 film. Joel McCrea starred as Wyatt in *Wichita*, a 1955 movie that focused on Earp as a lawman in the Kansas cattle town.

In 1957, Burt Lancaster and Kirk Douglas turned in bravura performances as Wyatt and Doc in *Gunfight at the OK Corral*, though the

30-second gunfight took ten minutes on film. Director John Sturges returned to the story ten years later, opening *Hour of the Gun* with an accurate version of the famous gunfight. Starring as Wyatt was James Garner, who returned to the role in 1988 in *Sunset*, in which an aging Earp teams up in Hollywood with Tom Mix, played by Bruce Willis. In 1971, the unsatisfactory *Doc* presented Stacey Keach in the title role and Harris Yulin as a sleazy Wyatt.

Far more satisfactory were two 1993 movies. *Tombstone* offered an accurate set and costumes, Kurt Russell as Wyatt, and Val Kilmer as a Doc who steals the film. *Wyatt Earp* starred Kevin Costner in the title role, while a cadaverous Dennis Quaid is the closest incarnation of Doc Holliday we will ever see on film.

Two nights later in Tucson, Wyatt, Warren, Doc Holliday, Sherman McMasters, and "Turkey Creek" Jack Johnson found Frank Stilwell, the chief suspect in Morgan's murder. Stilwell attempted to flee from the vengeful group, but he was headed off by Wyatt, wielding a shotgun. The entire party opened fire and riddled him with 30 slugs. Two days later, the vengeance-seekers located another prime suspect, Florentino Cruz, hiding at a wood camp near Tombstone and killed him with a volley of gunfire.

During that eventful year of 1881, Wyatt deserted Mattie for sultry Josephine Marcus. Wyatt married Josie the following year in San Francisco. Josie was Wyatt's companion until his death, and she lived until 1944.

Wyatt and Josie spent years wandering through the West. In 1883, he twice visited Dodge City, where he backed an old friend, gambler-gunfighter Luke Short, as a member of the celebrated Dodge City Peace Commission. He spent most of the next year in Idaho at the Coeur d'Alene gold rush, where he speculated with his brother James in mining claims and owned a couple of saloons. After jaunts to Wyoming and Texas, Wyatt returned to California, running a saloon in San Francisco until 1890, when he moved to San Diego to raise thoroughbreds.

In 1896, he refereed the Bob Fitzsimmons-Tom Sharkey prizefight and was widely accused of throwing the match to Sharkey. Attracted by the adventure and opportunities in Alaska at that time, he operated a saloon in Nome until 1901. For the next few years, Wyatt and Josie prospected in Nevada, visiting Virgil in the mining camp of Goldfield. Finally settling in Los Angeles, Wyatt tried to find someone to publicize his adventures, but he died in 1929 at the age of 80. Before he died, he worked as a technical consultant on Hollywood westerns, including those of cowboy movie star Tom Mix. A flamboyant, vain celebrity, Mix is said to have wept openly at Wyatt's funeral.

Two years after his death, Wyatt became the subject of more publicity than he could ever have imagined. Stuart N. Lake authored *Wyatt Earp: Frontier Marshal*, which presented him as an indefatigable gunfighter and a paragon of virtue. For many years afterward, books and films were laudatory about Wyatt Earp's life and career in the West, until revisionists tried to exploit every character flaw and rumor. Wyatt's most dedicated biographer, Glenn Boyer, collected documents, photos, and family testimonies for more than five decades. Boyer ridiculed Lake and other mythmakers, while systematically refuting detractors, leaving us with a human Wyatt Earp who marched combatively through an enormously adventurous life.

Throughout his career in the West, Wyatt Earp did prove himself to be tenaciously loyal and courageous—perhaps looming as a larger-than-life legend after all.

Earp (center) poses with Ed Englestadt and old friend John P. Clum in Nome, Alaska, around 1900.

DOC
HOLLIDAY

1851–1887

Doc Holliday. The name is magical to western enthusiasts, conjuring up an image of a cadaverous but dapper gambler who fatalistically courted gunplay because a bullet was preferable to slow death by tuberculosis. The captivating persona of this quintessen-

It was said that Holliday was "drilled in the art of dentistry, but for those who doubted his ability, he would drill 'em for free."

tial gambler-gunfighter belonged to John Henry Holliday, who was born in 1851 in Griffin, Georgia.

Holliday's father was a Mexican War veteran who became a prosperous landholder in Griffin. He served as a Confederate major during the Civil War until he was forced to resign because of illness. Holliday's fortunes collapsed with the Confederate dollar, and the family moved to Valdosta, Georgia, where John Henry's mother died in 1870. At this time, John Henry became Doc when he began to study dentistry, probably as the apprentice to a practicing dentist. Doc practiced briefly in Valdosta, then moved his dental business to bustling Atlanta. Soon thereafter he was di-

agnosed with tuberculosis and advised to move west because the drier climate might prolong his life. By 1873, he had opened an office in Dallas, in partnership with another Georgian, Dr. John Seegar.

Only occasionally did Holliday practice dentistry, however. More frequently he engaged in gambling, usually as a house dealer. Doc gravitated to numerous frontier boomtowns during their heydays, including Dallas and Fort Griffin in Texas; Cheyenne in Wyoming; Dodge City in Kansas; Denver, Leadville, and Pueblo in Colorado; and Tucson and Tombstone in Arizona.

Holliday drank heavily, which accelerated the deterioration of his health as well as his opportunities for trouble. Over the years, Doc engaged in eight shootings, killing two men and wounding various adversaries and bystanders. He also assisted in the assassination of two other men. He first traded shots with a Dallas saloonkeeper named Austin, but neither man was hit. Holliday's next gunfight, in July 1879 in Las Vegas, New Mexico, was more lethal. Doc and a partner operated a Las Vegas saloon, and one of their saloon girls was the mistress of Mike Gordon, a former army scout. Gordon tried to persuade the woman to quit her job, but when she refused, he decided to shoot up the place. Gordon triggered two rounds at the building before Holliday coolly stepped outside and dropped him with one shot. Gordon died the next day.

Holliday left town shortly thereafter. During his subsequent wanderings, he bullied a bartender named Charley White in Dodge City, causing White to leave town. White found employment in Las Vegas, and in June 1880, Doc drifted back into the New Mexico town and stopped off at the saloon to resurrect the old quarrel. Gunfire erupted and White was hit, collapsing behind the bar. Holliday departed, assuming White to be dead, but the wound proved to be superficial.

At this time, Holliday's female companion was a prostitute known as Big Nosed Kate. Frequently referred to as Kate Fisher, she was actually Katherine Elder from Davenport, Iowa. Born Mary Katherine Horony in Budapest, Hungary, in 1850, she migrated with her family to the United States during the 1860s. Kate lived until 1940, dying in the Arizona Pioneers' Home in Prescott.

Kate and Doc may have married in St. Louis in 1875, but their relationship ended in 1881 after Kate unkindly implicated him in the killing of Budd Philpot during a stagecoach robbery near Tombstone. Holliday was accused of the crime, but in one of several court appearances in the troubled year of 1881, he testified to his innocence. "Foresight is a virtue, they say," Holliday proclaimed at the time, giving insight into his constant readiness to do battle, "so I carried my .44 and a rifle in case some of my many admirers were unable to resist the desire to take a large chunk of my hair for a tender memento."

In Tombstone in April of that year, saloon owner Mike Joyce openly accused Holliday of participating in the stagecoach holdup. Doc angrily charged into the saloon with his revolver blazing, wounding Joyce in the hand and a bartender in the foot. In December,

Mike tried to shoot Doc, but he was arrested for carrying firearms within the city limits. A month later, on January 17, 1882, Holliday and John Ringo were arrested and fined 30 dollars on the same charge after bitterly quarreling on the streets of Tombstone. When Ringo, the West's most overrated gunfighter, was mysteriously shot dead and scalped on July 14, 1882, Doc was rumored to have killed him—but so were Buckskin Frank Leslie and Johnny-Behind-the-Deuce O'Rourke. A bizarre ruling of suicide officially cleared everyone.

A loyal friend to Wyatt Earp, Doc Holliday became deeply involved in the bitter feud between the Earp brothers and the faction led by the Clantons and McLaurys. Characteristically, Holliday helped push the trouble to a bloody end when, backed by Wyatt, Virgil, and Morgan Earp, he cursed an unarmed Ike Clanton in a Tombstone saloon. The next afternoon, October 26, 1881, Doc stood with Wyatt, Virgil, and Morgan against the Clantons and McLaurys outside the O.K. Corral.

As the firing commenced, Holliday pulled a shotgun from under his long overcoat and turned on Tom McLaury, who stood behind his horse unarmed except for a rifle in the saddle scabbard. Frank McLaury snapped off a shot that grazed Holliday in the side, but Doc blasted Tom McLaury with buckshot. He then drew his revolver and fired at unarmed Ike Clanton, who fled into a nearby doorway. Though only about 30 seconds had passed, the legendary gunfight was over, leaving

Tom McLaury was killed by a blast from Doc's shotgun during the Gunfight at the O.K. Corral.

COW TOWNS

In 1867, an Illinois-born entrepreneur named Joseph G. McCoy was looking for a place to gather and load cattle from Texas for rail shipment to the East. He settled on a small cluster of houses built around the railroad tracks in eastern Kansas. McCoy had stockyards, offices, a hotel, and holding pens erected near the railroad.

When cowboys drove 35,000 cattle up from Texas and through the streets the following summer, a new era began and a new kind of town was born. This was the first of the great cattle drives, and Abilene be- came the first of the Wild West towns known throughout the world for their hell-raising, gunfight- ing, whiskey drinking, and gambling.

For a time, Abilene held the distinction of being the wickedest city west of the Mississippi, but eventually the cattle drovers shifted the destination of their Texas herds to newer rail- head towns in the West. Abilene settled down and other cow towns assumed the mantle of lawlessness and violence.

First came Baxter Springs and Coffeyville, then Newton, Wichita, and Great Bend. The most noto- rious of the Kansas cow towns was probably Dodge City. The town was estab- lished in the summer of 1872 as a center for the buffalo hide trade. The great cattle drives began to reach Dodge City in 1875, and the town quickly became the largest mar- ketplace in the entire Southwest. Hand in hand with this rapid growth came its wild, lawless rep- utation. Said to attract men who were "as fearless as a Bayard, unsavory as a skunk," Dodge was home to at least 16 saloons, which sold only whiskey made on the premises.

Even Dodge City's time passed however, and by 1885, when new depots for cattle shipment were being created by the railroad's ever westward progress, the wildest town of the West was tamed.

Abilene became the first rip-roaring cow town when the Union Pacific established a railhead there for cattle drives. Abilene's heyday spanned the years 1867–1871.

Morgan and Virgil Earp wounded and Billy Clanton and the McLaurys dead.

In the ensuing months, Virgil and Morgan were ambushed. Virgil was severely wounded in December 1881, and in the following March, Morgan was killed. Wyatt and Warren Earp, Doc Holliday, Sherman McMasters, and "Turkey Creek" Jack Johnson promptly set out in search of the killers. Within two days, they found Frank Stilwell in Tucson, exacting vengeance with some 30 shotgun and bullet wounds. Returning to Tombstone, the five avengers found another suspect, Florentino Cruz, in a nearby wood camp. He was executed with 10 or 12 shots.

After these killings, Holliday, along with Wyatt and Warren Earp, fled Arizona for Colorado, but Doc was arrested on old charges stemming from the stagecoach robbery and murder. Wyatt Earp appealed for assistance to his friend, Bat Masterson, who, despite his dislike for Holliday, helped foil efforts to extradite Doc to Arizona. As long as he remained in Colorado, Doc was safe from Arizona courts. He drank and gambled steadily and contracted pneumonia, becoming even more emaciated and gaunt in appearance.

Two years later, Holliday was down on his luck in Leadville, Colorado. He borrowed five dollars from a bartender named Billy Allen, who shortly after threatened to beat up the frail gambler. On August 19, 1884, Allen followed Doc into Hyman's saloon, but the 130-pound mankiller angrily whipped out his revolver and snapped off two shots. The second slug struck Allen in the arm and knocked him off his feet, but he scrambled outside while a barkeep grabbed Holliday's gunhand. As with other gunfights, Doc won a legal acquittal.

The encounter with Allen proved to be Doc Holliday's final duel. Weakened by tuberculosis and alcoholism, he took a stagecoach to the Colorado health resort at Glenwood Springs, where he died at the age of 35 on November 8, 1887. On his deathbed, he reflected on the irony of such a peaceful end, as he gasped out his last words, "This is funny."

Despite his efforts to go out in a blaze of gunfire, Doc died in a sanitarium in Glenwood Springs, Colorado (bottom).

BASS REEVES

1840?–1910

In 1877, famed abolitionist Frederick Douglass became the first African American to receive appointment as a United States marshal. Two years earlier, however, another ex-slave, Bass Reeves, pinned on a badge for Judge Isaac Parker. In doing so, Reeves was probably the first African American to hold a deputy U.S. marshal's commission west of the Mississippi. For the next three and a half decades, Deputy Marshal Reeves battled badmen in lawless Oklahoma.

Bass was born around 1840, one of seven slaves on a farm near Paris, Texas. He grew into a big, powerful man, measuring six feet two inches and weighing 200 pounds. At some point during the Civil War, he left slavery behind him, apparently serving as a Union soldier in Indian Territory. By the end of the war, he had become an excellent shot, and he had learned to speak the Creek language as well as several other Native American dialects. When

Bass, or Baz, Reeves was one of several African-American lawmen who worked for Judge Isaac Parker, whose jurisdiction was the notorious Indian Territory.

the war ended, Reeves married and settled on a farm near Van Buren, Arkansas, where he and his wife eventually reared ten children.

In 1875, Isaac Parker became a federal judge operating out of Fort Smith, Arkansas. To quell the rampant outlawry in the Indian Territory, he appointed 200 deputy marshals—including Bass Reeves. A deputy U.S. marshal was unsalaried, receiving only mileage and fees, but like other deputies, Reeves counted on reward money as a primary source of livelihood.

The Oklahoma Native Americans disliked white men. Reeves, who could communicate in their own language, was able to readily uncover information that was unavailable to white officers. He was also clever at disguises and undercover work, and he often returned to Fort Smith with his prison wagon packed with prisoners.

Oklahoma homesteader Harve Lovelady remembered Reeves as "the most feared U.S.

marshal that was ever heard of in that country." Lovelady also mentioned that several times Reeves killed his prisoners. "He didn't want to spend so much time in chasing down the man who resisted arrest so he would shoot him down in his tracks."

Such an incident was related by Nancy E. Pruitt, a settler in the Creek Nation. "One time [Reeves] went after two mean Negroes and knew when he left that if he didn't kill them, they would kill him, for it would be impossible to bring them back alive." When Reeves located the fugitives, he lulled them with a ruse, then shot them dead before they could draw on him. "That looks like a cold blooded murder to us now, but it was really quick thinking and bravery," recalled Pruitt.

Reeves armed himself with a Winchester, a double-barreled shotgun, and a brace of revolvers, which he wore butts forward for a readier draw while mounted. His proudest accomplishment as an officer was halting the depredations of Bob Dozier, a farmer who had turned into a thief, rustler, and murderer. Reeves located Dozier in the Cherokee Nation, but the outlaw tried to shoot his way to freedom. After a sharp exchange of gunfire, Reeves collapsed into the mud, feigning a mortal wound while tightly gripping his cocked six-gun. Dozier emerged from his cover and walked toward Reeves, who suddenly sprang back to life and ordered the outlaw to surrender. Dozier tried to bring up his gun, but Reeves fired first, killing the fugitive with a bullet in the neck.

Dauntless in pursuit of criminals, Reeves proved cool and brave under fire. In 1884, while in pursuit of outlaw Jim Webb, Reeves rode into gunfire from the wanted man's Winchester rifle. The first shot clipped his saddle horn, the second tore a button off his coat, and the third round cut his bridle reins. Continuing to fire, Webb charged on foot, but Reeves unlimbered his own Winchester and pumped two bullets into the outlaw's chest.

Perhaps the most unusual entanglement in Reeves's career occurred a few months after he vanquished Webb. Reeves shot and killed his black cook, William Leach, after Leach threw hot grease onto Bass's dog. The lawman was eventually tried for murder, but he was acquitted.

Late in his career, Bass stated that he had killed 14 men. Not all of these executions can be substantiated, but without question, Reeves was an extremely competent and dangerous officer. His devotion to duty was tested when one of his sons, Benjamin, murdered his wife during a rage and then fled arrest. Reeves pursued and brought back Benjamin, who later earned a pardon and became a barber in Muskogee.

When Oklahoma became a state in 1907, federal jurisdiction gave way to local courts, and almost all of the deputy marshals relinquished their commissions. Reeves had served as a deputy marshal for more than 30 years. For two years after that, he walked a beat as a Muskogee policeman. Age forced him to use a cane, but he also carried a pistol on his hip and another in a shoulder holster. There was no crime on his beat.

At last failing health forced him to turn in his badge, and Bass Reeves died quietly on January 12, 1910. Hundreds of admirers and friends—black, white, and Native American—attended the funeral in tribute to a brave and dutiful man.

BILL TILGHMAN

1854–1924

Bill Tilghman enjoyed the longest and most varied career of any peace officer in the West. Tilghman's Wild West adventures began almost as soon as he was born on July 4, 1854. Bill was but a few weeks old when his head was grazed by an arrow during a Sioux attack.

Raised on the Kansas farm of his parents, he became an excellent shot. Taking advantage of his skill, he left home when he was 16 to hunt buffalo, killing nearly 12,000 beasts during the next five years. He also poisoned coyotes, wolves, and bobcats for bounties on their pelts, usually selling his harvest in Dodge City. Tilghman married in 1878 and began ranching near Dodge, but his place was burned during the large-scale Cheyenne uprising led by Chief Dull Knife. Moving into town, Tilghman served an occasional stint as a deputy, worked on railroad construction jobs to support his growing family, dabbled at ranching once again, and operated two Dodge City saloons.

In 1884, Tilghman's law enforcement career began when he was appointed city marshal of Dodge. During the next two years, Marshal Tilghman served Dodge efficiently. He also held a concurrent commission as a Ford County deputy sheriff, utilizing his intimate knowledge of the countryside to hunt down a succession of lawbreakers.

A still youthful Bill Tilghman belied his 58 years when he served as Oklahoma City's police chief in 1912.

Tilghman's parents are shown on the porch of the family home in Dodge City, with his brother Frank standing to the left. The girls are Tilghman's nieces.

From 1887 through 1888, Kansas was plagued by the County Seat Wars, in which towns fought each other for the privilege of being the county seat. Riots, gunfights, and raids ensued as hired guns battled each other on behalf of town fathers. Tilghman became involved in two violent county seat wars. He briefly served as a deputy sheriff at Farmer City, a hamlet between Leoti and Coronado, two towns that were rivals for the county seat. An exceptionally violent shoot-out had recently occurred in the area, and hard feelings were rampant among citizens of all three communities.

Later, Tilghman accepted $1,000 and another deputy sheriff's commission to lead the faction representing Ingalls, Kansas, against Cimarron in the war over the Gray County seat. On January 14, 1889, Tilghman and several other gunmen piled into a wagon. A little before noon, they arrived in Cimarron with the intention of hijacking the county seal and archives. Tilghman led his men into the courthouse, but local citizens discovered the invaders and opened fire.

Badly outnumbered, the men from Ingalls fired back and scrambled to escape. Shooting on the run, Tilghman tumbled into an irrigation canal and sprained an ankle. He was helped into the wagon, and the vehicle rattled away toward Ingalls. Four Ingalls men were trapped inside the courthouse, and after a brief siege, they surrendered, to be released later. Two Ingalls men were hit during the shoot-out, and four Cimarron citizens were wounded, one mortally. The governor of Kansas eventually called out the state militia, and the presence of the soldiers prevented further conflict.

Attracted to the spectacular Cherokee Strip land rush in 1889, Tilghman built a home in Guthrie and opened a saloon. Two years later, he sold his Guthrie property to join another Oklahoma land run. He established a homestead near Chandler and named his little horse ranch the Bell Cow. Shortly thereafter, he accepted a post as deputy U.S. marshal, and in 1893, he was assigned to supervise Perry, Oklahoma, following the last great land rush. During this period, Tilghman began working closely with two other Oklahoma officers, Heck Thomas and Chris Madsen, and this formidable trio of lawmen became known as the Three Guardsmen.

The lawless element in Perry became so threatening that city fathers of the boom-town hired Tilghman and Thomas as city marshal and assistant marshal, respectively. Marshal Tilghman, Deputy Thomas, and their police force engaged in a flurry of arrests, which rapidly tamed Perry. Early in 1894, U.S. Marshal E. V. Nix ordered the Three Guardsmen to concentrate on bringing in Bill Doolin and his gang.

Doolin's gang separated, but the lawmen arrested the gang's two teenage message carriers, Annie McDoulett and Jennie Metcalf—better known as Cattle Annie and Little Britches. On September 6, 1895, Tilghman cornered one of the Doolin gang, Little Dick Raidler, at a hideout. Raidler tried to flee, unlimbering his revolver and firing on the run, but Tilghman blasted him off his feet with a shotgun. Although riddled with six buckshot, Raidler survived to go to prison. Tilghman collected a $1,000 reward. With the money, Tilghman journeyed to Kentucky and bought two thoroughbreds, Chant, which won the Kentucky Derby in 1894, and Ceverton, victor in the Oakwood Classic. With these two splendid stallions, Tilghman operated a stud service.

Tilghman's most famous exploit as a law officer was his single-handed capture of Bill Doolin at an Arkansas hot springs resort.

Deputy U.S. Marshal Tilghman (left) poses with C. F. Colcord, a fellow deputy marshal, after being assigned to Perry, Oklahoma.

THE THREE GUARDSMEN

By the 1890s, the Old West had all but disappeared. Towns and cities were well established, range lands were largely fenced in, statehood was all the rage, and law and order had come to reign—except in the Oklahoma Territory. Formerly the Indian Territory, this area had only recently been opened for American settlers, and for the last decade of the 19th century, much of it remained as wild and wide open as the West had ever been.

A trio of U.S. marshals led the effort to bring order to this last frontier. Known as a crack shot with a rifle, Bill Tilghman had proven himself in the

Chris Madsen fought with Italian rebel Garibaldi.

streets of Dodge City, where he had served as marshal. Heck Thomas had been a courier in the Confederate Army as a boy, and he worked as a private detective before coming to Oklahoma in 1893. Chris Madsen, a Scandinavian, had seen military service under three different flags in earlier years, first in Italy, then as a member of the French Foreign Legion, and finally with the U.S. Cavalry. Working together to patrol the Oklahoma Territory, they came to be known as the Three Guardsmen.

While the Guardsmen would bring down a great many criminals in the 1890s, their most bitter and bloody quarry was the Doolin Gang. Led by Bill

Doolin, the gang included such dedicated criminals as Dan "Dynamite Dick" Clifton, "Arkansas Tom" Jones, George "Bitter Creek" Newcomb, "Tulsa Jack" Blake, and George "Red Buck" Weightman. Working from bases in the unsettled Oklahoma area,

Henry Andrew "Heck" Thomas was renown among outlaws as a man to avoid.

the outlaws targeted banks and trains throughout Kansas, Missouri, and Arkansas. The Guardsmen and other law officers hounded the Doolin Gang for years, following their trail of crimes, tracking them to various hideouts, and thinning their ranks in a number of bloody shoot-outs.

In the end, the Doolin Gang and most of the region's other badmen were brought to heel, and Oklahoma was brought into the Union. As the 19th century closed, the lawlessness that took its last refuge in the Oklahoma Territory was subdued, largely through the efforts of the West's last great law officers, the Three Guardsmen.

Troubled by chronic rheumatism and old wounds, Doolin sought relief at Eureka Springs, where Tilghman found him taking the waters and reading a newspaper on January 15, 1896. Tilghman got the drop on the outlaw and promptly took him by train to Guthrie. The capture of Doolin had a dime-novel ending. Tilghman's $5,000 reward vanished on July 5, 1896, when Doolin led an escape from the Guthrie jail. The following August 24, Heck Thomas located Doolin in Arkansas and killed him when he resisted arrest.

In 1897, Tilghman's wife, wracked by increasing physical and mental problems, filed for a divorce. Not long after the couple were divorced, she died. Bill served as the sheriff of Lincoln County in 1900, then moved his children to a two-story brick house in Chandler near the courthouse. Sheriff Tilghman won re-election in 1902, and the next year shortly after his 49th birthday, he married a 22-year-old schoolmarm, Zoe Agnes Stratton. The couple honeymooned in Kansas City, and Zoe learned that "Bill habitually slept with a loaded .45 under his pillow." Undaunted by his bedroom hardware, Zoe bore him three sons.

In 1908, Tilghman helped to make the film *The Great Bank Robbery*, persuading Heck Thomas, Chris Madsen, Chief Quanah Parker, and former outlaw Al Jennings to appear with him in the one-reeler. Two more one-reelers followed before the year ended.

Though Tilghman was elected to the State Senate in 1910, the next year he accepted appointment as police chief of Oklahoma City, now the state capital and a center of bootlegging, prostitution, and gambling. Selling his stud farm and resigning his Senate seat, Tilghman moved his family to Oklahoma City, then commenced a series of raids and other activi-ties to curtail lawlessness. He resigned in 1913, and for years, he tried unsuccessfully to attain an appointment as U.S. marshal.

In 1924, at age 70, Tilghman answered another call to duty at Cromwell, an oil boomtown plagued by crime. Chris Madsen advised his old friend not to take the assignment. "Better to die in a gunfight than in bed someday like a woman," shrugged Bill, adding, "I should have things straightened out in a month or so."

Tilghman made impressive progress, but on the night of November 1, a drunken prohibition agent named Wiley Lynn fired a shot on the street. Despite his age, Tilghman slammed Lynn against a wall and jammed his gun into Wiley's ribs. Lynn surrendered his pistol, and Tilghman released him. Lynn suddenly pulled another weapon and pumped two bullets beneath Tilghman's heart. The last great western lawman collapsed and died within minutes.

Incredibly, a jury acquitted Lynn. Eight years later, the prohibition agent became involved in another scrap, shot three men, and was fatally wounded by four bullets. Zoe Tilghman observed, "No jury on earth can acquit him now."

When Tilghman brought outlaw Bill Doolin in to Guthrie, citizens cheered Doolin. Tilghman never understood the general public's admiration for outlaws.

PAT GARRETT

1850–1908

When he triggered a bullet into the heart of Billy the Kid on the night of July 14, 1881, Pat Garrett won a permanent niche in the front rank of frontier lawmen. This spectacular success, however, was marred by unwanted but persistent criticism of the manner of the shooting, and Garrett's life went downhill after this legendary event in western history.

Born in 1850 in Alabama, Patrick Floyd Garrett was raised on a large Louisiana plantation. After the Civil War, his parents died, and the lanky teenager went west in 1869, spending the next several years as a Texas cowboy and buffalo hunter.

At a buffalo camp near Fort Griffin, Texas, in November 1876, Garrett made a remark that enraged a skinner named Joe Briscoe. Briscoe charged Pat with fists flying, but the six-foot-four Garrett quickly bested his smaller opponent. Furious at being beaten, Briscoe broke away and seized an ax, then charged Garrett again. Pat grabbed his Winchester and fired a slug into Briscoe's chest. Briscoe lasted less than half an hour, but just before dying, he reduced Garrett to tears by asking, "Won't you come over here and forgive me."

Garrett drifted to Fort Sumner, New Mexico, where he married in 1879. His teenaged bride died in premature childbirth, but Pat quickly remarried and began raising a large family.

By 1880, the Lincoln County War had been raging for two years. Garrett was elected county sheriff to restore order in general and to halt the crime spree of Billy the Kid in particular. The Kid was a daring killer and horse thief with many friends who helped him elude capture, but Sheriff Garrett launched a systematic, relentless manhunt.

After one series of arrests in December 1880, a belligerent hardcase named Mariano Leiva loudly proclaimed that " . . . even that damned Pat Garrett can't take me." Garrett slapped Leiva off a porch into the dusty street. Leiva palmed his revolver and snapped off a wild shot. Garrett pulled his .45 and fired twice, shattering Leiva's left shoulder blade.

A few days later, Garrett led a posse into Fort Sumner, launching an ambush when the Kid's gang rode in after dark. In the commotion that followed, Tom O'Folliard was mortally wounded, but the Kid and four other gang members galloped away into the darkness. Within four days, Garrett tracked the fugitives to a stone cabin at Stinking Springs. At dawn on December 23, 1880, Garrett and

With "journalist" Ashmun Upson, Pat Garrett penned *An Authentic Life of Billy the Kid.*

his men opened fire on Charlie Bowdre, who died on Pat's bedroll. The surviving outlaws surrendered that afternoon, and the Kid was quickly tried and sentenced to hang.

The Kid awaited execution in Lincoln. When Garrett was out of town on April 28, 1881, the Kid killed two guards and escaped. Garrett promptly resumed the manhunt, and on the night of July 14, he led two deputies into Fort Sumner. Leaving his men outside, Pat slipped into the bedroom of Pete Maxwell to ask the whereabouts of the Kid.

At that point, the Kid walked into the unlighted room. He had been with his Fort Sumner sweetheart and, deciding to eat a steak, had come to ask Maxwell for a key to the meat house. Hatless and in his stocking feet, the Kid was carrying a butcher knife but had a revolver stuck in his waistband. Passing the deputies, he pulled his gun and entered Maxwell's bedroom asking, *"Quien es? Quien es?"*

After Maxwell identified the Kid, Garrett whipped out his six-gun and pumped a bullet into his chest, killing him instantly. There was immediate criticism of the sheriff for shooting the Kid without warning and from the darkness. Garrett was forced to hire a lawyer to collect the reward money posted for the Kid. When election time rolled around, he was not even nominated for re-election to his post.

Garrett responded to his critics with a model statement of the deadly pragmatism of effective frontier peace officers. "I, at no time, contemplated taking any chances [with Billy the Kid] which I could avoid with caution or cunning. The only circumstances under which we could have met on equal terms, would have been accidental, and to which I would have been an unwilling party."

In the ensuing years, Garrett owned or managed several ranches, and he unsuccessfully tried to promote irrigation in the Pecos Valley. From 1884–1885, he headed a special group of Home Rangers against rustlers in the Texas Panhandle. In 1896, he returned to New Mexico as a territorial detective in charge of a search for the murderers of Judge Albert J. Fountain and his young son. Despite vigorous efforts and a wild shoot-out with suspects, the killers were never brought to justice.

Garrett (left) poses with John W. Poe (right) and James Brent (center). All served as sheriff of Lincoln County.

Finally moving his family to a ranch east of Las Cruces, Garrett was embroiled in a feud with a neighbor and was murdered on February 29, 1908.

TOM HORN

1860—1903

"Killing is my specialty. I look at it as a business proposition, and I think I have a corner on the market."

The lethal businessman who made this chilling statement was Tom Horn, one of the most mysterious and fascinating characters of the Old West. Horn possessed many of the most admirable traits of the traditional westerner. Repeatedly, he exhibited raw courage, tireless stamina, and unwavering loyalty. A man with a powerful physique, he was a superb horseman, a matchless roper, and a crack shot. But these attributes were offset by an inclination to drink, brag—and commit cold-blooded murder.

Born on November 21, 1860, in Memphis, Missouri, Tom was reared on the family farm. He often avoided farm work and school to roam the woods with a rifle and dog. Following a severe whipping by his father, the rebellious 14-year-old ran away from home to head to the West.

Working as a teamster, the strapping youngster made his way to Santa Fe, where

The life and times of shootist Tom Horn epitomize the image of the hired gun.

he learned to speak Spanish. He spent enough time on frontier ranches to master the cowboy skills, but by the early 1880s, he had signed on with the army as a packer in Arizona. His fluency in Spanish made him useful as an interpreter with the Apache who spoke Spanish, and he worked under the legendary scout Al Sieber.

In his famous but unreliable autobiography, Horn made exaggerated claims about his activities as an army scout during the Apache campaigns. His presence with the relentless General George Crook, however, testifies to his endurance and courage. In 1885, Captain Emmett Crawford selected Horn to lead the scouts in a pursuit of Geronimo. Horn was present at Geronimo's surrender in 1886 but was later discharged by the military during a sharp reduction of the scouting force.

In 1890, Horn joined the Pinkerton Detective Agency, working out of the Denver office. He left the Pinkertons four years later, declaring that he "never did like the work." That same year, he was hired by the Swan Land and Cattle Company as a range rider, or stock detective, to help eliminate rustling.

During this period, rustlers were often freed by sympathetic juries. This failure of the legal system irked the powerful cattle barons, who turned to hired guns to hunt down and kill cattle thieves. For the next several years, Horn worked for big Wyoming ranches, prowling the ranges to eradicate rustling. Working closely with such ranchers as John Coble, who ran the Iron Mountain Cattle Company northwest of Cheyenne, Tom Horn acquired a reputation for gunning down rustlers who refused to leave the country.

Horn's reputation was built on such episodes as the killings of William Lewis and Fred Powell. Lewis, who held a 160-acre homestead near the Iron Mountain ranch, bragged about stealing Iron Mountain cattle. He received a warning to pull out of the territory, but he did not heed it—at least not in time. In August 1895, his corpse was found riddled with three bullets fired from a range of 300 yards. Powell, a known confederate of Lewis, worked a homestead ten miles away. Defiantly, Powell invited cowboys from the nearby KYT Ranch to come to a supper consisting of their own beef. Shortly thereafter, a large rider shot Powell to death. Horn, who stood over six feet and weighed more than 200 pounds, was the obvious suspect in both killings, but everyone was wise enough not to accuse him publicly.

When not investigating stock thefts, Horn worked cattle on the ranches that employed him. He always carried a 40-foot lariat and liked to show off his roping skills. Horn usually packed a revolver along with a rifle, and he readily demonstrated his marksmanship.

A cowboy for the Swan Land and Cattle Company was sometimes asked to toss tin cans in the air for Horn, who would drill them twice with revolver bullets before the can would strike the ground. Horn's two primary enjoyments were participating in rodeos and drinking in a good saloon in Cheyenne, Laramie, or Denver. He drank heavily whenever in town, and when he was drunk he talked boastfully, often about his murders and gunfights. Much of this drunken boasting fell into the category of classic frontier exaggeration, but his murderous braggadocio doubtless added to his increasingly sinister reputation.

Horn roamed through much of Wyoming and Colorado, "working the pastures," as he called it. Though the range was mostly fenced, he would still be out for a week or two at a time, riding across the vast holdings of his employers. He also checked the smaller pastures belonging to the nesters who were likely to brand mavericks or rustle branded cattle.

Horn interrupted his career as a range rider during the Spanish-American War, serving in Cuba as a chief mule packer. When he returned to Wyoming, he was welcomed back by the big ranchers, who had become increasingly pressured by nesters and sheepmen. In 1900, he ventured into Brown's Park, a notorious haunt of outlaws. Yet, even in outlaw country, Horn proved to be a formidable figure, later bragging that "I stopped cow stealing there in one summer."

By 1901, Horn was once again working for John Coble at Coble's ranch north of Laramie. It seems Coble and the other large cattlemen were thoroughly disgusted with Kels Nickell. Nickell was a small cattle rancher who was suspected of having ob-

RANGE WARS

As soon as the open range was exhausted in the American West, the stage was set for range wars. When one rancher strung

During a range war in Custer County, Nebraska, circa 1885, a group of masked riders prepare to cut barbed wire on the Brighten Ranch.

wire that separated his neighbor's cattle from water, hostilities usually followed, often resulting in death and destruction on both sides.

Another type of range war occurred because of the intense hatred that cattlemen held for sheep and their owners. Sheep ruined the range, according to the cattle ranchers, and shouldn't be allowed anywhere near cows. Not so, replied the sheepherders, who maintained that their stock had as much right to graze the vast grasslands of the West as anybody.

The Pleasant Valley War of the 1880s became an example of the growing animosity between cattlemen and sheep owners. Although ill feelings had existed between the Tewksbury and Graham families for several years, it was the introduction of sheep to the Arizona range by the Tewksburys that resulted in several murders by both groups. On September 4, 1887, at Holbrook, Arizona, in one of the most famous gunfights in history, Sheriff Commodore Perry Owens singlehandedly slew several Graham employees accused of killing John Tewksbury and a friend. In 1892, Tewksbury's brother was convicted of killing one of the Graham brothers.

Wyoming's Johnson County War had its beginnings in 1892. Frustrated members of the Wyoming Stock Growers' Association hired several "range detectives" to put a halt to rustling. Calling themselves the Regulators, the detectives invaded Johnson County and killed two suspected rustlers, Nate Champion and Nick Ray, in a dramatic 12-hour shootout. Concerned neighbors formed a 200-man posse and surrounded the Regulators at a ranch near the town of Buffalo. The U.S. Cavalry rescued the Regulators and escorted them to Cheyenne, where they stood trial. None of the Regulators were ever prosecuted for any crimes, and the dispute eventually subsided. In the long term, the Johnson County War hurt the local economy for several years and greatly affected the state's political makeup.

tained his herd through rustling. He then compounded the tension by switching to sheep. Another small rancher, James Miller, and his sons had been feuding with Nickell for years. On July 18, 14-year-old Willie Nickell, clad in his father's hat and coat as protection against a rainstorm, was murdered at a fence gate by a rifleman from a distance of 300 yards.

At first it was thought that Willie's murder was the result of the feud, and the Millers were subsequently questioned. Seventeen days later, Kels was wounded by a fusillade from concealed riflemen. Shortly thereafter, four riders killed about 75 sheep pastured by Nickell. The unfortunate rancher eventually sold his spread and moved away. Although blame might rest with the Millers, public suspicion began to center on the notorious Tom Horn.

Though attention surrounding the case had begun to fade away, detective Joe LeFors refused to give up the investigation. He laboriously deceived Horn into thinking his services as an assassin were needed by a Montana rancher. Pretending to be a middleman, LeFors lured Horn into an incriminating conversation, with a deputy sheriff and a court reporter listening from concealment. The resulting "confession" would not be admitted in a modern court, but the controversial transcript resulted in his arrest. Horn later insisted he was guilty only of drunken boasting.

Although the cattle barons provided Horn with an expensive legal team, Horn's lawyers were badly outdueled by the prosecution during the spectacular two-week trial in October 1902. Horn was declared guilty and sentenced to hang; all legal appeals were denied. On August 9, 1902, Horn escaped from jail, but he was quickly caught and beaten into submission. To the end, the famed shootist denied that he had killed Willie Nickell.

In Cheyenne, on November 23, 1903, he ate a hearty breakfast, smoked a final cigar, and met his end impressively. Even if Horn had been innocent of the murder of Willie Nickell, there was a general certainty that he had gunned down four other men. There were also the rumors that he had slain countless others. Many people felt that Horn was a throwback to a more primitive and lawless era and that the West was well rid of an old-fashioned hired killer.

A jury deliberated only five hours before finding Tom Horn guilty of the murder of Willie Nickell.

BUFFALO
BILL CODY

1846—1917

More than any single historical figure, Buffalo Bill Cody has stood as the epitome of the Old American West. Eighty years after his death, his image remains indelible—a tall, handsome man dressed in fringed and beaded buckskins, gauntlets, and hip-high boots, with shoulder-length hair flowing from his wide-brimmed sombrero as he sat on a snow-white horse.

Between 1870 and the World War I era, an estimated 1,700 dime novels provided an eager public with lurid, totally fabricated tales of Buffalo Bill's exploits. These, together with Cody's spectacular record as an internationally beloved showman, overshadowed his genuine accomplishments as a frontiersman, Pony Express rider, scout, Indian fighter—and Indian friend. This triumph of myth over reality has resulted in a layer of varnish so thick that it must be scratched deeply to see what lies beneath it.

Born near Leclaire, Iowa, on February 26, 1846, William Frederick was the third of eight children of Isaac and Mary Ann Laycock Cody. Young Billy continued his country school education when the family moved to Kansas in

Bill Cody was quite conscious of the myth surrounding his life and readily embellished it through tall tales and grand posturing.

1854. Among the first families to settle in the newly opened territory, the Codys homesteaded in the Salt Creek Valley, a few miles east of Fort Leavenworth.

Within months of their settlement in Kansas, Isaac Cody was the victim of a violent incident that shaped the future of his oldest son. A religious man and an outspoken abolitionist in a pro-slavery district, Isaac was stabbed in the chest in a political argument. He survived the attack, but his health was broken. He died in 1857. Mary Ann took in boarders to make ends meet and took her son, then age 11, to Leavenworth to find him a job.

Billy landed work as a messenger for Russell, Majors and Waddell, the newly established but already important freight company. In his brief association with the outfit, young Cody had the first of a lifetime of adventures. He was among the horseback messengers who took instructions and orders from wagon to wagon when Russell, Majors and Waddell shipped supplies to the army in its expedition to Utah in 1857 to quell the Mormon rebellion. Brigham Young's troops attacked the caravan in Wyoming and captured many of its wagons.

In the three years that followed, Cody made several freighting trips to Forts Kearny and Laramie and learned the rudiments of mining and trapping. At age 15, he returned briefly to the Leavenworth freight company's employment for a stint as a Pony Express rider on the 116-mile run between Red

Buttes on the North Platte River and the Sweetwater in Nebraska.

In 1861, Cody joined a band of jayhawkers—Union guerrillas fighting Confederate sympathizers. The group stole horses from secessionists in Missouri and drove them back across the Kansas line. The next year, he worked as a scout for the 9th Kansas Volunteers on the Santa Fe Trail in Comanche-Kiowa country, and in 1863, he worked as a teamster. While en route to Denver, he received word of his mother's grave illness. He returned to Leavenworth in time to be at her bedside when she died that November. Thereafter, he credited Mary Ann Cody as guiding the course of his life.

While waiting to be mustered out of the army in St. Louis, he met Louisa Maude Frederici, three years his senior. After his discharge, Cody found work with Ben Holliday's Overland Stagecoach Line in Kansas, but he returned to St. Louis in the spring of 1866 and married Louisa. The marriage endured for 50 years, until Cody's death, despite being somewhat of a mismatch. The prim, temperamental, and jealous Lulu—as Cody called her— disliked the West, her husband's friends, his fame, and above all his inability to stay put long enough to have a stable family life. For his part, Will—as Louisa called him—remained a gregarious, free-spending, hard-drinking, philandering nomad, who was unwilling to conform to Louisa's homebody existence.

Cody made one half-hearted attempt at domesticity. He and Louisa returned to the

Perhaps no other western figure was the subject of more dime novels than Cody.

Salt Creek Valley area soon after their wedding and opened a hotel, the Golden Rule House. Yet this mundane existence quickly debilitated Cody. "It proved too tame employment for me," he later wrote, "and again I sighed for the plains." Despite a promise made to his wife, who soon returned to St. Louis, the restless adventurer headed west.

Cody received his celebrated moniker, Buffalo Bill, around 1867–1868 when he began hunting buffalo for the eastern division of the Union Pacific Railroad, later the Kansas Pacific. A Hays City company, the Goddard Brothers, held the contract to feed the U.P.'s track gangs. Cody, who had a well-known skill with his .50 caliber Springfield breechloader, was hired at the handsome salary of $500 a month to supply the meat. He later estimated that he killed 4,280 buffalo in the 18 months at this job.

By July 1868, Buffalo Bill Cody was employed once again as a scout for the United States Army. In one daring exploit, he rode 65 miles from Fort Larned to Fort Hays to deliver to General Philip Sheridan news of the huge camp of Comanche and Kiowa that had sprung up near Larned. Sheridan then sent the scout on a 95-mile journey to Fort Dodge, carrying vital dispatches over a trail on which several other couriers had been killed. Cody made the trip unscathed, took a brief nap, and climbed back in the saddle. He rode into Larned, rested, and then returned to Hays—riding 350 miles through hostile country in under 60 hours. Sheridan, a man who was never easily impressed, called Cody's ride "an exhibition of endurance and courage" and appointed him chief of scouts for the 5th Cavalry at Fort Hays.

In the fall of 1868, the 5th fell to the command of Major General Eugene A. Carr and moved to Fort McPherson in central Kansas. There Cody had a fateful encounter with a 46-year-old New York writer named Edward Zane Carroll Judson. An author of dime novels and sensational magazine serials, Judson is best known by his penname, Ned Buntline.

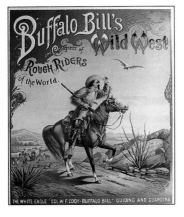

Cody's real-life exploits as a young man became the basis for some of the acts in Buffalo Bill's Wild West show. Other acts were based on other famous western events.

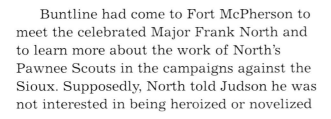

Buntline had come to Fort McPherson to meet the celebrated Major Frank North and to learn more about the work of North's Pawnee Scouts in the campaigns against the Sioux. Supposedly, North told Judson he was not interested in being heroized or novelized

and pointed to Cody, sleeping under a nearby wagon, saying, "There's the man you're looking for." Judson spent some time with Cody and returned home to write the first in a series of hair-raising adventures about his new-found hero, *Buffalo Bill, King of the Border Men*.

Between scouting assignments for the army, Cody served as a guide for various hunting expeditions, including a memorable one arranged for the Grand Duke Alexis, son of Czar Alexander II of Russia. This expedition also included General Sheridan, Lieutenant Colonel George A. Custer, and Spotted Tail, chief of the Brulé Sioux, who gathered 100 of his warriors to put on a war dance for the visiting nobleman.

On May 22, 1872, Cody was awarded the Congressional Medal of Honor for his gallantry as an army scout. The Medal was revoked in 1917, along with 910 others, in a purging of the award and retroactive tightening of the rules. Cody was declared to have been a civilian and therefore ineligible for the Medal. In 1989, 72 years after his death, the rules were rewritten once again, and the Medal was restored to him.

Cody journeyed east during that eventful year of 1872 with fellow scout J. B. "Texas Jack" Omohundro after repeated appeals from Buntline. The prolific writer wanted them to appear in his melodrama, *The Scouts of the Prairies*. The play opened in Chicago's Nixon

NED
BUNTLINE

Ned Buntline, the king of the dime novelists, was born Edward Zane Carroll Judson in New York in 1823. After serving at sea for a few years, Buntline participated in the Second Seminole War before choosing a literary career at age 21. A born prevaricator and ne'er-do-well, he had a knack for spinning entertaining yarns around just a handful of facts.

Buntline's first writing effort was *Ned Buntline's Magazine*, published for only two issues in New York City. Next, he founded the *Western Literary Journal and Monthly Review*. In order to save the magazine from failure, Buntline decided to set his sights toward the South for both contributions and subscriptions. He reorganized the magazine and renamed it *The South-Western Literary Journal and Monthly Review*. Unfortunately, it did little better than his earlier efforts.

A prolific writer, Buntline is best-known for his wild yarns about Buffalo Bill Cody.

Buntline's life sometimes resembled the melodrama he was so good at fabricating. While promoting his fledgling magazine in Nashville, Buntline became involved with a married woman. The liaison caused quite a stir among Nashville society. After a preacher had observed the pair talking in a local cemetery, the woman's husband tracked Buntline down and shot at him several times. He missed, but Buntline did not. When a lynch mob attempted to capture the rakish novelist from authorities, he jumped out of the third story window of the City Hotel. He was recaptured and actually hanged on Nashville's Public Square, but friends were able to rescue him before the hangman's knot did its job. Finally, when a grand jury heard his plea of self-defense, he was freed. Buntline left Nashville immediately, never to return.

Untouched by his brush with death, Buntline returned east to continue his literary career. He gradually built his reputation and improved his income, which at $20,000 per year made him the highest-paid writer in the United States.

For many years, it was assumed that Ned commissioned the Colt's firearm factory to customize several 1873 Single Action Army revolvers to carry a 12-inch barrel and be fitted with a detachable walnut stock that converted the pistol into a rifle.

These mementos, called Buntline Specials, were supposedly given to several eminent lawmen, including Wyatt Earp, Bat Masterson, and Bill Tilghman. Recent research, however, has disproved parts of this story, yet the gun remains a major part of the lore and legend of Buntline.

Buntline was a prodigious writer, and before he died in New York in 1886, he wrote several hundred books, pamphlets, articles, and stories under both his own name and a variety of pseudonyms.

Amphitheater on December 17 to a packed house. The Chicago *Times* reported, "Such a combination of incongruous dialogue, execrable acting . . . scalping, blood and thunder, is not likely to be vouchsafed to a city for a second time—not even Chicago." But the participation of the *real* Buffalo Bill and Texas Jack gave the ludicrous play a semblance of authenticity, and audiences loved it. By the time the traveling melodrama's first season ended in New York, Cody had earned $6,000. He and Omohundro argued with Buntline over their earnings and soon parted company with the writer.

Looking out of place in a Venetian gondola, Buffalo Bill and a few of his cast members catch the sights while in Europe in 1890.

The cast of the retitled *The Scouts of the Plains* continued to perform the melodrama in the East and Midwest for several years, with a new manager. At the end of each season, Cody would rejoin Louisa and their growing family—daughters Arta and Orra and son Kit—in St. Louis and then report in at Fort McPherson for army duties. In the fall, he would gather with the rest of the cast to resume theatrics.

In the summer of 1876, Cody cut his theatrical season short and announced to his audiences that he was returning west to fight Indians once again. He rejoined the 5th Cavalry in Cheyenne, where he served under Major General Wesley Merritt.

In July, about 800 Cheyenne fled the Red Cloud Agency at Fort Robinson in northwest Nebraska. Merritt's command located the renegades about 30 miles from the agency on Hat Creek, strung out along a wide front. With Merritt's permission, Cody and eight troopers and scouts rode out to intersect one band of Cheyenne as they advanced on an army wagon train. In the skirmish that ensued, Cody fought with the Cheyenne chief Yellow Hair (often mistakenly called Yellow Hand). The experienced scout shot the chief's pony only to have his own horse stumble. Cody escaped a bullet that just missed him, returned the fire, and shot the Cheyenne through the head. He took Yellow Hair's scalp, and this grisly scene was depicted on countless garish posters, playbills, books, and magazines. It was even written into a five-act melodrama. The scalp and the Cheyenne chief's warbonnet became standard props in Cody's performances thereafter.

For the most part, the service with Merritt marked Cody's last official duty with the army. After two decades as a teamster, scout, buffalo hunter, and Indian fighter, he turned full-time to a career as showman, a calling he pursued the last 40 years of his life.

The open-air-extravaganza that became the internationally renowned Buffalo Bill's Wild West debuted at an Independence Day celebration in North Platte, Nebraska, on July 4, 1882. The show was officially launched in Omaha the following May, then moved eastward to Boston, growing in popularity with each performance.

Over its 25-year run, Buffalo Bill's Wild West underwent many script changes as the show traveled the United States and Europe, but certain features remained standard. The show almost always featured a Pony Express race, the Deadwood Stage attacked by bandits, Custer's last fight, the Battle of Summit Springs, Native American attacks on covered wagons, and a reenactment of the Yellow Hair duel. Also included were trick riding and roping, and appearances by frontier notables. The *pièce de résistance* was always Buffalo Bill himself. A grand figure, Cody would wave his wide-brimmed hat, bow to the audience, and race his snow-white horse around the ring.

Because of financial difficulty, Cody merged his Wild West show with a similar show owned by Gordon W. "Pawnee Bill" Lillie in 1908. The Buffalo Bill Wild West & Pawnee Bill Great Far East Show collapsed in Denver in 1913. Buffalo Bill became associated with the Sells-Floto circus and then with 101 Ranch Wild West Show, performing regularly up to two months before his death. Despite the many years of success and acclaim, Cody was not a wealthy man. He had gone through several fortunes, making bad investments, trusting too many people.

Near the end, he was also not a healthy man. Before each show, a member of the cast had to help the old man onto his horse. He would sit slumped in the saddle until the curtain parted. Then, as his assistant said, "Ready, Colonel," Cody would ride out into the arena, standing tall in the saddle with his back straight and chin held high. He would doff his white Stetson hat to the cheering audience and then gracefully bow just as he had done in the old days.

Yet Cody's lack of financial acumen, ill health, and hard times ultimately matter very little. As the champion purveyor of western lore and legend, he perpetuated the spirit of the Wild West just as his image captured the essence of the mythic frontier hero. For millions of people who never set foot west of the Mississippi, he provided the excitement and adventure of a time and place that had passed all too quickly. Buffalo Bill Cody died on January 10, 1917, and was buried on Lookout Mountain above Denver.

A crowd of 18,000 attended his funeral.

Though not a wealthy man when he died, Cody was beloved around the world as witnessed by the 18,000 mourners at his funeral.

ROY BEAN

1827?–1903

In 1892, ten years after Roy Bean had set up his saloon-courtroom in Langtry, Texas, he received a letter from his putative boss, Governor James Hogg. Hogg was concerned that Judge Bean had not been turning over to the state a share of the fees and fines he collected. Bean's response to the Texas chief executive formed, in a dozen words, the sum of his entire professional philosophy: "Dear Governor: You run things up in Austin and I'll run them down here. Yours truly, Roy Bean."

For two decades, Bean did just that. From his headquarters at Langtry, a speck on the map a few miles west of where the Pecos River empties into the Rio Grande, he was the law in a vast and trackless territory that extended westward 350 miles to El Paso.

The Texas Rangers, the only other law in Bean's domain, loved him for the lightning justice he meted out. State officials were dubious of him because he was a mere justice of the peace, yet he was forever superceding his authority. And miscreants of every stripe—from simple drunks to killers—feared the bang of his six-shooter gavel that often dispensed unpredictable verdicts and capricious punishments.

One other feature of Bean's career is that he kept few records. He wrote no journal or memoir, scribbling only a handful of letters during his lifetime. Most of what we know of his early life derives from what Bean told others. Much of what we know of his Langtry career has been unearthed by folklorists who dote on him more for his peculiarly Texan sense of humor than for his outrageous administration of frontier law, though the two are perhaps inseparable.

Despite trying cases involving serious crimes, Roy Bean (foreground) was only a justice of the peace.

Born on the Ohio River in Macon County, Kentucky, in about 1827, Bean supposedly ran away from home at age 16. He visited New Orleans but seems to have gotten into some kind of trouble there. He claimed to have enlisted for the Mexican War and said that he drove ammunition wagons for General Zachary Taylor in northern Mexico.

With his brother Sam as partner, Bean gathered a wagonload of trade goods and journeyed from Westport, Missouri, to Santa Fe in 1848. He took the profits from this venture and continued south through the wild Trans-Pecos region of West Texas into Chihuahua. There, according to Bean, he killed a Mexican in an argument and had to flee the country, hiding in a wagonload of buffalo hides.

He made his way to San Antonio, where he ran a dairy for a time before abruptly leaving for California. One story about his sudden departure is too good not to be told but too good to be believed. Bean supposedly had been diluting his milk with water from the Rio Grande, a tactic that succeeded until a customer found a minnow in her milk.

He made his way to San Diego, where his brother Joshua operated a saloon. On February 24, 1852, Bean fought a duel on horseback with another man and wounded his opponent. The incident was written up in a local newspaper, representing a rare instance of being able to verify a story about Bean. He was jailed briefly but escaped and made his way to Los Angeles, where Joshua had just opened the Headquarters Saloon. Two years later, Joshua was murdered, probably over a woman, and Roy inherited the Headquarters.

According to Bean, he fell afoul of the father of a Spanish girl he was courting and came within a literal inch of being lynched for the indiscretion. The rope stretched, he claimed, and he had to stand on tiptoe to stay alive until his girlfriend cut him down. The story may be apocryphal, but, according to friends, Bean had a scar around his neck and could not turn his head independently of his body.

He turned up in Mesilla, New Mexico Territory, in 1858, where his brother Sam owned a hotel-saloon. During the Civil War, Roy claimed to have operated with Confederate irregulars serving with General Henry H. Sibley. He returned to San Antonio in 1863, and for 20 years, he worked as a bartender, saloonkeeper, and teamster. During this period, he married and fathered four children.

Bean was enamored with actress Lily Langtry. A world-famous beauty, she was once the mistress of King Edward VII.

Perhaps because of debts, unhappiness in his marriage, or simple wanderlust, Bean crossed the Pecos in 1882. With a wagonload of whiskey and canned goods, he opened a saloon along the Southern Pacific Railroad tracks at a place called Vinegaroon, which is the name of the ugly whip scorpion indigenous to the area. Soon after, he moved his establishment a few miles northwest to Eagle's Nest Springs. He supposedly renamed the village Langtry after an English actress named Lily Langtry. But once again, it is difficult to tell fact from folklore. The place may have been previously named Langtry, after a railroad contractor with that name. However, the possibility that Bean named it for his beloved actress makes better sense and most certainly a better story.

At Langtry, where he was named justice of the peace a few weeks after he moved there, Bean built his saloon. Made of roughly hewn boards, it was a boxlike building measuring 20 feet long by 14 feet wide, with a porch across the front. Inside there was a cast iron stove, two poker tables, a bar at the far end, and a rough courtroom table with two benches for defendants, lawyers, and witnesses. Bean rarely employed juries, but when he was forced to have one, he brought in a third bench.

He named his establishment the Jersey Lilly, a slight misspelling of the name of the woman whose visage he had seen in a magazine and doted on thereafter. He subscribed to theater magazines to follow Langtry's career, tacked up pictures of her over his bar, and stoutly defended her honor. When a visitor examined a picture of her over the bar and rudely likened Lily to a range heifer, Bean fined the man $20 for slander.

The signs over the Jersey Lilly proclaimed Judge Roy Bean a notary public, justice of the peace, and

the Law West of the Pecos. Another large sign read, "Ice Beer." From August 1882 to the end of his life, he dispensed whiskey, beer, and his personal brand of justice from the Jersey Lilly, tending bar and holding court, often simultaneously. He would trade his bar apron for an alpaca coat and use his six-shooter as a gavel. Frequently he could be found on the Lilly's porch, wearing a huge Mexican sombrero and playing cards with cronies.

Langtry never had a population above 150, but the the Jersey Lilly did a thriving business as a saloon and particularly as a courtroom. Judge Bean knew little about the law, and most of what he did know came from the single law book he owned, *Revised Statutes of Texas, 1878.* He took care of minor infractions such as drunkenness, assaults, and petty theft, but he also handled serious crimes, which were far outside his jurisdiction, including cattle rustling, horse theft, and murder. He never ordered a convicted person to prison because it would have involved state authorities, and this was a bother Bean avoided assiduously. His verdicts ranged from ordering a defendant to buy drinks for the house to ordering the accused to be hanged.

Bean holds court on the porch of the Jersey Lilly around the year 1900. He is supposedly trying a horse thief.

He kept no records of the transactions of his court, but some of his most memorable moments behind his makeshift bench were preserved by his Langtry friends, visitors, and lawyers. For example, Bean once held an inquest over the body of a railroad worker who had died in a fall from a bridge. In the victim's belongings were a pistol and $40 in cash. Judge Bean fined the corpse the $40 for carrying a concealed weapon, confiscated the weapon for use by the court, and gave the $40 to the railroader's friends to bury him.

In another inquest, in which the victim had been found with a bullet hole between his eyes, Bean declared the man had met his death "at the hands of a damned good pistol shot." He once threatened to fine a lawyer for using profanity in court when the attorney said he intended to obtain a writ of habeas corpus on behalf of his client. He performed weddings and granted divorces, the latter granted when he found that the marriages "didn't take." He once freed an Irishman accused of killing a Chinese railroad worker after consulting his law book and determining the statutes "did not say it was against the law to kill a Chinaman."

In February 1896, Bean put together one of the strangest events in sports history when he staged a heavyweight championship prizefight between Bob Fitzsimmons and challenger Peter Maher. Prizefighting was illegal in Texas, but Bean was undeterred. The 200 fight fans paid $12 per ticket, came to Langtry on a train from El Paso, and were led by the judge to the Jersey Lilly for prefight imbibing. He then directed them to a rickety pontoon bridge made of beer kegs and scrap lumber and guided them across the Rio Grande to a sandbar on the Mexican side of the border. The ring had been constructed on the sandbar, and spectator benches cut into the river bank. While Rangers stood on the American side to enforce Texas law, the fight began on schedule. Fitzsimmons knocked out Maher in 90 seconds, after which the crowd filed back across the river to Bean's now-famous saloon for libations and all-night postfight speculation.

The small burg of Langtry finally got on the map, or at least in the newspapers, in the 1890s when Bean wrote a letter to Miss Langtry to inform her that he had named the town for her. She wrote back, graciously thanking him for the honor and offering to finance the erection of a drinking fountain in the town square. Appreciative of her offer, the judge responded, saying he didn't think it would be necessary. "If there's anything these hombres of Langtry don't drink, it's water," he said.

Roy Bean died in his room at the Jersey Lilly on March 16, 1903, close to the age of 78 years. He had become such a national character by this time that newspapers across the country carried his obituary and recounted some of his expoits as the Law West of the Pecos. He was buried in nearby Del Rio.

Ten months after his death, Lily Langtry, on a tour of the United States, visited the town named for her. A celebration was held in her honor, and she was presented with a pistol that belonged to her long-time admirer. The Jersey Lily remembered Judge Bean when she published her memoirs, *The Days That I Knew*, in 1925. She regretted never meeting him and spoke of his "ready wit and audacity."

BAT MASTERSON

1853–1921

He was born Bartholomiew Masterson in Canada in 1853. The American version of his name was Bartholomew, but later he changed his name to William Barclay Masterson. Still later, he became famous as Bat Masterson, a sobriquet that inspired as many yarns and tall tales as the events of his life. He may have acquired the nickname because it was short for Bartholomew, or maybe because he struck lawbreakers over the head with a cane, or perhaps because he was known to be a battler.

However it developed, few western names were better known in the late 19th century than Bat Masterson. The second of seven children of Thomas and Catherine Masterson, Bat lived with his family on a succession of farms in Canada and the northern United States. Finally, Thomas established a permanent home at a claim near Wichita, Kansas. Bat and his older brother, Ed, helped their father for a few months, then left home to seek adventure on the nearby frontier. Ed was 19 years old; Bat was a mere 17.

The Masterson brothers spent several months skinning hides for buffalo hunters. In the buffalo camps, Bat met Wyatt Earp, and he began to learn the art of gambling while drinking. In mid-1872, Bat and Ed undertook a grading contract for the Atchison, Topeka & Santa Fe Railroad. The job took them into a new town that was to be named Dodge City.

Their toil seemed to be for naught after contractor Raymond Ritter skipped town owing them $300. The Masterson brothers returned to hunting buffalo to restore their fortunes. When Ritter returned to Dodge on April, 15, 1873, he descended from the train to be met at gunpoint by Bat. The daring young man forced Ritter to hand over the $300, then treated a crowd of admiring onlookers to drinks. "He was a chunk of steel," observed noted scout and buffalo hunter Billy Dixon, "and anything that struck him in those days always drew fire."

By now a superb rifle shot, Bat resumed hunting buffalo, joining a party that ventured into the Texas Panhandle. On July 27, 1874, 20-year-old Bat was the youngest of 29 defenders at the famous Battle of Adobe Walls. There were two sod stores, a sod saloon, and a picket blacksmith shop at Adobe Walls to serve the buffalo hunters who swarmed through the Panhandle. The profusion of hunters and the resulting reduction of the buffalo herds inspired the Plains Indians to ally against the men who threatened to destroy their way of life. A combined force of several hundred Comanche, Kiowa, and Cheyenne warriors

In legend, Bat Masterson killed 27 men; in truth, he killed one.

planned to sweep through the Panhandle, beginning with a dawn attack on the congregation of white men (and one woman) at Adobe Walls.

When the big war party galloped toward the little cluster of buildings, the hunters scrambled for their Big Fifty Sharps buffalo guns. Forted up behind thick walls, the professional marksmen repulsed one charge after another. Masterson fought impressively.

The Battle of Adobe Walls opened the Red River War. When the army launched a major convergence on the Panhandle, Masterson signed on as a scout with the column of Colonel Nelson A. Miles. Later in the campaign, Bat worked as a teamster out of Camp Supply.

After the Native Americans were driven onto reservations, a new Panhandle community, Sweetwater (quickly renamed Mobeetie), was founded to service the hunters and soldiers stationed at nearby Fort Elliott. At the Lady Gay, a Sweetwater saloon and dance hall, Masterson notched his only fatality in a gunfight. Trouble erupted between Bat and Corporal Melvin A. King over a saloon girl named Molly Brennan. On the night of January 24, 1876, Corporal King apparently barged into the Lady Gay, found Bat and Molly together, and opened fire. As the story goes, Molly attempted to save Bat by throwing herself in front of him. Molly and Bat were hit, but as Masterson fell, he managed to shoot King, who had paused to cock his pistol. King died as a result of his wounds, and sadly, so did Molly. During his long recovery, Masterson used the cane that may have inspired his famous nickname.

Bat's brother, Ed Masterson, was gunned down in the line of duty.

Bat eventually returned to Dodge City, where he opened a saloon. On June 9, 1877, Masterson brawled with City Marshal Larry Deger. Deger had arrested a small man named Bobby Gill and was marching him to jail. Periodically, he kicked Gill in the backside to make him move faster. Masterson became angered at the display and grabbed the marshal around the neck, which helped Gill escape. With the help of a few bystanders, the 300-pound lawman pistol-whipped and arrested Masterson. Gill was rearrested the next day, and he was eventually fined $5.

Bat, who had made the mistake of resisting arrest, was fined $25. A short time later, Bat secured an appointment as undersheriff of Ford County—and subsequently relieved Marshal Deger of his concurrent commission as a deputy sheriff. In the fall, Masterson and Deger ran against each other for the office of county sheriff, with Bat edging his massive nemesis, 166–163.

Bat's jurisdiction as sheriff of Ford County ranged 100 miles from east to west and 75 miles from north to south. Just a couple of weeks after assuming office, Masterson led a posse in pursuit of a band of six train robbers. Outmaneuvering two other posses and the bandits themselves, he set a trap and captured two of them right away. Eventually, he found and captured three of the remaining four, which helped secure Masterson's reputation as an able lawman.

Ed Masterson had been appointed city marshal of Dodge in June 1877. Ed and Bat had differing approaches to maintaining law

Masterson's letter to the Dodge City *Times* appeared on November 15, 1879. This type of tough-sounding rhetoric maintained his reputation as an effective lawman.

and order. Bat had already developed a reputation as a gunfighter.

Consequently, he rarely had to fire his guns during an encounter, because his opponents did not want to shoot it out with him. He constantly practiced his shooting skills, a habit that was made well known to the public. He filed the notch of the hammer off his gun so that the weapon would go off at the slightest touch.

Ed did not have the reputation that Bat did, and his easy-going manner and gentle ways contrasted Bat's tendency to be on the edge of trouble. Ed's policy was to keep his gun holstered as much as possible in order to talk out any difficulties with lawbreakers, a tactic that proved too tame for Dodge. As the raucous cow town grew, it attracted con men, rowdy soldiers, and petty thieves. Saloon brawls and midnight robberies increased, and Ed found his job more and more taxing. Bat tried to warn his older brother that he needed to instill fear amongst the rising tide of lawbreakers and desperados, but his warnings went unheeded. Ed was fatally wounded in a wild gunfight with two drunken cowboys outside a saloon on April 9, 1878. Dodge City mourned their marshal by closing down business the next day and

draping doorways with black crepe. His body lay in state in the parlor of the Dodge City Fire Company, because Ed had been a member. The firemen conducted the funeral, and 60 uniformed volunteers followed Bat to the military cemetery at Fort Dodge, where Ed was buried. Although griefstricken, Bat continued to lead posses and capture horse thieves, confidence men, jail escapees, and train robbers.

He garnered additional authority in January 1879 by accepting appointment as a deputy U.S. marshal. Two months later, Masterson temporarily left Dodge to hire his gun to the Atchison, Topeka & Santa Fe Railroad. He led a large posse of gunmen to back up the railroad in a dispute with the Denver & Rio Grande line over the right-of-way through Colorado's Raton Pass. This profitable diversion from his duties may have worked against him, because he was decisively defeated during his re-election bid for sheriff the following November.

After leaving office in January 1880, Masterson drifted into Colorado and then Nebraska. In Ogallala, Nebraska, he helped rescue gunman Billy Thompson, younger brother of gunfighter-lawman Ben Thompson. Local citizens were in a lynching mood over a gunfight involving Billy, who continually needed his brother's help in escaping trouble. Bat disliked Billy, who had been wounded in the altercation, but he loyally responded to the call for help from his friend Ben.

Early in 1881, Bat joined Wyatt Earp at the Oriental Saloon in Tombstone, Arizona Territory. While he was gambling in Arizona, his younger brother, Jim, became mired in dangerous difficulties in Dodge. In April, Jim exchanged gunfire with a business partner and an employee, A. J. Peacock and Al Updegraff. No one was hit, but Jim telegraphed Bat in Tombstone.

Bat's train arrived in Dodge at 11:50 A.M. on April 16, 1881. As he stepped off the train, Bat spotted Peacock and Updegraff walking together, and he aggressively made his way through a crowded street. "I have come over a thousand miles to settle this," shouted Masterson from a distance of twenty feet. "I know you are heeled—now fight!"

All three men drew guns. Bat dove behind the rail bed, while Peacock and Updegraff darted around the corner of the city jail. Bullets began to shatter windows and thud into the walls of surrounding buildings as two men from a nearby saloon (probably Jim Masterson and a friend) joined the gunplay. One slug kicked dirt into Bat's mouth before ricocheting and wounding a bystander. Updegraff was struck in the right lung, possibly by Bat or maybe by one of the men in the saloon.

When the antagonists paused to reload, the mayor and sheriff marched onto the scene brandishing shotguns. Updegraff was carried away to recover. Bat paid a small fine, then boarded the evening train out of town. At the age of 27, he had fought in his last shoot-out.

Masterson drifted around the West for several years, involving himself in minor altercations. In 1883, he returned to Dodge to answer a call for help from his friend Luke Short, but the widely publicized "Dodge City War," in which Short was pitted against reformers over his saloon and gambling operation, proved to be decidedly nonviolent. It seems Short had been arrested when shots were exchanged during a run-in with a local policeman. Forced to leave town, he headed

for Topeka, where he spoke to the press and spread the word that he was in trouble. The press speculated about what dire circumstances might occur if Short's friends, including Wyatt Earp, Bat Masterson, and Charlie Bassett, should appear on the streets of Dodge in defense of their associate. When Earp, Masterson, Bassett, W. F. Petilon, M. F. Mclain, and Neil Brown did arrive in Dodge, the town leaders quickly backed down, and Short returned to his business interests. In honor of the occasion, a photo was taken of Short and his friends titled "The Dodge City Peace Commission."

Later, Bat was present but uninvolved when Short killed Longhair Jim Courtwright in Fort Worth in 1887. In 1892, Masterson apparently served briefly as a peace officer in Creede, but he was never embroiled in bloodshed in the Colorado boomtown. In the course of drinking and gambling, Masterson sometimes became involved in altercations, but his early reputation tended to restrain adversaries from going for their guns.

During these years, Masterson became increasingly active as a sportsman, especially as an official and promoter of horse races and prizefights. Headquartering in Denver, he pursued those activities around the West. In 1896, he was part of the sporting crowd that accompanied heavyweight champion Peter Maher and challenger Bob Fitzsimmons as they tried to stage a championship bout. Frustrated repeatedly by reformers and do-gooders who attempted to ban boxing in many states, the crowd finally took a special train to Langtry, Texas, where Judge Roy Bean arranged to have the fight across the Rio Grande in Mexico.

A natty dresser, Masterson cut quite a figure with the ladies. On one occasion in 1886,

MASTERSON
ON HOLLIDAY

By the time Bat Masterson moved to New York City, he was making his career as a newspaper columnist. He became a sports writer for the New York *Morning Telegraph* just after the turn of the century. He also wrote about the gunfighters and Wild West characters he had known in the Old West in a series of articles for *Human Life* magazine in 1907. Bat wrote fondly of his old friend Wyatt Earp, but he clearly disliked Earp's friend, Doc Holliday.

"Holliday had a mean disposition and an ungovernable temper, and under the influence of liquor was a most dangerous man. . . . I have always believed that much of Holliday's trouble was caused by drink and for that reason held him to blame in many instances.

While I assisted him substantially on several occasions, it was not because I liked him any too well, but

In his later years, Masterson wrote about his Wild West acquaintances from days long past.

on account of my friendship with Wyatt Earp who did.

"Holliday had few real friends anywhere in the west [*sic*]. He was selfish and had a perverse nature—traits not calculated to make a man popular in the early days of the frontier.

"Physically, Doc Holliday was a weakling who could not have whipped a healthy 15-year-old boy in a go-as-you-please fist fight, and no one knew this better than himself, and the knowledge of this fact was perhaps why he was ready to resort to a weapon of some kind whenever he got himself into difficulty. He was hotheaded and impetuous and very much given to both drinking and quarreling and, among men who didn't fear him, was very much disliked. . . ."

Perhaps the most eloquent part of Masterson's reminiscences on Holliday involved Doc's devotion to Earp.

"His whole heart and soul were wrapped up in Wyatt Earp and he was always ready to stake his life in defense of any cause in which Wyatt was interested. . . . Damon did not more for Pythias than Holliday did for Wyatt Earp."

he drew his pistol and struck the husband of Nellie Spencer. Bat and Nellie ended up running off together, but the union did not last long. Soon thereafter, he began a permanent relationship with an actress named Emma Walters. The couple married in 1891, though they never had children.

Masterson had dabbled in newspaper writing since the 1880s. In the late 1890s, he became a sports editor for a Denver newspaper. Sadly, as time passed, Masterson turned to the bottle more and more. By the early 1900s, he was frequently drunk and disorderly and considered a troublesome frontier relic. He was asked to leave Denver.

A move to New York City in 1902 improved his lot considerably, because he became something of a celebrity in the big city. He cultivated friendships with heavyweight champions Jack Johnson, Jess Willard, and Jack Dempsey, as well as with writer Damon Runyan, newspaper columnist Louella Parsons, and owner of the New York Giants, Charles Stoneham. President Theodore Roosevelt hosted Masterson in the White House and offered him an appointment as U.S. marshal for Oklahoma. When Bat declined to return to western law enforcement, Roosevelt appointed

him deputy U.S. marshal in New York at a handsome annual salary of $2,000.

When Masterson was named sports editor of the New York *Morning Telegraph*, he resigned his deputy's commission and happily immersed himself in sporting events and New York night life. On the morning of October 25, 1921, he arrived at his newspaper desk to catch up on his work. He wrote, "There are those who argue that everything breaks even in this old dump of a world of ours. I suppose these ginks who argue that way hold that because the rich man gets ice in the summer and the poor man gets it in the winter things are breaking even for both. Maybe so, but I'll swear that I can't see it that way. . . ." These became the last words that Masterson ever wrote. As he worked on his column, Bat Masterson slumped over his desk with pen in hand and died of a heart attack.

During the 1890s, Masterson worked as a sports editor in a rapidly expanding Denver. But, considered a drunken relic of the Old West, he was asked to leave around 1902.

JUDGE ISAAC PARKER

1838–1896

"During the 20 years that I have engaged in administering the law here, the contest has been one between civilization and savagery, the savagery being represented by the intruding criminal class."

The criminal class intruded so rapidly into Indian Territory after the Civil War that lawlessness reigned unchallenged—until Isaac Parker was appointed federal judge with unlimited powers and no appeals, even to the Supreme Court. Parker tirelessly championed the cause of civilization against savagery, almost immediately becoming known as the "Hanging Judge." Undeterred by this unflattering appellation, Parker tried 13,490 cases in 21 years on the bench, securing 9,454 convictions and handing down 162 death sentences, of which 80 were carried out.

The Hanging Judge was born in Ohio on October 15, 1838. Reared on a farm, he was instilled with the stern moral principles of

Judge Isaac Charles Parker maintained a crushing schedule of cases throughout his career but still made time for civic activities.

the Methodist Church, and as an adult he readily battled evil in the cause of righteousness. As a young man he taught school, then studied for the bar, and in 1859 opened a law office in St. Joseph, Missouri. The next year, he was elected city attorney, and in 1861 he married Mary O'Toole, who would bear him two sons. After serving briefly as a Union corporal during the Civil War, Parker became prosecuting attorney for the Twelfth Judicial Circuit in 1864, then won election as judge of this court in 1868.

Two years later, he was elected to the first of two congressional terms as a Republican representative. In 1875, President Ulysses S. Grant appointed Parker chief justice of Utah Territory, but within two weeks, Parker decided he would be more useful as the ruling jurist of the lawless Indian Territory. Rustlers, murderers, thieves, and fugitives from other areas congregated in growing numbers in Indian Territory, rendering the region unsafe for honest settlers and travelers. Parker's judicial predecessor was corrupt, and it had become open season on law officers who dared penetrate the West's most lawless area.

At the age of 36, Parker was the youngest federal judge in the nation, but he arrived at judicial headquarters in Fort Smith, Arkansas, unintimidated. A tall, imposing, 200-pound man, he spent the rest of his life there ruling his court with a total commitment to crushing outlawry.

Because of the unprecedented degree of criminal activity in Indian Territory, Judge Parker was permitted to utilize the services of 200 deputy U.S. marshals, far more than in any other jurisdiction. So dangerous was Indian Territory that these officers often traveled in groups of four or five. Still, 65 of Parker's deputies were slain over the years. The deputies were unsalaried, collecting only mileage, fees, and rewards. And Parker would not pay arrest fees for dead fugitives unless there was a dead-or-alive reward. Despite the meager incentive, Parker's army of deputies fanned out into Indian Territory, hauling vast numbers of fugitives in prison wagons to Fort Smith.

The first session of Judge Parker's court lasted eight weeks, during which he tried 91 defendants. He sentenced eight murderers to hang simultaneously, although one, because of his youth, had his sentence commuted to life in prison, while another was killed trying to escape. On the morning of September 3, 1875, a crowd estimated at 5,000 jostled for a view of the massive gallows Parker had constructed. Big enough to accommodate a dozen felons, the gallows was 20 feet long and built of heavy timbers. In a ceremony that lasted over an hour, the sentences were read, hymns were sung, prayers were said, and farewell statements were made. Then, six black hoods were set in place, and six murderers plunged to their fate. A few months later, on April 21, 1876, five more killers were hung *en masse.*

Parker opened court at eight o'clock in the morning six days a week, and sessions often lasted into the night. Because of this staggering caseload, there were some years in which Parker's court was in recess no more than ten days. For 14 years, there was no appeal from his decisions, which dealt harshly with felons. Outside the region, however, there was criticism of the Hanging Judge, and in 1889 murderers he had sentenced to death were permitted to appeal to the U.S. Supreme Court. "I attribute the increase [in murder] to the reversals of the Supreme Court," complained an exasperated Parker in 1895. "These reversals have contributed to the number of murders in Indian Territory."

Parker dispensed law from this jail and courthouse at Fort Smith. Parker's jurisdiction included Indian Territory, where outlaws and killers escaped the restraints of white law.

As early as 1883, his jurisdiction began to be reduced in size, primarily to relieve his workload. Still, he maintained a crushing judicial schedule. Suffering from overwork and diabetes, Parker died at age 57 on November 17, 1896. The advance of civilization had made his swift, harsh style of justice obsolete, but the West had lost the most effective judge in frontier history.

NAT LOVE

1854—?

About one out of every three cowboys was of African-American or Mexican descent, a fact seldom reflected in western novels, films, or television series. Nat Love was born a slave in Tennessee in 1854, but after the Civil War, his imagination was fired by the colorfully dressed, free-spirited cowboys of the West.

In 1869, 15-year-old Nat left the South to become a cowboy, making his way on foot to Dodge City, where he was attracted to a Texas outfit with several black cowboys. Offered a job if he could ride a rank beast named Good Eye, Love, who had broken colts for a neighbor at ten cents apiece, was able to stay aboard. He began his career as a cowboy. Booted and spurred, sporting a bright bandanna and a broad-brimmed white hat, he worked as a cowhand, driving Texas longhorns to Kansas for several years.

After the Civil War, more than 8,000 black cowboys, including Nat Love, made their way west and worked the cattle drives. In 1876, Nat Love helped trail a herd from Arizona to the

Nat Love looks every bit the adventurer he claimed he was in his autobiography.

In 1876, Nat Love arrived in the mining town of Deadwood, South Dakota, where he showed off his cowboy skills during their centennial celebrations.

Dakota gold-mining boomtown, Deadwood, where he entered the centennial Independence Day celebrations. Love related that he won a roping competition and a shooting contest. "Right there," he reminisced, "the assembled crowd named me 'Deadwood Dick' and proclaimed me champion of the Western cattle country."

Love thereby laid claim to having been the inspiration for the famous dime novel character, Deadwood Dick. The immensely popular dime novel was the creation of Erastus Beadle, a Buffalo, New York, publisher who envisioned that the development of the steam-powered, high-speed printing press made

AFRICAN-AMERICAN COWBOYS

Although African-American cowboys were already at work west of the Mississippi River before the Civil War, thousands of emancipated slaves from the South turned their eyes westward when the great conflict ended in 1865. The age of the great cattle drives was about to begin, and hard-working men—regardless of color—could earn a fair if rough living wrangling the millions of Texas longhorns. Despite the ever-present threat of frontier violence, blacks were safer in the West than in the South, which averaged over 150 lynchings per year into the 1890s.

Although segregated bunkhouses were the norm on most ranches, African-American men found a readier acceptance on the frontier and far more integrated conditions in western towns than in southern communities. Cowboys judged each other by how well they could ride, shoot, tend cattle, and stand on their own. Family, breeding, nationality, and race mattered less amid the demands and dangers of a cattle drive. Although most African Americans worked as regular cowboys—watching after the herd, busting broncos, and the like—they also took on positions of authority, such as ranch foreman, trail boss, or ram-

A talented bronco-buster, Isom Dart was one of the many black cowboys.

rod. For the time, such a thing was remarkable; even in the most liberal parts of the North, it was all but impossible for a black man to find work supervising whites.

One of the most famous of all black cowboys was Bill Pickett. Born in Texas in 1860, Pickett is said to have been hired at age 13 at the famous 101 Ranch in Oklahoma. When he was about 20 years old, he created the sport of bulldogging, in which a rider leaps from his horse and wrestles a full-grown steer to the ground. As he perfected his bulldogging technique over the years, Pickett found that he could get a struggling steer to submit more quickly if he bit its upper lip. In the early 1900s, when the 101 Wild West Show was organized, Pickett accompanied such well-known cowboy stars as Will Rogers and Tom Mix on the wide-ranging show circuit. He performed in Madison Square Garden and in Europe before returning to Oklahoma and the 101 Ranch. In 1971, Pickett became the first African American ever inducted into the National Cowboy Hall of Fame in Oklahoma City.

NAT LOVE, COWBOY

"In the spring of 1876 orders were received at the home ranch for 3,000 head of three-year-old steers to be delivered near Deadwood, South Dakota. This being one of the largest orders we had ever received at one time, every man around the ranch was placed on his mettle to execute the order in record time. . . .

"Our route lay through New Mexico, Colorado and Wyoming, and as we had heard rumors that the Indians were on the war path and were kicking up something of a rumpus in Wyoming, Indian Territory and Kansas, we expected trouble before we again had the pleasure of sitting around our fire at the home ranch. Quite a large party was selected for this trip owing to the size of the herd and the possibility of trouble on the trail from the Indians. We, as usual, were all well armed and had as mounts the best horses our ranch produced, and in taking the trail we were perfectly confident that we could take care of our herd and ourselves through anything we were liable to meet. We had not been on the trail long before we met other outfits, who told us that General Custer was out after the Indians and that a big fight was expected when the Seventh U.S. Cavalry, General Custer's command, met the . . . Indians . . . who had for a long time been terrorizing the settlers of that section and defying the Government. . . .

"We arrived in Deadwood in good condition without having had any trouble with the Indians on the way up. We turned our cattle over to their new owners at once, then proceeded to take in the town."
—from *The Life and Adventures of Nat Love*, 1907

it possible to reach mass audiences with inexpensive "steam literature."

Beadle's writers had little or no first-hand acquaintance with the West, but they still produced volumes on the subject. Formula writers such as Prentiss Ingraham, who churned out over 600 novels, described the fantastic exploits of imaginary heroes, as well as using the names of such real westerners as Wild Bill Hickok, George Armstrong Custer, Kit Carson, and Buffalo Bill Cody. In 1887, another of Beadle's prolific novelists, Edward L. Wheeler, introduced the genre's first outlaw hero: *Deadwood Dick, The Prince of the Road; or, The Black Rider of the Black Hills*.

This first book established the premise that Deadwood Dick had been victimized by powerful establishment figures, which vengefully pushed him into seeking justice. Wearing a black hat, a "jetty black" buckskin jacket, and a black mask "through the eyeholes of which there gleamed a pair of orbs of piercing intensity," Deadwood Dick took on a variety of powerful villains. A working-class readership that was oppressed by political bosses and robber-baron industrialists responded enthusiastically. Indeed, the popularity of Deadwood Dick spawned imitations, including characters based on Frank and Jesse James, who acquired a Robin Hood image as good badmen. The character of Deadwood Dick was instrumental in establishing the heroic outlaw as a staple of countless movies, novels, and television series.

There were 33 Deadwood Dick dime novels, as well as 97 Deadwood Dick, Jr., sagas. Titles ranged from *Deadwood Dick's Protegee; or, Baby Bess, the Girl Gold Miner* to

Deadwood Dick, Jr., in Chicago; or, The Anarchist's Daughter. Since there were so many dime novels with heroes who sported the names of actual frontiersmen, some Deadwood Dick fans assumed that he was a real westerner.

By this time in the real West, the trail drives were ending, the nature of ranching was changing dramatically, and large numbers of black cowboys were trying to find more stable work. During the era of open range ranching, most cowboys were employed only seasonally, during roundups and trail drives. By the 1880s, the cowboys of Nat Love's generation no longer were footloose teenagers in search of adventure and excitement; many men decided it was time to settle down and raise a family.

Nat Love gave up cowboying in 1890 and became a Pullman porter, the most reliable and renumerative job generally available to African Americans of that period. In 1907, he published the only book-length autobiographical account of a black cowboy: *The Life and Adventures of Nat Love, Better Known in the Cattle Country as 'Deadwood Dick.'* In addition to his claims about being the prototype for the famous fictional shootist, Love stated that he was a friend of Bat Masterson and that he had met Billy the Kid in 1877 and had various experiences with the

The first Deadwood Dick story described the title chracter as "an interesting specimen of young, healthy manhood."

Kid and Pat Garrett during the Lincoln County War. Love fearlessly endured two decades of harrowing escapades: "I gloried in the danger." He related a series of sensational adventures, from skirmishes with Native Americans (one nation supposedly adopted Love after capturing him), to cattle stampedes, to wild animal attacks, to gun battles. "I carry the marks of 14 bullet wounds on different parts of my body, most any of which would be sufficient to kill an ordinary man," he boasted, "but I am not even crippled." His book reads somewhat like a Deadwood Dick novel, and in *Sixguns and Saddle Leather,* the peerless western bibliophile Ramon Adams details "the author's many preposterous statements" and concludes that Love "either had a bad memory or a good imagination."

Perhaps Nat Love was not the inspiration behind the fictional Deadwood Dick. He spent most of his life as a cowboy rather than a daring shootist, but he was an adventurous man who went west to become a cowboy during the heyday of that captivating profession. And he was an African American who spearheaded the movement of his race into the last West, embellishing the deeds of his eventful life with the good-natured exaggeration that characterized entertaining frontier storytelling of every era.

WILD BILL
HICKOK

1837–1876

Frontier adventurer Wild Bill Hickok became the West's most famous gunfighter. A tall man with an athletic physique, he was a flamboyant dresser who affected shoulder-length hair and sweeping mustaches. "He always had a mistress," reminisced old friend Charlie Gross. Hickok was also acquainted with almost every noted westerner of his era. He pinned on a badge in several reckless frontier towns; he served as a daring scout during the Indian campaigns and the Civil War; at various times, he earned his living as a gambler, teamster, stagecoach driver, and Wild West show performer. And Wild Bill was the Prince of Pistoleers.

A fine shot with either hand, Hickok the dandy carried two revolvers tucked into a colorful sash with butts forward. In addition to Civil War combat, he engaged in at least eight

Wild Bill Hickok lives up to his name as he dons this dandified suit while working as a scout in Rolla, Missouri, circa 1864.

shoot-outs and killed seven or more adversaries during his short life.

"As to killing," he once reflected, "I never think much about it. I don't believe in ghosts, and I don't keep the lights burning all night to keep them away. That's because I'm not a murderer. It is the other man or me in a fight, and I don't stop to think—is it a sin to do this thing? And after it is over, what's the use of disturbing the mind."

This formidable character was born on May 27, 1837, in Homer (later Troy Grove), Illinois. James Butler Hickok was the fourth of six children of a Vermont couple who moved to Illinois the year before he was born. His father established a way station for the Underground Railroad, and young Jim often helped whisk away fugitive slaves.

By the time he was a teenager, Jim had become an excellent marksman. An older brother, Oliver, left home for the California gold fields, fueling the wanderlust that would come to characterize Hickok. His restlessness surfaced in 1852 after his father died. Upon leaving home, Jim adopted his father's name, Bill.

By 1855, 18-year-old Hickok had drifted into Kansas. "Bleeding Kansas" was torn by strife over slavery, and Hickok spent a year in the Free-State Militia of Jim Lane. A couple of years later, he began working his homestead claim. He often hired out as a laborer in Monticello Township, where he was elected constable in March 1858. This first brief tenure as a peace officer was perhaps too peaceful, and by 1859, Hickok was working for Russell, Majors and Waddell as a teamster on the Santa Fe Trail. He began acquaintanceships with other frontier notables: While in Santa Fe, he met Kit Carson, and he encountered 12-year-old Bill Cody at Leavenworth.

At Raton Pass, Hickok was mauled by a bear, although he managed to kill the beast with pistols and a knife. Russell, Majors and Waddell sent him to Kansas City for medical treatment, then assigned him to light duties at their Rock Creek Station in Nebraska, a Pony Express post along the Oregon Trail. Hickok worked as a stock tender under station manager Horace Wellman. Wellman's common-law wife was present, along with stable hand Doc Brink.

Across the creek, Dave McCanles lived with his family, and in a bold move, he installed his mistress, Sarah Shull, in a house nearby. McCanles began insulting Hickok by calling him Duck Bill, a slur upon his facial features, and hermaphrodite, a slur upon certain other features. Hickok retaliated by secretly seeing Miss Shull. McCanles also caused trouble with other employees, as well as with the company, and the festering situation came to a head on the afternoon of July 12, 1861.

McCanles told Sarah Shull that he was going to the station to take care of the people there. He appeared at the station backed up by his cousin, James Gordon; his 12-year-old son, Monroe; and an employee, James Woods. As Gordon and Woods headed toward the barn, McCanles exchanged angry words with the Wellmans. Spotting Hickok standing behind a curtain partition, McCanles threatened to drag Duck Bill outside.

"There will be one less son-of-a-bitch when you try that," challenged Hickok ominously. The 24-year-old frontiersman had never been involved in a shoot-out, but he boldly readied his weapon.

When McCanles stepped toward the curtain, Hickok pumped a slug into his chest. Staggering outside, McCanles died in the arms of his son as Gordon and Woods ran toward the sound of the gunshot. When Woods approached the kitchen door, Hickok shot him twice, then turned to wing Gordon, who had suddenly appeared at the front door. Woods and Gordon tried to flee, but Wellman and Brink, armed respectively with a hoe and a shotgun, gave chase. Brink killed Gordon with a blast from his shotgun, while Wellman easily caught Woods and hacked the life out of him.

Hickok had shot three men, at least one fatally. Tales about the gory fight spread rapidly, embellished with typical frontier exaggeration. In February 1867, the popular *Harper's New Monthly Magazine* published an article by Colonel George Ward Nichols entitled "Wild Bill." Wild indeed was

Nichols's account of the fight at Rock Creek Station, where Hickok, armed with a revolver, rifle, and bowie knife in the story, was attacked by Dave "M'Kandlas" and nine members of his "party of ruffians." Hickok supposedly told Nichols, "I was wild and I struck savage blows, following the devils from one side to the other of the room and into the corners striking and slashing until I knew that every one was dead."

J. W. Buel, who had been personally acquainted with Hickok while reporting for the Kansas City *Journal*, also wrote that Wild Bill killed ten outlaws, but in return he suffered four bullet wounds, a skull fracture, numerous knife gashes, and a slash to the head that left his scalp hanging across his eyes. In *Wild Bill, The Pistol Deadshot*, dime novelist Colonel Prentiss Ingraham stated that Hickok was shot 11 times while wiping out the McCanles gang.

Hickok lived for a decade and a half after first achieving notoriety, and during that time, he added immensely to the legend of Wild Bill. By the time of the Rock Creek fight, the Civil War had begun, and Hickok headed east to associate himself with the Federal army for the duration of the conflict. He experienced combat at Wilson's Creek, Missouri, and at Pea Ridge, Arkansas, and he served as a scout and spy under General Samuel P. Curtis. During the war he received his famous

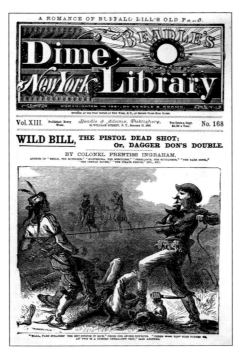

Colonel Prentiss Ingraham churned out many dime novels about Wild Bill, including this one in 1882.

nickname, and reputedly Wild Bill was involved in one dangerous scrape after another.

After the war, Hickok became a gambler in Springfield, Missouri, where he clashed with Dave Tutt over the affections of a girl named Susanna Moore. Hickok and Tutt, a former Union soldier, quarreled angrily over a card game at the Lyon House, then challenged each other to a duel the next day.

The dramatic showdown on a dusty main street that is a staple of western movies and novels almost never occurred in the real West. However, at six o'clock in the evening, as an excited crowd of onlookers jostled for a view, Hickok and Tutt confronted each other in the town square. At a distance of 75 yards, Hickok shouted "Don't come any closer, Dave!"

But Tutt defiantly drew a revolver and squeezed off a shot that went wild. Hickok steadied his own revolver in his left hand, then fired a ball squarely into Tutt's chest. Tutt pitched onto his face, dead in an instant. Wild Bill surrendered to the authorities, but he was tried and acquitted.

Following this cool display of courage under fire, Hickok ran unsuccessfully for the office of chief of police in Springfield, Missouri. On January 1, 1867, he began a six-month enlistment at $100 monthly to scout for Custer's 7th Cavalry. Though later in the

A GAMBLER'S TOOLS

E. N. Grandine of New York manufactured "readers"—marked cards—and shipped them to gamblers throughout the West for $1.25 per pack or $10 per dozen. Sometimes every card in a deck was altered, but more often only certain cards were marked, which reduced the chances of detection.

Aside from tiny markings on cards, a color compound might be applied to indicate selected cards, or edges might be trimmed slightly. Gamblers kept their hands soft, sometimes sandpapering their fingertips for extra sensitivity, so that they could detect the slightest alterations.

In addition to marked cards, Grandine's of New York manufactured various "advantage tools" for gamblers. Gamblers were experts at handling cards and dealing to improve their odds, but advantage

A gambler's game box might hold cards, chips, and a derringer, along with dice and items for other games. Note that this derringer fits into a fake book.

tools offered a further edge. Grandine's was only one mail-order house that sold marked cards and advantage tools. Other catalogs were sent out from New Orleans, Chicago, and—by the 1880s—San Franscisco's Will and Finck Company.

Professional gamblers eagerly perused these catalogs for devices that would improve their chances at the card table. For instance, dime-sized reflectors were inserted in poker chips or in the bowl of a pipe, and when one of

these items was placed on the table, a dealer could see the underside of the cards as they were passed out. Less conspicuously, special coins provided this same advantage, as did highly polished cufflinks or pocket watches.

Mail-order catalogs advertised a variety of mechanical holdouts for gamblers. A sleeve holdout, for example, buckled around the cheater's bare arm and sent a card into the palm when the elbow was extended. A wide shirt cuff was necessary, and a rub-

ber band retained the device when the gambler straightened his arm.

A breastplate holdout required a long cord that stretched to the gambler's shoe or boot. The breastplate was sewn to the gambler's shirt. By bending or extending his leg, cards would be sent to his hand or made available inside a bag that was strapped under a gambler's waist and was also manipulated by a long cord. But if a holdout was discovered by a cardsharp's victims, there was no explaining these mechanisms, and the consequences tended to be severe.

Suspicions also were aroused by those wearing blue-tinted glasses. Cards could be marked with phosphorescent ink, and while these marks were invisible to the naked eye, they could be read through blue-tinted glasses.

year Hickok was defeated in the sheriff's race in Ellsworth County, Kansas, he did obtain a commission as a deputy U.S. marshal, chasing army deserters and thieves of government livestock. On March 30, 1868, Wild Bill arrested 11 deserters who were operating as horse rustlers, and he engaged Buffalo Bill Cody to help him bring in the gang.

From left: Hickok, Texas Jack Omohundro, and Buffalo Bill Cody all worked as scouts on the Great Plains.

Hickok continued his haphazard career in law enforcement, despite his proclivity for hard drinking and rough living. In 1869, he was elected interim sheriff of Ellis County, Kansas. The county seat was Hays City, which, because of raucous buffalo hunters and reveling members of the 7th Cavalry stationed at Fort Hays, was as wild a town as any in the West.

On August 24, 1869, shortly after taking office as county sheriff, Hickok encountered an intoxicated ruffian named Bill Mulvey. Mulvey was accompanied by several equally drunken friends, and the gang was shooting up the town. Mulvey reacted belligerently when Wild Bill tried to arrest him. Sheriff Hickok shot Mulvey, who collapsed and died the next morning. About an hour past midnight on September 27, Sheriff Hickok and Deputy Peter Lanihan were called to John Bitter's Beer Saloon, where a local troublemaker named Samuel Strawhun and several drunken cronies were taking the place apart. When Strawhun turned on Hickok, the sheriff shot him in the head, killing him instantly and stopping the riot.

Instead of favorably impressing the electorate, Hickok's two killings in five weeks alarmed enough voters to give the November election to Deputy Lanihan, 144–89. On July 17, 1870, an inebriated ex-Sheriff Hickok became involved in a brawl at Drum's Saloon with five drunken troopers from the 7th Cavalry. The soldiers threw Hickok to the floor, and one trooper tried to shoot him, but the cap misfired. Wild Bill desperately pulled out his own guns and opened fire, wounding Private Jerry Lonergan in the knee and wrist and hitting Private John Kile in the torso. The other soldiers backed away, giving Hickok the opportunity to flee the town. The wounded soldiers were taken to the Fort Hays hospital, where Private Kile died the next day.

With commendable foresight but a lack of showbiz acumen, Hickok staged a Wild West show at Niagara Falls entitled The Daring Buffalo Chase of the Plains. When the show flopped financially, Wild Bill returned to the West and his career as a lawman. In April 1871, he was hired to be city marshal of Abilene at $150 per month plus a percentage of fines.

Abilene was just as raucous and raw as other cow towns of the period. Texas gamblers Phil Coe and Ben Thompson opened the Bull's Head Saloon and decorated it with a clearly depicted symbol of masculinity, which offended Abilene's respectable citizens. On instructions from the city council, Marshal Hickok ordered the alteration of the sign. Coe resented this interference, and trouble brewed between the two men.

On the night of October 5, 1871, Coe led about 50 Texas cowboys on a drunken spree through Abilene. Hickok was one of several citizens compelled to buy drinks, but the marshal warned the rowdies to control themselves, and he alerted Deputy Mike Williams. When a shot rang out at nine o'clock, Hickok ordered Williams to stay put and then hurried to investigate.

Hickok elbowed his way through the crowd and confronted Coe, who, along with several other Texans, brandished a revolver. When Hickok went for his guns, Coe, standing just eight feet away, snapped off a shot that cut through Wild Bill's coattails. Hickok's first slug tore through Coe's stomach and out his back. As Coe collapsed, he fired another wild round. Suddenly Mike Williams broke through the cowboys, intending to help Hickok. Glimpsing the movement amid a hostile crowd, Hickok whirled and fired, killing Williams with a bullet in the head.

An agonized Hickok scattered the crowd and shut down the town. One or two bystanders were treated for flesh wounds, while Phil Coe was carried away to die a lingering death three days later. Hickok paid Mike Williams's funeral expenses. After accidentally killing his deputy, Wild Bill Hickok was never seen firing a shot at another man.

During the next couple of years, Hickok traveled through the East with Buffalo Bill's troupe, somewhat ineptly performing in a production billed as *The Scouts of the Plains*. In 1872, he took time to join a royal Russian buffalo hunt in Kansas, and in 1874 he went back to the West, drifting from place to place as a gambler. His eyesight began to fail, perhaps as a result of gonorrhea, and on several occasions he was arrested for vagrancy.

By this time, he had renewed an old acquaintance with Agnes Lake, now a 50-year-old circus proprietor. The couple married on March 5, 1876, in Cheyenne, Wyoming. Shortly thereafter, Wild Bill left Mrs. Hickok for the Black Hills mining boomtown of Deadwood, where he was a regular at the gambling tables of the No. 10 Saloon.

On August 2, 1876, a young man named Jack McCall walked into the No. 10 Saloon and shot Hickok in the back of the head as he played cards at a table. As Hickok fell dead, McCall triggered the gun at the crowd, but every other cartridge was defective. McCall was quickly apprehended, and he was later tried and hung. Murdered at the age of 39, Wild Bill clutched a pair of black aces and a pair of eights, a poker combination immortalized as the Dead Man's Hand.

Hickok's gravesite in Deadwood, South Dakota, has long been a tourist attraction. Its appearance has been "improved" many times.

WOMEN IN THE WEST

Courage. Stamina. Fortitude. Endurance. Resourcefulness. These qualities were exhibited repeatedly by brave, rugged settlers of the West. Many western men also had these qualities.

Pioneer women, like their men, had to endure hardships and dangers on the frontier. But the women of the West did not enjoy the same political privileges and rights as men. Until 1918, anyone in Texas could vote "except imbeciles, idiots, aliens, the insane, and women." But women were in short number on the frontier, and in order to attract a greater female population, western states were the first to award women the right to vote and to sit on juries.

Women reacted to frontier conditions in the same ways as their male counterparts. Few men were better shots than Annie Oakley, and few had a more notorious reputation than Belle Starr. Stagecoach driver Charley Parkhurst never had an accident and once shot three would-be robbers. Only after she died was it realized that Charley's name was Charlotte Parkhurst.

Fueled by an interest in Native American culture, Alice Fletcher expanded her horizons by taking a job directing the allotment of lands for Plains Indians.

CALAMITY JANE

1844—1903

Calamity Jane was born Martha Jane Cannary in 1844, according to the census of 1860. Other birth dates have been suggested, and with a vanity not typical of Calamity Jane, she reduced her age by claiming to have been born on May 1, 1852, in Princeton, Missouri.

Calamity Jane gained fame as a "character" but solidified her legend as a scout with General George Crook.

When Martha Jane was an adolescent, her family moved from Missouri, most probably to Calamus, Wisconsin. Her father, Robert Cannary, was a heavy drinker, and she left home after the Civil War to escape an intolerable home life. Martha Jane went west and supported herself as a prostitute in Wyoming. Shortly thereafter, she became known as Calamity Jane, although it is unclear how she acquired the famous sobriquet. Calamity Jane became a colorful frontier character of the first order. Although Calamity continued to work as a sporting lady from time to time, she decided that men had a better life. As her once-trim figure filled out to husky proportions, Calamity chopped off her hair and donned soiled buckskins and a slouch hat.

Calamity loved to belly up to the bar with the boys. She chewed tobacco and drank to excess. She cussed like a teamster and even worked as one on occasion. She enjoyed nothing better than spending a boisterous evening in a loud, smoky saloon, drinking and gambling, even though she was a poor gambler. In 1876, she was jailed in Cheyenne, and as the years went by, there were other arrests for rowdiness. During one raucous revelry, she reportedly bet everyone within earshot that she could enter a bordello, engage a prostitute, and, until a certain delicate moment, pass herself off as a man. Calamity swaggered into a red-light house

PROSTITUTION

It was inevitable that prostitution thrived in the West, where the ratio of men to women was ten to one. The cattle towns, the mining camps, and the military posts were all locales dominated by single males.

Many prostitutes were foreign-born, alone in a strange country with no other means of support: Chinese women on the West Coast, Mexican señoritas in New Mexico, and African-American ladies in the larger cities. These and other women added their individual personalities to a well-established business that boomed in the West when the first Texas cowboys arrived at Abilene soon after the end of the Civil War.

In one of the early cattle towns—Ellsworth, Kansas—the city fathers, rather than outlaw the profession, actually profited from it. A local newspaper of the times explained:

"The city realizes $300 per month from prostitution fines alone. . . . The city authorities consider that as long as mankind is depraved and Texas cattle herders exist, there will be a demand and necessity for prostitutes, and that as long as prostitutes are bound to dwell in Ellsworth it is better for the respectable portion of society to hold prostitutes under restraint of law."

Prostitutes were categorized into four groups. The streetwalker, the lowest rung on the ladder, solicited anyone from any social strata who could pay. Next came the saloon girl, who entertained the customers in the bars and saloons. The crib girl worked out of her crib, that is, a small room or residence. Crib girls catered to out-of-town visitors and guests. At the top of the scale were the women who worked in the large city parlors, often bestowing their talents on the town's leading citizens.

With such colorful names as Molly b'Damn, Contrary Mary, and Velvet Ass Rose, the prostitutes contributed much to the lore of the Wild West regardless of the moral stigma associated with them.

Prostitution thrived where there were lonely men and ample money. Some say Julia Bulette earned $1,000 a night at the Comstock Lode in Nevada.

and, with witnesses strategically positioned, proceeded to win the bawdy wager.

Calamity sometimes found employment as a bullwhacker, cracking a whip over teams of oxen. Posing as a male teamster, she accompanied the 1875 geological expedition of Professor Walter P. Jenney into the Black Hills. Supposedly, the next year she marched with George Crook's column into Montana, but when she went bathing with troopers and her gender was revealed, Calamity was ordered to return to civilization.

Civilization—of a sort—could be found in Deadwood, South Dakota, where she turned up not long before Wild Bill Hickok was murdered on

Calamity Jane's legend was enhanced by fallacious stories by *Beadle's* and other dime-novel accounts of the West. She did, however, live unconventionally for a woman of her time.

August 2, 1876. Claiming a long and intimate association with the famous gunfighter, Calamity stated in her spurious autobiography that they had wed, then divorced so that Wild Bill would be free to marry Agnes Lake. She also claimed that she had borne Wild Bill a child.

She may have given birth to a son around 1882, although nothing further is known about this offspring. A daughter was born on October 28, 1887, but was deposited with St. Mary's Convent in Sturgis, South Dakota, eight years later. Thereafter, the little girl disappeared from history. The girl's father was El Paso cab driver Clinton Burke, who apparently married Calamity Jane in 1885. There were other husbands, perhaps of the common-law variety, in other places. Few documented details exist on Calamity Jane's attempts at romance, love, and family life.

Calamity drifted all over the West, gravitating to cavalry outposts, cattle towns such as Miles City in Montana, and boomtowns on the order of Deadwood. In Deadwood, she displayed a classic heart of gold by assuming the unlikely role of nurse. Working at times without pay, she cared for a stabbing victim, a smallpox patient, a dying girl, and a premature baby.

Her features coarsened, a reflection of her outdoor life and years of carousing. Calamity Jane eventually became an alcoholic and her habits were rough, but she was tough and resilient. She had to be to survive such a hard lifestyle.

With a ghost writer, she produced an autobiography, which put into print a boastful collection of falsehoods, including the claims that she had campaigned with Custer, married Wild Bill, and helped capture his killer. In 1896, Calamity made stage appearances as "the Famous Woman Scout," and at the 1901 Pan-American Exposition in Buffalo, New York, she appeared on the midway as a buckskin-clad cowgirl.

By this time, however, Calamity had sagged into alcoholic addiction. She was discovered sick and drunk in an African-American bordello in Horr, Montana, and she grumbled an uncharacteristic wish that people should "leave me alone and let me go to hell my own route." That route kept taking her back to Deadwood, where she fell ill at Terry, a nearby mining town. Delirious, she spoke lamentably of her daughter and then died on August 1, 1903.

Insisting that Calamity's dying wish was to be buried next to Wild Bill Hickok, her friends arranged to have her interred only 20 feet from his grave. They even changed the date of her demise to August 2, 1903, the 27th anniversary of Hickok's death.

Just 20 years later, a silent movie titled *Wild Bill Hickok* included the story of Wild Bill and Calamity Jane. Her character would continue to appear in the profusion of films about Hickok that followed. Calamity's tall tales and Hollywood had managed to insinuate a closeness between Martha

Jane Cannary and the Prince of Pistoleers that really never existed while Wild Bill was alive. This identification helped her become the most recognizable woman in frontier folklore.

Yet, Calamity Jane earned this fame and notoriety, if not for a supposed relationship with a legendary gunfighter, then for having the nerve to live as she pleased. The West was a man's world, and she entered that world not only by wearing the garb of a frontiersman but also by working at the occupations of a man and roistering in saloons, the western man's clubhouse. Calamity Jane was adventurous, rugged, courageous, strong-minded, and flamboyant, earning a place in the front rank of legendary western characters.

Calamity Jane visits the Deadwood, South Dakota, grave of Wild Bill Hickok around 1900. Her wish of being buried beside him was fulfilled after she died in 1903.

CHARLEY
PARKHURST

1812?—1879

Sometime between Christmas 1879 and New Year's Day 1880, the celebrated stagecoach driver Charley Parkhurst was buried in the Odd Fellows Cemetery near Wat-

Some speculate that Charley Parkhurst began her illusion as a male to succeed in her escape from an orphanage.

sonville, just east of Monterey Bay, California. It was entirely appropriate that Parkhurst, who had long been active in the local lodge of the International Order, be buried there: Charley was the oddest fellow in the graveyard. In fact, until Charley was embalmed, no one knew she was not a fellow at all.

Charley was born Charlotte Darkey Parkhurst (or Pankhurst, the record is not clear) in Lebanon, New Hampshire, in about 1812. In her teens, after abandonment by her parents, she ran away from an orphanage in Massachusetts and found work in a livery stable in Worcester owned by Ebenezer Balch.

There is no dependable historical record of Parkhurst's movements and work in the 20 years that followed her debut as a stagecoach whip under the tutelege of Balch, but there are some random facts and clues about these years. From her earliest days of learning to drive a coach-and-six, she called herself Charley and began wearing men's clothing. She worked in Providence, Rhode Island, for a time, then drifted to Georgia. There is no clue as to what she did or for how long in any of these ventures, but in 1849 she was back in Providence. There she learned about the gold rush north of Sutter's Fort on the American River in northern California.

One of Parkhurst's coach-driving colleagues in Providence, a man named James Birch, had quickly departed for California, intending to start up a coach line from the goldfields to Sacramento. He urged Parkhurst to follow, promising her employment.

She made the arduous six-month voyage to San Francisco via the Isthmus of Panama. In 1851, she made her way to the goldfields, where Birch hired her to drive coaches in the Mother Lode country around Georgetown,

Hangtown, and Coloma. By 1854, when Birch organized the California Stage Company, Parkhurst was one of his chief drivers. She was familiar with the entire Sierra Nevada foothill country, from as far north as Sacramento and Stockton to as far south as Monterey. Her regular runs were to San Francisco and Oakland.

Stories—some no doubt apocryphal—abound about her exploits during the period she worked as a stagecoach whip in California. The most notable instance involved a highwayman known as Sugarfoot, whose outsized feet wrapped in burlap sacks accounted for his unusual moniker. Sugarfoot stopped her coach, stuck a shotgun in her face, and ordered her to throw down the strongbox. Parkhurst did as she was told but warned the bandit, "Next time, I'll be ready for you."

She took to wearing six-shooters after this robbery. A year later, Sugarfoot and his gang held her up again. This time she began blazing away at them as they drew up to her coach. She whipped up her horses and flew down the trail. When a posse returned to the site, Sugarfoot was found dead, with two of his gang wounded.

Other dangers faced by Parkhurst as a stage driver involved the forces of nature as opposed to the follies of man. One of her stage routes crossed a dilapidated

The stagecoach was uncomfortable to ride in and just as arduous to drive. There were few private stops along a line, yet Charley Parkhurst was able to conceal her gender for years.

bridge over the Tuolumne River. While on this run during a severe rainstorm, Charley grew apprehensive about crossing the bridge. Her fears proved founded when the stage drew up to the Tuolumne and she saw a raging, rain-swollen torrent beneath the swaying, creaking bridge. She gritted her teeth, laid the whip to her team, and bolted across the bridge at full speed. Just as the stage touched the other side, the bridge tore loose from its anchors and was washed down river by the swift floodwaters.

Despite taking a daring risk now and then, Parkhurst approached her job with great seriousness and professionalism. She did not drink while on the job and was highly critical of those who did. She maintained that stage accidents, particularly wrecks, were mainly the result of "whiskey or bad driving." She was openly affectionate with her horses, calling them her beauties and lavishing them with loving care. A good scrapper in a fight, she made short work of anyone who dared mistreat a horse or other animal in her presence.

Parkhurst retired from the rigors of the stage routes in the early 1860s, making her farewell run from San Jose to Santa Cruz. She was particularly proud of the fact that none of her passengers had suffered an injury, despite some hair-raising close calls.

STAGECOACH MARY

The stagecoach driver stood six feet tall and weighed 200 pounds, smoked cigars, drank whiskey, never ducked a fight, and packed a .38 in addition to a double-barreled shotgun.

The stagecoach driver was named Mary Fields.

Fields was born into slavery in 1832 in Tennessee. When the Civil War ended—or perhaps during the conflict—she made her way north to Ohio, where she found work at a Catholic mission school.

Mary became close to an Ursuline nun named Mother Amadeus. When the Ohio school closed, Mother Amadeus was sent to Montana Territory in 1884 to help establish a mission school for Native American women, and she brought her big, loyal friend along to help out. St. Peter's Mission School was built near Cascade,

about 60 miles north of Helena.

Mary was over 50 when she arrived in Cascade, but for eight years she worked at hauling freight and performing heavy chores. Locals called her "Black Mary." At first, the sight of Fields driving her wagon with a cigar and a jug of whiskey intimidated and alienated some of the townsfolk.

Although liked and appreciated by the nuns for her steadfast contributions to their work, Mary tended to clash with the workmen at the mission. Once, Mary and an antagonist went for their guns and exchanged gunfire. Although no one was wounded, the bishop in Helena directed Mother Amadeus to discharge her pugnacious friend.

Mother Amadeus helped Mary establish a restaurant in Cascade. Mary was a good cook but

Although Mary Fields's first years in Cascade, Montana, were turbulent, she eventually became an honored citizen.

fed everyone regardless of their inclination to pay, and she went broke. Despite this, the locals were won over by Fields's determination, independence, and inherent kindness to those less fortunate.

"Black Mary" became "Stagecoach Mary" by riding shotgun and working as a driver on an area stagecoach line. When a mail route was established

between Cascade and St. Peter's Mission, Mother Amadeus aided her 63-year-old friend in securing the position of carrier. Mary drove the route for eight years, becoming perhaps the second woman in history to deliver U.S. mail.

When Mother Amadeus was transferred to a mission in Alaska, Mary felt she was too old to follow her longtime benefactor. Now in her 70s, she operated a laundry, babysat, and celebrated her birthdays by handing out candy to children. The New Cascade Hotel gave her free meals, and friends helped her build a house. When her home burned, townspeople helped her rebuild.

By the end of her life, Mary Fields was revered as a local legend. Supposedly, Cascade's public schools were closed to honor her birthday. Mary died in 1914.

In 1856, Parkhurst was living in the lumber town of Searsville when she was kicked in the face by a horse she was shoeing. She lost the sight in her left eye and wore a black patch, which added to her rough appearance. She acquired the nickname One-Eyed Charley as a result.

After her retirement, she purchased land in Rancho Soquel, near Monterey, raised some cattle, and grew vegetables. In 1867, she registered to vote in the local and state elections, listing herself on the voter rolls as: "Parkhurst, Charles D., age 55, Occupation farmer, Native of New Hampshire." The next year she voted in a federal election. About 43 years after Parkhurst voted in these elections, suffrage came to California!

In what proved to be her last venture, Parkhurst bought 25 acres of land in the Watsonville area in the 1870s. She took on a partner, Frank Woodward, and operated a small cattle ranch. Parkhurst became crippled by rheumatism and debilitated by cancer of the tongue. She died on her ranch on December 28, 1879. The physician who pronounced her dead and performed the autopsy was the first to discover Charley's secret.

Word of the decades-long masquerade quickly leaked out, with newspapers carrying the story all over the West. Reporters tended to embellish the story with outlandish speculation and exaggerated versions of her exploits. The doctor who examined her revealed that she had given birth to at least one child, but no record exists as to when or where this occured.

No one, not even her partner, seems to have ever questioned her gender, although she was only five feet seven inches tall, her face was suspiciously clean-shaven, and she spoke but a few words. She limited her speech to avoid suspicion, speaking in a voice described as a "whiskey tenor." She often wore pleated shirts over outsized trousers, and she was never seen without her leather gauntlet-like gloves in public. She tended to sleep in the stable with her horses while on the road and never bathed in a public bath house. Whenever an unsuspecting widow or single woman took a romantic interest in Charley, Parkhurst made sure her route was switched. To offset these peculiarities and ground her identity as a male, she swore like a longshoreman, smoked cigars, chewed tobacco, and was said to have known the inside of numerous saloons frequented by teamsters.

The question remains as to why Charlotte Darkey Parkhurst became One-eyed Charley. The challenge of keeping up the masquerade year after year seems daunting while the sacrifices involved were extreme. Friendships had to be kept to a minimum, while relationships with the opposite sex were not possible. Rumors that she was a cross-dresser and lesbian were spread at the time of her death, but the truth seems more complicated. In a male-dominated society, perhaps Charlotte became Charley to earn a decent wage and work at an occupation that offered excitement and challenge. Stage drivers were considered kings of the road, and many were celebrated for their daring as well as their skill.

In 1954, long after her original headstone had been stolen from the Odd Fellows Cemetery in Watsonville, her grave was rediscovered. A local historical society placed a new marker on the plot. The inscription reads: "Charley Darkey Parkhurst (1812–1879). One-Eyed Charley, the first woman to vote in the U.S., November 3, 1868."

ANNIE
OAKLEY
1860–1926

Though arguably America's greatest female sharpshooter, Annie Oakley was never an outlaw, a hellraiser, nor even a westerner.

Phoebe Anne Oakley Moses was born on August 13, 1860, in a log cabin in Patterson Township, Darke County, Ohio. She was the fifth of seven children of Jake and Susanne Moses.

From an early age, Little Annie seemed a natural at shooting a gun. "I was eight years old when I made my first shot," Annie related to an interviewer, "and I still consider it one of the best shots I ever made." Spotting a squirrel perched on a fence in front of her house, the child impulsively climbed onto a chair, dragged down a loaded rifle, then rested the gun on the porch rail. Remembering to shoot a squirrel in the head so as not to spoil the meat, Annie triggered "a wonderful shot, going right through the head from side to side." Annie's frightened mother refused to let her touch the gun again for eight months, but it wasn't long before the little girl was putting meat in the family pot.

Phoebe Anne Oakley Moses was dubbed "Annie" by her four older sisters.

Annie was offered a schooling opportunity if she assisted a housewife whose husband was superintendent of the county prison farm. It was while sewing for the inmates that Annie became fascinated by needlework. Eventually the quality of her embroidery would reach the level of art. When offered wages above the cost of schooling in return for babysitting duties, Annie moved to a farm 40 miles from her home. Unfortunately, she was underfed and sometimes beaten. Two years later, Annie broke away and made her way home.

By the time she was a teenager, Oakley was a dead shot. To help earn a living, she supplied game to a general store. The storekeeper began shipping her surplus to a Cincinnati hotel. The hotel keeper, Jack Frost, met Annie when she visited a married sister in Cincinnati. Frost set up a Thanksgiving Day shooting match between Annie and a traveling exhibition sharpshooter named Frank Butler. Butler always issued a challenge to local marksmen. Frost put up $50 on a 15-year-old girl wearing a sunbonnet and a pink gingham dress. Annie outshot Butler by one clay pigeon. The mighty marksman was so impressed that when he went on the road with his act, he began a correspondence. On June 22, 1876, Frank and Annie were married.

Butler, an Irish immigrant with a failed marriage in his past, was about ten years older than his young wife, but they became a devoted and inseparable couple. Butler and another crack shot named Billy Graham performed between acts of a traveling stock company, but when an ill Graham missed a performance, he was permanently replaced by markswoman "Annie Oakley."

Frank Butler and Annie Oakley toured the vaudeville circuits, then joined the Sells Brothers Circus. When Sells Brothers played New Orleans in 1884, Buffalo Bill's Wild West was also in town. Frank and Annie took in Cody's show, then asked the legendary westerner for a job. The Wild West had other shooting acts, but Butler offered to perform without pay as a tryout. Cody gave Frank and Annie a trial in Louisville early in 1885, and a crowd of 17,000 responded immediately to sweet-natured, beautiful Annie Oakley.

Oakley, a natural showman and crowd-pleaser, became one of the primary assets of Cody's Wild West. Annie traveled with Cody for 17 years but found it unnecessary to sign a contract with the old frontiersman, stating "His words were more than most contracts." Cody affectionately called her Little Missie, audiences regarded her as America's Sweetheart, and Chief Sitting Bull, who joined the Wild West shortly after Annie and Frank, gave her the name *Watanya Cicilia*—Little Sure Shot.

Annie lived up to Sitting Bull's nickname in performance after performance. She was a

shooting machine with a rifle or shotgun. The year before she joined Cody's Wild West, she shot 943 out of the 1,000 glass balls tossed in the air by Butler in a Tiffin, Ohio, exhibition. In Cincinnati in 1885, she fired a shotgun for over nine hours to register 4,772 hits out of 5,000 for 95.4 percent. In 1888 at Glouscester, New Jersey, $5,000 was wagered that Annie could not hit 40 of 50 clay pigeons, but Little

Annie Oakley was a star attraction in Buffalo Bill's Wild West for 17 years; she also was the star in other shows before and after her association with Cody.

Sure Shot hit 49. The next day she was challenged by the champion of New Jersey, Miles Johnson, whom she defeated by again hitting 49 of 50.

Oakley's act consisted of more than just shooting clay pigeons and glass balls. For a touch of showmanship, she liked to wait until two clay pigeons were released, then vault over a table, snatch up her gun, and shoot both targets. Other parts of their act featured Butler shooting an apple from the head of a trained dog. At 30 paces, Annie would shoot a dime from Butler's fingers or a lighted cigarette from his lips. She could also hit a dime tossed in the air or slice a playing card in half. Sometimes, Butler would toss a card with a picture of Oakley inside a heart-shaped bull's eye into the air, and Little Sure Shot would drill it six times.

Prominently advertised as The Peerless Wing and Rifle Shot, Oakley appeared second on Cody's bill of 19 acts. Following the grand entrance of riders, the diminutive Annie paraded in, bowing, and throwing kisses. In addition to her immense popularity, her early appearance was designed to accustom the audience to the constant explosion of firearms that accompanied the remainder of the show.

Annie Oakley was known the world over for her skill as a trick-shot artist.

Cody utilized several shooting acts, starting with himself. There were also Lillian Smith, a teenager who could break 495 out of 500 glass balls, and Johnny Baker, who consistently lost face-offs with Little Sure Shot. Audiences enjoyed the rivalry, and for those who thought that Baker always let the show's headliner win, he later admitted that he was never able to beat Oakley.

In 1887, Buffalo Bill's Wild West performed at Queen Victoria's Golden Jubilee in London, then launched a triumphal tour of Europe. In Berlin, Crown Prince William, later Kaiser Wilhelm II, horrified everyone except the confident Little Sure Shot by insisting that she shoot the ashes from a cigarette held in his lips. As always, she was successful. Cody's company numbered 640 performers and workers, as well as hundreds of animals and vehicles. The loading and unloading from trains and the feeding of the Wild West animals and crew had been perfected to a science, which impressed the military-minded Germans. "We never moved without at least 40 officers of the Prussian Guard standing all about with notebooks, taking down every detail . . . " wrote Oakley. Years later, when Kaiser Wilhelm was the detested villain of World War I, Annie stated that she should have missed the cigarette and shot the Kaiser.

Oakley, whose career was managed by Butler, broke away from Cody's Wild West to conduct a solo tour of European capitals, which immensely expanded her fame. Back in the United States, she appeared in a melodrama, *Deadwood Dick*, and in a variety act in New York City. Oakley and Butler joined Pawnee Bill's Wild West show, and Little Missie was reunited with Cody when Pawnee Bill and

Buffalo Bill merged their operations. Numerous competing Wild West shows capitalized on an enormous public appetite for the loud, colorful, exciting western extravaganzas, but aside from Cody himself, the most popular star during the long heyday of the Wild West shows was Annie Oakley.

On October 28, 1901, as Cody's show left Charlotte, North Carolina, for its final performance of the season in Danville, Virginia, their train collided head-on with a freight train, killing 110 horses. Oakley represented the most serious human casualty, suffering from severe internal injuries and partial paralysis. She underwent several operations, and her hair turned white. It looked as though Annie Oakley's career had ended.

After months of recovery, however, she resumed performing. She toured in 1902 and 1903 with the melodrama *The Western Girl*. Though her vigor was somewhat diminished, she demonstrated her old-time marksmanship in exhibitions. Annie Oakley never again appeared with Cody's Wild West, but in 1911 she began three seasons of touring with a show called Young Buffalo Wild West. In 1915, Annie and Frank joined the staff of the Carolina Hotel in Pinehurst, North Carolina, where they taught and

Later in her life, Annie Oakley taught rifle and shotgun shooting in Pinehurst, North Carolina, as well as in army camps during World War I.

demonstrated rifle and shotgun shooting. During World War I, they toured army camps, giving instruction as well as performances.

Offstage, Annie was quiet and prim, devoting herself to crafting her exquisite needlework and to reading the Bible. Although she sipped an occasional beer with the hard-drinking Cody, her favorite beverage was lemonade. Annie and Frank didn't have children, but she supported and educated 18 orphan girls.

In 1921, Oakley was crippled in an automobile accident. She and Butler moved to Greenville, Ohio, in her home county, where she died at age 66 on November 3, 1926. Butler passed away three weeks later, on November 23, and he was buried beside her in the Brock Cemetery near her birthplace.

Annie Oakley was not a westerner, and, except for her performance tours, she never experienced the Old West. However, through her countless exhibitions with Buffalo Bill's Wild West and other shows, and then later exposure in comic books, movies, television, and, most notably, Rodgers and Hammerstein's *Annie, Get Your Gun*, Annie Oakley became indelibly identified with the Wild West.

NELLIE CASHMAN

1850?—1925

"Pretty as a Victorian cameo and, when necessary, tougher than two-penny nails," wrote Nellie Cashman's biographer, Suzann Ledbetter. Ledbetter describes in down-to-earth terms this remarkable frontier woman who was known during her lifetime by such heavenly appellations as Frontier Angel, Miner's Angel, Angel of the Cassiar, Angel of Tombstone, and Saint of the Sourdoughs.

Born in Queenstown, County Cork, Ireland, around 1850, her formal name may have been Ellen, but from childhood, she was called Nellie. It appears she and her sister Fannie emigrated to the United States in the 1860s and settled in Boston. Years later, in an interview with a writer, Nellie reminisced about those years. She recalled that she worked as a bellhop in a prominent Boston hotel, a job she acquired because of the shortage of available working men during the Civil War.

During this period, she not only had the honor of meeting General Ulysses S. Grant, but she actually had a chance to chat with the Civil War hero. Grant must have been impressed with her for

The Angel of Tombstone, Nellie Cashman had a fine business sense but never let the pursuit of money overshadow her love of helping others.

he advised her to go west. "The West needs people like you," he supposedly told her.

Cashman took Grant's advice and used her hard-earned savings to travel with her sister to San Francisco in 1869. Within a year, Fannie married a man named Cunningham and began raising a family. Nellie hired out as a cook in various Nevada mining camps, including Virginia City and Pioche. With her savings from her months as a cook, she opened the Miner's Boarding House at Panaca Flat, Nevada, in 1872.

Forever footloose and willing to follow the gold scent, Cashman joined a party of 200 Nevada miners journeying north to the Cassiar gold strike around Dease Lake in northern British Columbia. Dressed in a colorful mackinaw, miner's trousers, boots, and fur hat, Cashman looked like a female Nimrod of the North among the prospectors who came to her boarding house near the diggings. Periodically, she came out of the wilderness to the city of Victoria, and during one of these visits, she learned that a scurvy epidemic had broken out among the miners at Dease Lake. She enlisted the help of six men, loaded pack animals with 1,500 pounds of supplies, including the antiscorbutics potatoes and lime juice, and began the long trip back to the Cassiar. The overland journey took 77 days.

Much of the time, the group had to sleep in the snow and subsist on short rations. One

Virginia City, Nevada, was home to Nellie Cashman when she was just starting her adventure in the West.

night, her tent was pitched on the side of a steep bank where the snow was ten feet deep. When someone tried to bring her coffee the next morning, Nellie was nowhere to be found. Nellie, her tent, and her belongings had disappeared. The men finally found her about a quarter of a mile down the hill. During the night, a small snowslide had carried her downhill and buried her under the snow.

United States officials at Fort Wrangel had tried to talk her out of making what she admitted was a "mad trip," but their advice failed to deter her. When reports leaked back to the fort that she and her party had perished on the trail, a detachment of men set out to find her. They did, relaxing with her partners beside a campfire on the Stikeen River. She politely offered her rescuers a cup of tea. Cashman's rescue party eventually reached the miners' camp in time for her to nurse 75 men back to health.

After the Cassiar strike, Cashman went to Tucson, Arizona, where she opened the Delmonico Restaurant in 1879, the first business in the town owned by a woman. The venture was a success despite her propensity for feeding down-and-out miners gratis. The next year, she moved to Tombstone, following the silver rush in the San Pedro Valley. She opened a boot and shoe store, sold it, and launched a restaurant. She sold the latter just before a fire gutted the entire Tombstone business district. Her last restaurant venture in Tombstone was the Russ House, which was named after the original in San Francisco. There, Nellie offered good meals for 50 cents. She advertised with the plain-spoken declaration that "there are no cockroaches in my kitchen and the flour is clean."

Cashman was a devout Catholic but also a pragmatist. While Nellie lived in Tombstone, a Reverend Endicott Peabody arrived in town. He had been educated in Cheltenham in England and graduated from Oxford University. Reverend Peabody did not have a church where he could hold his services, so Nellie prevailed upon the owners of the Crystal Palace saloon to lend him their premises. Nellie thought preaching in a den of iniquity was preferable to not holding services at all, so the barroom nudes were covered and faro games put away while Reverend Peabody attempted to turn sinners into saints.

The Crystal Palace saloon in Tombstone, Arizona, served whiskey and beer—and, on Sunday mornings, a measure of Christian services, thanks to Nellie Cashman.

During her years in Tombstone, Cashman became a prominent and revered local figure as she helped raise money to build the Sacred Heart Church and scrounged funds for the Salvation Army, Red Cross, Miner's Hospital, and for amateur theatricals. She also took up collections for individuals who had been injured or found themselves in trouble. In her missions of mercy, she often sought the assistance of the inhabitants of Tombstone's red-light district, because she found them sympathetic and willing to lend a helping hand. One Tombstone resident recalled, "Nellie Cashman always called for help from Black Jack, known as the queen of the red-light district, and Nellie said her greatest help came from the back street which had no name on the map."

In an unusual use of her nurturing tendencies, she served as an impromptu officer of her church in hearing the confessions of two of the five men who were to be hanged for the Bisbee Massacre of December 1883, in which four Bisbee townspeople were killed during a store robbery.

Cashman didn't always take the side of the miners and the downtrodden; she took the side she believed to be the right one. When a group of miners wanted to hang mine owner E. B. Gage during a strike, Nellie rode into the middle of the foray in her buggy and rescued Gage from the lynching party. She escorted Gage from Tombstone to Benson, where he boarded a train for Tucson. Gage became one of Cashman's lifelong supporters.

Cashman joined a gold-seeking party on a futile expedition to the Golo Valley in the vicinity of Guyamas, Mexico, on the Gulf of California. The story goes that a dying Mexican arrived in Tombstone one day with his pockets stuffed with gold nuggets. He stumbled into the front of a hotel and then fell over, mumbling something about Mulege. Mulege was on the Baja Peninsula, so the gold would have been located in desert

POKER ALICE

"I would rather play poker with five or six experts than to eat," reflected Alice Ivers, known simply as Poker Alice.

Ivers was born on February 17, 1851, in Sudbury, England. The family eventually moved to Colorado, where Alice married mining engineer Frank Duffield. When he spent evenings at a card table, she stood behind him and watched. Alice began to sit in on games while Frank was at work, and she quickly demonstrated an affinity for poker. When Frank was killed in a dynamite explosion, she turned to the tables for a living, and soon the miners and other gamblers began calling her Poker Alice.

Like other gamblers, Alice moved from one promising western community to another. In Colorado, she worked gambling rooms in Alamosa,

Central City, Georgetown, and booming Leadville before heading south to Silver City, New Mexico. At Silver City, she bucked the tiger at a faro table and broke the bank, then left for New York City to enjoy her winnings.

Blue-eyed and fair-haired, Alice dressed fashionably but also puffed on small black stogies. Because of her religious upbringing, she refused to play on Sundays, an unprofitable quirk.

Like most professional gamblers, Alice went heeled, packing a .38 on a .45 frame. She left Creede for Deadwood, South Dakota, where she took a job as a dealer in the saloon of a character named Bedrock Tom. The dealer at the next table was W. G. Tubbs, and one night a drunken miner pulled a knife on him. Alice deftly palmed her .38 and pumped a slug into

Alice Ivers received a fortune when she "bucked the tiger"— successfully predicting the winning cards at faro.

the miner's arm, thereby triggering a romance between Tubbs and herself. Alice Ivers Duffield married Tubbs in 1907, and the couple abandoned the tables for a homestead north of Deadwood.

In 1910, Tubbs contracted pneumonia and died in Alice's arms during a blizzard. Alice drove his frozen corpse in a sled 48 miles to Sturgis, where she had to pawn her wedding ring

to get the $25 to pay for her husband's burial. She promptly took a table in a gambling hall and resumed her old profession. With her first winnings, she reclaimed her ring.

While she gambled in Sturgis, she hired George Huckert to tend her sheep. He continually proposed to her, and when his back wages totaled $1,008, she married him. Alice noted, "It would be cheaper to marry him than pay him off."

During Prohibition, Alice opened a house near Fort Meade, west of Sturgis, offering liquor, gambling, and girls. But after she shot and killed a trouble-making trooper, her establishment was shut down, even though she was acquitted at a jury trial.

Alice spent her last years quietly in a Sturgis house that today is open to tourists. She died in 1930.

HARVEY GIRLS

Fred Harvey purchased a small lunch counter in the Topeka train depot in 1876. A few years after his purchase, Harvey persuaded officials of the Atchison, Topeka & Santa Fe Railway to allow him to open restaurants in depots along the main line.

Before the Harvey empire closed during the late 1950s, more than 100,000 women between the ages of 18 and 30 had been hired. The ladies became known as the Harvey Girls. Dressed in starched black and white uniforms, the Harvey Girls were regarded as symbols of hospitality throughout the Southwest.

Harvey Girls were never called waitresses. They were Harvey Girls, plain and simple. They lived by a strict code of conduct passed down by Fred Harvey himself. Even their personal lives were subject to scrutiny. As their historian, Lesley Poling-Kempes, has written, "They were expected to act like Harvey Girls 24 hours a day. They were told where to live, what time to go to bed, whom to date, even what to wear down to the last detail of makeup and jewelry."

The Harvey Girls were the mainstay of a restaurant chain that stretched from San Francisco to Chicago.

country. Unfortunately, the party underestimated the amount of water they needed to make the trip. When the group was perilously close to running out of water, Nellie volunteered to go for help alone. She came across a Catholic mission and organized a search party to find her companions. The gold-seekers were rescued and decided to abandon their quest.

Soon after Nellie's return, her widowed sister, who had been living in Tombstone in a cottage Nellie built for her, died of tuberculosis, leaving Nellie in charge of five children. She sold Russ House and took the children with her as she wandered mining camps in Wyoming and Montana and in the New Mexico and Arizona Territories. The youngsters, who never suffered for care and education, remembered their Aunt Nellie with great fondness. All grew up to lead successful lives, and one became a banker who managed his aunt's affairs.

In 1898, Cashman had her last adventure as an argonaut when she joined the gold rush to the Klondike in Canada's Yukon Territory. With a party of prospectors, she sailed to Skagway, port of entry to the goldfields far to the north. She made her way across Chilkoot Pass to the lakes leading to the Yukon River, then to Dawson, which was the center of the Klondike diggings. In Dawson, she engaged in several pursuits. She opened a short-order restaurant for a time and later a mercantile store. Always thinking of her beloved miners, she set aside an area in her store known as the "Prospector's Haven of Retreat," where the weary placer miners could write letters home, read, and smoke the free cigars she made available.

Many women might have been reluctant to reside in the rugged mining camps, which were dominated by rough and hardy men. But Cashman scoffed at the idea that she or her virtue were ever in any danger. Nellie told a reporter, "I never have had a word said to me out of the way. The 'boys' would sure see to it that anyone who ever offered to insult me could never be able to repeat the offense."

After years of helping miners and learning from their experiences, Cashman sometimes tried her hand at mining. While in Dawson, one of her claims along the Bonanza River panned out and garnered her more than $100,000. However, she spent most of that money either looking for or buying up other claims.

Cashman lived in Dawson from the most hectic period of the strike to its exhaustion. In those seven years, she became known as one of the greatest figures of the gold rush. Her champions included everyone from the richest of the Bonanza Kings to the lowliest of failed prospectors as well as such celebrated figures as Jack London, Joaquin Miller, Captain Jack Crawford, and Robert W. Service.

Around 1907 or 1908, Cashman's wanderlust took her farther north. She established herself at Fairbanks, Alaska, while running the Midnight Sun Mining Company in the wild Koyukuk region, only 60 miles from the Arctic Circle. She owned and operated 11 mines in the Koyukuk, but none of them paid particularly well. Still in excellent shape and full of life in old age, she once took a dog sled across 750 miles of rugged Alaskan wasteland.

In 1923, she retired to live in Victoria, British Columbia, where she died on January 25, 1925. Nellie Cashman never married, and if she had any lovers, she kept that information to herself. Once, during an interview with the *Arizona Star*, a reporter asked her about her lifelong status as a bachelor woman. She

This photo shows Nellie Cashman going down the Yukon River aboard the steamship *Casca* in 1921, a few years before she retired.

responded, "Why child, I haven't had time for marriage. Men are a nuisance anyhow, now aren't they? They're just boys grown up."

ADAH ISAACS
MENKEN

1835?—1868

"**S**he is the most undressed actress now tolerated on the American stage," fumed an outraged reviewer. One of her starring vehicles, the racy melodrama *French Spy,* was branded a "leg show," and another critic stated that her stage assets were limited primarily to "*them limbs* and *that bust.*" A wide-eyed reviewer, offended after viewing her in her most popular role—as a Tartar prince in *Mazeppa (or the Wild Horse of Tartary)*—once announced, "Prudery is obsolete now."

Who was this controversial performer who stirred up such extravagant reactions? She was a bold actress who became famous across the early mining frontier as Adah Isaacs Menken. Born around 1835 in the living quarters of her family's general store near New Orleans, she was christened Adah Bertha Theodore. According to one story, she was quite the well-rounded woman; Adah learned to ride and shoot in addition to experiencing a good education. Her schooling included instruction in the languages, poetry,

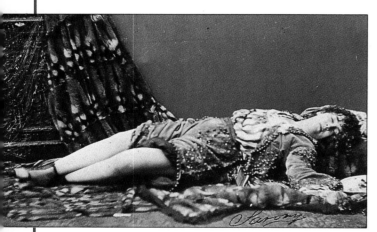

Beloved by mining audiences throughout the Southwest, Menken reclines seductively in costume as Prince Ivan Mazeppa.

dance, and voice. She made her stage debut as a child in a New Orleans ballet performance. Later, she said she danced in Texas and Cuba. Unfortunately, after her father died, Adah had to support her ailing mother with nontheatrical occupations.

In 1856, she wed Alexander Isaac Menken, the son of a wealthy Cincinnati manufacturer. Alexander Menken helped his wife join a small traveling troupe of performers, and she assumed the stage name Adah Isaacs Menken. She kept the name but not her husband, and she moved to New York City in pursuit of grander theatrical ambitions. In New York, she found another husband, a prize fighter, but not many roles. Adah divorced the pugilist, who was the second of four husbands, and found work as an assistant to the famed acrobat Blondin. She also managed to work up a vaudeville act of her own.

Producer James Murdoch learned of her riding ability and signed her to the role she would play for the rest of her life—Mazeppa. Ivan Mazeppa was a Tartar prince who fell in love with the betrothed daughter of a Polish nobleman. When Prince Ivan's overtures to his daughter were discovered, the nobleman had Mazeppa stripped naked and lashed "to a fiery, untamed steed." The steed galloped through the mountains to Tartary, where the king, outraged at his son's humiliation, organized a punitive expedition to march into

Poland. Prince Ivan rode—still unclad—to the rescue of his Polish princess.

In portraying Prince Ivan, Menken wore flesh-colored tights, but she was well-endowed, and her gender was obvious. However, it was not unusual for 19th-century actresses to play men's roles. The great Sarah Bernhardt, for example, appeared as Hamlet. Menken opened as Prince Ivan Mazeppa in 1861 in Albany, New York. *Mazeppa* proved to be a sensation, although a New York *Tribune* critic was unimpressed by Adah's acting ability, "Her talent is like gold in quartz veins—all in the rough."

Tom Maguire, a San Francisco theatrical impresario, knew that masculine audiences in gold mining country would be impressed by more than her thespian gifts. Western theaters in general provided enthusiastic receptions for melodramas and other performances. Adah Isaacs Menken was a spectacular hit in *Mazeppa,* and she toured throughout mining country. In Virginia City, Nevada, Samuel Clemens, beginning his writing career for the *Territorial Enterprise,* appreciated Adah as a "shape artist," penned a rave review, then spent a memorable evening with the star at her room in the International Hotel.

The dark-haired actress proved to be captivating company. Menken loved to gamble; she was one of the first women to smoke in public; and she was a delightful conversa-tionalist who enjoyed reading her own poetry and listening to the verse of others. She counted among her friends Walt Whitman, Charles Dickens, the elder Alexandre Dumas, hedonistic English poet Algernon Charles Swinburne, and French novelist George Sand. Sand, who smoked cigars and enjoyed wearing men's clothing, was another daring woman of her day.

Menken met these European literary figures when she starred in *Mazeppa* across the Atlantic. She toured Britain, then played in Paris. Sadly, she developed complications

from an injury sustained while performing in the role that made her famous, and she died in Paris at the age of 33. A notable woman, Adah Isaacs Menken created a sensation when she toured the mining region of California and Nevada, where westerners recognized and relished a fine-looking woman—and a kindred spirit—when they saw one.

The well-rounded Menken wrote poetry and consorted with, among others, Samuel Clemens, Walt Whitman, and Charles Dickens.

BELLE
STARR

1848–1888

"The ghost of Belle Starr still rides the Indian Territory." These words appeared in the *St. Louis Republican* in 1910, 21 years after Belle was shotgunned from ambush. They remain applicable today. Among the women of the Wild West, only Calamity Jane attained the degree of notoriety afforded Belle Starr, the Bandit Queen.

The "female Jesse James," as she would later be called, started life as Myra Maybelle Shirley on February 5, 1848, in Carthage, Missouri. Her father, John Shirley, prospered as a farmer and owner-operator of the Carthage Hotel. Called May by her family, she was educated at Carthage Female Academy, becoming quite well read. She was also a competent pianist. During the Civil War, her brother, Bud, rode as a Southern guerrilla until he was slain in 1864. Within a few months, John Shirley, sick over the loss of his son and the disruption of his business, sold his property and moved to Texas, where another son, Preston, had settled near Dallas. The Shirley family traveled to Texas in two Conestoga wagons, one driven by 16-year-old Myra Maybelle.

Belle Starr was accused of many transgressions in her life, such as robbery and rustling.

After the war, Myra fell in love with Jim Reed, a former family acquaintance from Missouri whose credentials included service as a guerrilla raider. Married in Collin County, north of Dallas, on November 1, 1866, Myra and Jim moved to the Reed home in Bates County, Missouri, a year later. In September 1868, Myra Reed gave birth to a daughter. Though the girl was christened Rosie Lee, she was always called Pearl.

Jim Reed exhibited more interest in horse racing and gambling than in farming, and he became involved with Tom Starr's gang of rustlers. Starr, a Cherokee, was a hulking desperado who trafficked in stolen livestock and illegal whiskey from a family stronghold. His favorite accessory was a rawhide necklace strung with the dried earlobes of men he had killed, and he was emulated by his admiring son, Sam. The family stronghold was located in the Cherokee Nation at a place Starr dubbed Youngers' Bend, because outlaw Cole Younger often sought refuge there. Younger visited Dallas about the time the Shirleys moved to Texas, and there were stories that he was Belle's first love and

Pearl's father, but he always denied any such connection.

With such wild companions, Jim Reed engaged in rustling, whiskey running, and a killing or two. When warrants were issued for his arrest, Jim fled to California, where he was joined by his wife and daughter. On February 22, 1871, the Reeds had a son, whom they named James Edwin after his father and his mother's slain brother. A month later, Jim was charged with passing counterfeit currency, and he bolted out of California. Lugging along her two babies, Myra followed Jim back to Texas.

The Reeds settled on a Bosque County farm set up for them by John Shirley, but Jim, a wanted man, could not stay out of trouble. In November 1873, Reed and two confederates ventured into Arkansas and brutally robbed Watt Grayson. During this period, Reed was unfaithful to Myra, and she and the children moved in with her parents near Scyene, Texas. The following April, Reed was part of another small gang that pulled a stagecoach holdup, and the reward money for Jim Reed quickly mounted. He shot his way out of an arrest attempt in Collin County and fled north to Indian Territory. He escaped from a posse and headed back to Texas, where he was finally killed near Paris on August 6, 1874. Myra testified that her husband "left me in a destitute condition."

The young widow rented her farm but realized no profit, although she found the means to send Pearl to school in Dallas. Myra's father died in 1876, and she drifted into Indian Territory, where she married Sam Starr, a handsome man who was four years younger than Belle, as she was now called. Because she was married to a Cherokee,

Above: Some said that Belle's daughter, Pearl (right), was fathered by Cole Younger. **Left:** In this pose, Belle looks as if she deserves her reputation as an outlaw.

Belle Starr was a citizen of the Cherokee Nation.

Sam built a log cabin on a timbered knoll at Youngers' Bend. The approach to the Starr home followed a narrow defile that they called Belle Starr Creek. Jesse James later hid out at remote Youngers' Bend, causing Belle to complain that "My home became known as an outlaw ranch. . . ." She also complained, "I am the constant theme of slanderous tongues . . . " supposedly because of her refusal to let her neighbors hunt game on the Starr property.

Some of these slanderous tongues apparently belonged to ladies of a higher station, whom she avoided. "So long had I been estranged from the society of women (whom I thoroughly detest) that I thought I would find it irksome to live in their midst." Despite these protestations, Belle sometimes tended sick neighbors and occasionally shared favorite recipes with other women.

Uncovering the personality of Belle Starr from the facts and episodes of her life is not a simple task. Belle maintained her solitude, wandering off with a pillow and books for a day of reading, or after acquiring a piano, happily staying at the keyboard for hours. Belle's relationship with her children often seems contradictory. She doted on Pearl, but when her daughter later had an illegitimate baby, Belle arranged for the infant's adoption without Pearl's knowledge. Her son, Eddie, spent much of his boyhood with the Reed family. As an adolescent, he apparently stayed with Belle, and she often flogged him with a riding quirt.

Blue Duck and Belle Starr: This photo fueled rumors that they were lovers and that Starr hired the lawyer who helped get Blue Duck's sentence commuted.

In 1882 or 1883, Belle and Sam Starr were arrested for the theft of two horses and bound over to the Fort Smith court of the famous "Hanging Judge," Isaac Parker. Because of Belle's previous marriage to a criminal and the appearance of Jesse James at her home, sensationalized stories were printed that purported her to be the "queen" of a band of horse thieves. The courtroom was packed during the four-day trial, and Belle and Sam were declared guilty.

Because there had been no previous convictions, Judge Parker leniently sentenced Belle and Sam to one year in the House of Corrections in Detroit. Steadfastly refusing to permit Pearl to appear as a defense witness, Belle arranged for her daughter to stay with relatives. Belle wrote a long and reassuring letter to Pearl, promising "that never again will I be placed in such humiliating circumstances and that in the future your little tender heart shall never more ache. . . ."

Belle and Sam were released after nine months. Returning to Youngers' Bend, they resumed farm work. Belle became more solitary and withdrawn than ever. She brought Pearl and Eddie home. Belle hired a piano teacher for her children, but Eddie was indifferent. According to Belle, Pearl "tried hard, but had little talent."

By 1885, Sam returned to robbery and horse rustling. He hid out around Youngers' Bend where he was sheltered by relatives and friends. He also might have fled to New Mexico. As an ex-convict, Belle naturally was viewed with suspicion, and various charges were leveled against her in 1886.

That year, Belle consented to pose for a photograph in Fort Smith with a convicted murderer named Blue Duck. Belle was told that it would make Blue Duck feel better as he marched to the gallows, but his lawyer really hoped to call further attention to his client. The stratagem apparently worked, because Judge Parker later commuted the sentence to life imprisonment. A photograph of Myra Maybelle Reed that was taken when she was 22 years of age portrays a young woman with pretty features, but when Belle Starr posed with Blue Duck, she looked far older than her 38 years, revealing the toll exacted by a hard life.

In September 1886, while Belle was in Fort Smith winning acquittal from theft charges, Sam Starr was jumped by a posse as he rode his wife's mare, Venus, near Youngers' Bend. Venus was killed, and Sam was wounded. He escaped, but Belle persuaded him to surrender, and his trial was postponed until the next year. During this period, Sam's father, old Tom Starr, was sent to prison for whiskey running. Considering all of his bad luck, Sam was in a foul mood when he encountered a longtime enemy, Frank West, at Youngers' Bend. At a Christmas dance on December 17, 1886, Starr and West went for their guns. Both men inflicted fatal wounds, and Belle became a widow once more.

With Sam dead, Belle's claim to their Youngers' Bend property was in jeopardy under Cherokee law.

Belle Starr's body was returned to her daughter by a passerby. Pearl had Belle's tombstone engraved with an elegy, which ends, "The gem . . . sparkles yet."

Belle solved the problem by acquiring another Native American husband, Jim July. Tom Starr had taken July under his wing, even calling the young man Jim July Starr. July was 15 years younger than Belle, which did not please her children. Both children began to fall into trouble. Pearl turned to prostitution, and Eddie was arrested for horse stealing.

On Saturday, February 2, 1888, while riding on an errand, Belle was blasted out of her saddle in an ambush. As she tried to rise, the bushwhacker finished the job with the second barrel of his shotgun. The likeliest suspect was Edgar Watson, a neighbor who had clashed with Belle, but he was acquitted, and the killer was never officially determined.

Belle was buried near her cabin with no religious ceremony. She had spent her life in areas wracked by violence and lawlessness, and her taste in men linked her with thieves and killers. Her relationships with her children were troubled ones, and even though her reputation as a bandit queen was wildly exaggerated, she did serve time as a convicted felon. "It seems as if I have more trouble than any other person," she once lamented in a letter. Yet she brought on most of her trouble herself, which paints a picture of the West's most notorious female as more melancholy than nefarious.

NATIVE AMERICANS

"**I** thought God intended us to live, but I was mistaken," reflected Standing Bear, a Ponca chief from Nebraska Territory. "God intends us to give the country to white people, and we are to die."

Standing Bear became philosophical as his people faced the overwhelming westward sweep of a numerically and technologically superior race of conquerors. But other tribal leaders fought back with defiant courage. Crazy Horse was a fearless and aggressive Sioux chieftain. He outdueled General George Crook and 1,300 soldiers, then a few days later played a major role in the triumph over George Armstrong Custer.

Sitting Bull and Red Cloud also provided inspired leadership to the Sioux. Few American leaders of any race have displayed greater eloquence or nobility than Chief Joseph of the doomed Nez Percé. Quanah Parker, half-Comanche and half-white, proved himself a fierce warrior. And a middle-aged Apache known as Geronimo stubbornly refused to relinquish his wild, free life, conducting a masterful guerrilla campaign against incredible odds until he became the last chief to surrender to the U.S. Army.

Crow Indians such as these shared a similar economy with other Plains groups but saw themselves as culturally distinct from their neighboring Sioux and Blackfoot enemies.

SITTING BULL

1831?—1890

"I hate all white people. You are thieves and liars. You have taken away our land and made us outcasts." This hard-bitten view was expressed by an uncompromising Sioux war chief and medicine man called Tatanka Iyotake—Sitting Bull.

His father, a mystic and warrior named Returns-Again, had originally named the boy Slow because his habits were so deliberate. Born around 1831 near South Dakota's Grand River, the young Hunkpapa Sioux developed his own intimate association with the spirit world. He became devoutly religious, with the soul of a prophet, but he also possessed the ferocious instincts of a warrior and the leadership gifts of a general.

The Hunkpapa, a part of the Teton division of Sioux, were unsurpassed as fighting men. Slow grew up lusting for the prestige and honors of a warrior. When he was 14, he accompanied a war party who encountered a band of Crows. Slow raced ahead on his horse, rode over a Crow brave, and counted first *coup*, establishing himself as a warrior.

On the battlefield and at the negotiating table, Sitting Bull led the Hunkpapa Sioux in their fight to remain free.

His father, who had renamed himself Sitting Bull because of a dream, immediately gave the name to his only son.

Subsequent raids proved young Sitting Bull to be a daring warrior, and he was admitted to the elite military society, Strong Hearts. While his prowess as a warrior grew, he also developed a reputation as a visionary. His special ties to the spirit world were said to bring him guidance and insight into the future.

His exploits and engaging personality eventually brought him nine wives, several taken from other warriors, which was an accepted custom. It is notable that none of his wives were taken from Sitting Bull. He fathered at least nine children.

During an 1856 battle with Crows, Sitting Bull dueled with a chief who shot him in the left foot. Despite the injury, Sitting Bull felled the Crow leader with a ball from his muzzle loader and then limped forward to finish him with his knife. This impressive display of courage sent the other Crows galloping away from the battlefield.

Witnessed by 100 Hunkpapa warriors, the incident helped establish Sitting Bull as leader of the Strong Hearts, a position that included the responsibility of organizing buffalo hunts for his people. This responsibility proved to be a major one, as his tribe required as many as 30,000 buffalo each year. Sitting Bull's permanent limp from his encounter with the Crows was a constant reminder of his bravery in battle, and within a few years he became chief of the Hunkpapa.

Sitting Bull was a staunch opponent of the whites. He observed their unstoppable movement onto the lands of other tribes, and he sensed the danger of any contact between his people and whites. He began his lifelong struggle against the white man in 1863, skirmishing with soldiers of General H. H. Sibley who had attacked his hunting party.

Over the next two years, he frequently fought against American soldiers, and the fame of Sitting Bull as a war chief grew rapidly. He directed the Sioux in the Battle of Killdeer Mountain on July 28, 1864. With 2,000 men and eight artillery pieces, General Alfred Sully held the braves at bay.

Later that summer, during a brief clash with 600 of Sully's men, Sitting Bull was wounded at point-blank range by a soldier on foot. The pistol ball entered at his left hip and exited at the small of his back, but the chief stayed on his horse and galloped to safety. Sitting Bull scorned Sully's invitations to talk peace, and in September 1865, he and 400 warriors relentlessly badgered a 2,000-man column under Colonel Nelson Cole and Lieutenant Colonel Samuel Walker.

Feeling the pressure of the continued interference of the army, the Teton Sioux decided to coordinate their tribes under one chief.

Sitting Bull was the overwhelming choice for this unprecedented position. The chief began a campaign of harrassment against Fort Buford, a stockaded fort recently built in North Dakota. His warriors stole cattle and horses and picked off a few soldiers in skirmishes. When the sawmill at the fort was completed, Sitting Bull led a

When Sitting Bull surrendered at Fort Buford, the number of his followers had been reduced to less than 200, including these members of his family.

raiding party, stole the circular blade, and used it for a tom-tom.

The Hunkpapas were troubled by other Native American nations as well as by the encroaching whites. Late in 1869, 30 Crows killed a young Hunkpapa hunter, and Sitting Bull promptly led 100 warriors through the snow in pursuit. The Crows forted up at a rocky knoll now called Crow Rock, Montana, and conducted a fierce defense. The Hunkpapas overwhelmed the Crows and wiped them out in hand-to-hand fighting, but 13 Hunkpapa warriors died and 18 more were wounded. Sitting Bull counted three *coups*, adding to the total of 63 that he accumulated in his active years as a warrior.

Not long afterward, Sitting Bull directed an attack on a Flathead village on the Musselshell River. A small party of young braves drew 100 Flathead warriors in pursuit, whereupon 400 Hunkpapas launched an ambush that routed the surprised and outnumbered Flatheads. While leading a charge, Sitting Bull took either an arrow shaft or a bullet through his arm, adding to his honors.

Late in 1875, all the Sioux were ordered by the government to report to the reservation by the end of January 1876. Sitting Bull ignored the reservation directive. He was already angry that gold prospectors had been swarming into the sacred Black Hills, which had been promised permanently to the Sioux by treaty. A week after the deadline, the War Department was notified that Sitting Bull was hostile and should be dealt with by force.

Sitting Bull sent messengers to the Sioux, Arapaho, and Cheyenne, including bands living on reservations. He urged them to unite against the white threat. More than 10,000 Native Americans gathered, and with Sitting Bull's spiritual power and courage widely recognized, he was chosen war chief of all the camps combined. Three columns of soldiers converged on the northern plains. "We must stand together or they will kill us separately," counseled Sitting Bull. "These soldiers have come shooting; they want war. All right, we'll give it to them."

Sitting Bull did his best to arm his warriors, although at least half had no guns, and most of the firearms were obsolete. To provide numerous mounts for his unprecedented number of warriors, Sitting Bull sent small parties of young braves in search of horses to steal. "Listen, young men," he directed. "Spare nobody. If you meet anyone, kill him, and take his horse. Let no one live. Save *nothing!*"

Enormous organizational skills were required to keep more than 10,000 people and their animals fed and watered, and the huge camp had to be moved to new pasturage every few days. Sitting Bull presided over these demanding activities with his usual affable authority, though he radiated a fearful sense of purpose.

In preparation for the coming conflict, Sitting Bull underwent a ceremony. Each of his arms were sliced 50 times from wrist to shoulder. He then rose, blood dripping from his arms, and performed the sun-gazing dance, in which he stared all day into the sun as he chanted. The ceremony continued through the night and into the next day until Sitting Bull collapsed. During the ordeal, he received a vision of a great victory by his people over the whites.

On the evening of June 16, 1876, scouts rode into camp with reports that the nearby valley of the Rosebud River was filled with soldiers. General George Crook, at the head of 1,300 men, was on the march to make first contact with the rebellious Native Americans. A vanguard of warriors equaling Crook's numbers quickly assembled and rode through the darkness to the Rosebud. Having endured the bloodletting ritual three days earlier, Sitting Bull was too weak to take an active part in the fighting on June 17. Crazy Horse of the Oglala Sioux was the most prominent leader during the six-hour Battle of the Rosebud. When the Native Americans finally withdrew, perhaps hoping to lure the soldiers into an ambush, the fighting ended with nine dead troopers and 21 more wounded. Crook was so stunned by the unexpected size of the resistance that he went into camp for two months.

Sitting Bull's powerful dream had revealed great numbers of soldiers falling, but the limited casualties at the Rosebud did not seem to be the fulfillment of his vision. The big Native American camp was

Sitting Bull declined Buffalo Bill's offer to join a tour to England in 1887. Sitting Bull said that it was "bad for me to parade around" when there were negotiations to be settled regarding Sioux lands.

moved to promising hunting grounds along the Little Bighorn River. Sitting Bull was still expecting a major victory.

On June 25, Lieutenant Colonel George Armstrong Custer led his 7th Cavalry in search of the encampment. First, Major Marcus Reno and two companies crossed the Little Bighorn and attacked the southern end of the camp. Sitting Bull buckled on his cartridge belt, seized his .45 revolver and 1873 Winchester carbine, and mounted a black war pony.

Vast numbers of warriors also armed themselves and mounted war horses, and Reno's advance was checked, then thrown back into the river. As these desperately outnumbered soldiers were about to be overwhelmed, Custer approached the middle of the Indian encampment with five companies. While a few warriors stayed on the southern end of the camp to hold the ford, the mass of braves galloped to counter this new threat. As many as 3,000 armed braves battled Custer's 215 troopers, and within an hour, the so-called "last stand" ended with the death of all of Custer's soldiers. By this time, Reno's companies had been joined by others, and they dug in to present a determined defense.

Sitting Bull moved the Hunkpapa camp downriver, away from the bloating corpses of Reno's men and horses. He and his warriors then rode toward the defensive position, with the chief himself participating in some of the charges. After engaging in some sniping throughout the night, the warriors resumed fighting the next day. Yet Sitting Bull did not organize an all-out assault, feeling that enough of his braves had fallen. The victory was already enormous, with

more than 200 soldiers dead and many guns and horses captured. As another column of soldiers advanced from the north, the Native American camp was moved. A few days later, a new camp was set in the Bighorn Mountains, and a victory dance was held.

Eventually, the triumph over Custer proved hollow as hordes of soldiers descended upon the Native Americans, defeating almost all the nations by policy as well as by the gun. The murderous efforts of the buffalo hunters destroyed the Native Americans' major food source, a factor that aided the military in rapidly driving bands onto the reservations.

Sitting Bull fought to keep his Hunkpapas free. He engaged in unproductive conferences with Colonel Nelson A. Miles, and then fought the soldiers for two days before artillery fire sent the warriors into retreat. Miles pursued and forced the surrender of 2,000 Sioux, but Sitting Bull escaped with 400 Hunkpapas.

Top: Sitting Bull places a stone on a pedestal during ceremonies at the Standing Rock Reservation. **Bottom:** The Sioux police guard was sent to arrest Sitting Bull in December 1890.

In May 1877, Sitting Bull crossed the border into Canada. The Canadian government refused to assume responsibility for the Indians and urged the United States to persuade Sitting Bull to return. Sitting Bull refused to leave, though hunting was poor in Canada. When his band dwindled to less than 200 ragged followers, he reluctantly submitted to United States authority. Surrendering at Fort Buford on July 19, 1881, he was confined as a prisoner of war for two years, then released to the Standing Rock Indian Agency.

Lionized by the American populace as a legend of the Wild West, Sitting Bull made some public appearances and even traveled with Buffalo Bill Cody during the showman's 1885 tour. He wrestled unsatisfactorily with the government over the sale of traditional tribal territories. When a newspaperman asked him how Indians felt about giving up their lands, Sitting Bull growled contemptuously, "Indians! There are no Indians left but me!"

When the mystical Ghost Dance craze spread through the reservations, Sitting Bull refused to embrace the new religion. Despite his lack of interest, authorities ordered that he be taken into custody. They were concerned about the restlessness of the Native Americans under their charge and realized the influence a man of Sitting Bull's stature might have on them. Sioux policemen surrounded his cabin on December 14, 1890, but the chief's followers swarmed to his support. Fighting erupted, and there were a dozen casualities. Among them was Sitting Bull, shot through the torso and head by the Sioux police. He was buried in the military cemetery at Fort Yates, his coffin filled with quicklime. It was an end that the greatest of Sioux chieftains would have expected from his white enemies.

THE GHOST DANCE

As Native Americans faced cultural eradication, mystical religions that blended native beliefs and Christian-like concepts developed. Among those messianic movements was the Ghost Dance, a nonviolent cult inspired by a Paiute named Wavoka in the 1880s. Ghost Dance followers prayed, chanted, and danced to bring the return of the old world, in which dead relatives would come back, and the land would return to its original state—with the buffalo but without the white man.

Wovoka's message spread among several nations, including the Sioux, Arapaho, and Cheyenne. As it spread, the Ghost Dance took on added mysticism and its peaceful message was downplayed. White government agents near the Sioux reservations misinterpreted the religion and feared it might incite rebellion—a volatile situation that indirectly led to the Battle of Wounded Knee.

Wovoka prescribed nonviolence, ceremonial purification, and abstinance from alcohol for the followers of his religion, which whites called the Ghost Dance.

CRAZY HORSE

1841?–1877

Daring, aggressive, and courageous, Crazy Horse led devastating attacks against Sioux enemies and defended his lifestyle with fierce heroism.

Born most likely in the fall of 1841, Crazy Horse was first called Curly or Light-Haired

A work in progress, the Crazy Horse monument in South Dakota was designed by Korczak Ziolkowski. No known photos of Crazy Horse exist.

Boy. His mother was a sister of Spotted Tail, who became a magnificent warrior chief. His father was named Crazy Horse, a respected medicine man of the Hunkpatila band of the Oglala Sioux. Curly's hair and complexion were lighter than those of other Native Americans, although his eyes were black. He was a quiet boy, but he eagerly participated in the training activities that prepared young men for war.

Curly was out of camp on September 3, 1855, when a large column led by General William S. Harney launched an attack. Harney's assault on the Sioux encampment left 86 dead. Many of the casualties were women and children. Harney also marched off with 70 female captives. Stunned at the slaughter of his friends and relatives, Curly became a staunch foe of white men.

In 1858, Curly rode with a war party against an Arapaho village in central Wyoming. A small band of Arapaho warriors forted up behind some boulders on a hill and stood off the Sioux for a couple of hours. Suddenly, Curly's fighting qualities possessed him, and the youthful brave rode his pony at the Arapaho position. As their arrows whizzed by him, he counted *coup* on two Arapaho before pulling back. Twice more he charged the enemy, and when two warriors rode out to challenge him, he killed them both with arrows. When he dismounted to scalp the fallen braves, another Arapaho fired an arrow into his leg, but he managed to limp to safety.

At the victory dance celebrating his feat, Crazy Horse proudly gave Curly a new name—his own. Crazy Horse was a common name among the Sioux, but in more than two decades of valiant deeds, the fearless brave made it his own. The name came to symbolize the proud courage of the Native Americans of the last days of the Old West.

THE SIOUX

Fierce warriors and masters of their lands, the Sioux represent the prototype of the Plains Indians, and indeed of Native Americans in general.

The Sioux nation consists of three subgroups, the Eastern or Santee group, the Central or Yankton group, and the Western or Teton group. The word Sioux can be traced back to the Chippewa word for the tribe, *nadowe-is-iw*, which means adders, or enemies. This term was then corrupted by French *voyageurs* into *nadouessioux*. While Sioux remains the popular designation of this nation, the word Dakota, which is Siouan for allies, is a more correct term. In the Santee dialect, the tribe referred to itself as the Dakota. In the Teton dialect, it was the Lakota, while in the Yankton dialect, it was the Nakota. The name the Sioux nation used to refer to themselves was *Ocheti shakowin,* which

means the seven council fires.

The aboriginal homelands of the once agricultural Sioux were the forests east of the Mississippi River. Conflict with other Native American nations, particularly the Chippewa, resulted in the migration of some of the Sioux sub-

A Dakota couple stands outside their tepee. Covered in buffalo hide, it was waterproof, easily transportable, and well ventilated.

groups across the Mississippi. Once settled on the Plains, the Sioux turned away from agriculture. When they acquired horses, they became master buffalo hunters, gallant horsemen, and bold warriors.

Like other Plains Indians, the Sioux lived in tepees, or *tipis* (a Dakota

word). Within Sioux tribes or divisions, a number of societies existed that performed various functions. Military societies performed policing duties and presided over the buffalo hunts; other societies were shamanistic. Men acquired prominence within their tribe by committing brave acts during warfare.

The most westward-dwelling and largest subgroup of the Sioux was the Teton. It consisted of several divisions: Brulé, Hunkpapa, Minniconjou, Oglala, Two Kettle, San Arcs, and Blackfoot (no relation to the Blackfoot nation). The wealth built up by the Teton in terms of fine horses as well as stores of food and hides to trade resulted in the Teton becoming the most powerful of the Sioux and thus the principal threat to whites. From the Teton came the Sioux's great leaders—Sitting Bull, Crazy Horse, and Red Cloud.

THE OTHER SIDE
OF THE STORY

Native Americans had their own stories to tell in regard to the Sioux campaign of 1876 and the Battle of the Little Bighorn. In drawings and in first-person accounts, warriors who participated in the fighting that summer offer different points of view. Skirmishes never reported in U.S. military accounts are detailed in Cheyenne drawings, for example, while some Sioux depictions of the Little Bighorn mention no last stand or offer any focus on Custer.

Flying Hawk was an Oglala Sioux warrior who participated in the Battle of the Little Bighorn when he was 24 years old. Sitting Bull was his uncle by marriage, and Crazy Horse was his cousin and best friend. Sometime during the 1920s, Flying Hawk dictated his version of Custer's last stand.

"When we got them [the soldiers] surrounded the fight was over in one hour. There was so much dust we could not see much, but the Indians rode around and yelled the war-whoop and shot into the soldiers so fast as they could until they were all dead. . . . We got off our horses and went and took the rings and money and watches from the soldiers. We took some clothes off too, and all the guns and pistols. Then we went back to the women and children and got them together that were not killed or hurt. . . . It was a big fight; the soldiers got just what they deserved this time. No good soldiers would shoot into the Indian's tepee where there were women and children. These soldiers did, and we fought them for our women and children. White men would do the same if they were men."

The introspective Crazy Horse joined a medicine society called the Thunder Cult, and he regularly sought visions. His mystical side fueled his warrior's instincts with confidence and dedication.

In 1865, Crazy Horse, who had counted a total of 240 *coups* by this point, was selected as one of four new chiefs by the Oglalas. Almost immediately, he assumed a prominent role under Sitting Bull in the harassing of a 2,000-man column of soldiers led by Colonel Nelson Cole and Lieutenant Colonel Samuel Walker. A year later, he played an even larger role in Red Cloud's War, which was a massive campaign against army possession of the Bozeman Trail.

During a fight near Fort Phil Kearny on December 6, 1866, Crazy Horse initiated an ambush by dismounting within sight of a detachment of soldiers, who eagerly charged the vulnerable warrior. Suddenly, other braves materialized to ambush the soldiers, killing two and wounding five others. This aggressive but impulsive reaction convinced Crazy Horse, Red Cloud, and other chiefs that a major force could be lured out of the fort and into a fatal trap.

On the frigid morning of December 21, 2,000 warriors concealed themselves on both sides of the road north of Fort Phil Kearny where the Bozeman Trail descended down a ridge to Peno Creek. A diversionary attack on a wood-cutting party drew a company of soldiers from the fort. Then, Crazy Horse and his party of ten decoys—two Cheyenne warriors, two Arapaho, and two each from the Oglala, Brulé, and Minniconjou Sioux—appeared within view of the post. An artillery round sent the decoys scrambling as though frightened, and Captain William J. Fetterman marched out with 80 cavalrymen and infantrymen.

Egotistical and scornful of Native Americans, Fetterman once snorted, "With 80 men I could ride through the Sioux nation." With fatal irony, he pursued the decoys with 80 men, defying orders by plunging out of sight of the fort. Concealed braves launched a barrage of 40,000 arrows and charged against a desperate defense. All 81 soldiers were slain and mutilated. Until the Battle of the Little Bighorn, the Fetterman Massacre was the army's worst defeat in the West.

On August 2, 1867, Crazy Horse led decoys against a group of woodcutters near Fort Phil Kearny. The soldiers were armed with new breechloaders and remained inside a barricade of wagon beds, successfully repelling an enormous war party during more than four hours of combat. Soon after this Wagon Box Fight, Crazy Horse was made war chief of the Oglalas.

Crazy Horse tried unsuccessfully to decoy George Armstrong Custer and his 7th Cavalry into traps during a Montana expedition in 1873. Custer's soldiers were too well disciplined to be ensnared, but during a skirmish, Custer's horse was shot out from under him.

In 1876, the army sent three large columns against unsubmissive Sioux and Cheyenne. The first clash occurred on June 17, 1876, at Montana's Rosebud River, where General George Crook's column of 1,300 men met an Indian force of approximately the same size masterfully led by Crazy Horse. Crazy Horse kept the soldiers off balance with a series of attacks and counterattacks, sending Crook back into camp for nearly two months. Eight days later, on June 25, Crazy Horse rode into combat against Custer's 7th, providing inspired leadership during the most famous battle of the Indian Wars.

These triumphs proved empty as the buffalo—the Plains Indians' major source of food—soon disappeared from the prairies. By 1877, Crazy Horse was forced to bring his starving people onto the reservation, after battling Nelson A. Miles, Ranald Mackenzie, and other noted soldiers. Assigned to the Nebraska reservation at Fort Robinson, Crazy Horse was constantly under watch as a potential escapee. On September 5, 1877, he

This illustration from *Leslie's Illustrated Newspaper* depicts Crazy Horse leading the Sioux to a reservation in 1877.

was arrested. When he realized he was to be confined in Fort Robinson's guardhouse, he went for a knife. Seized from behind, the valiant warrior was bayoneted through the kidney, and he died that night. His parents buried their 36-year-old son in a secret place.

For more than two decades, Crazy Horse had ridden as a Sioux warrior, counting hundreds of *coups*. He fought Crows, Shoshonis, and the white soldiers, leading his warriors with devastating skill in the West's largest conflict between the army and Native Americans.

CHIEF
JOSEPH

1840—1904

"From where the sun now stands, I will fight no more forever." Chief Joseph pronounced these oft-quoted words in 1877, at the climax of an epic campaign in which his Nez Percé battled the U.S. Army with such skill and unity that they won the admiration of everyone familiar with the history of the West.

During the first half of the 19th century, the Nez Percé, whose homeland was the Pacific Northwest, had traded with fur trappers and had proven open to the Christian missionaries. An important convert was Tuekakas, later called Old Chief Joseph, a noted leader, warrior, and hunter of the southerly Wallowa band of the Nez Percé. Baptized shortly after a mission was founded at Lapwai in 1836, he was christened Joseph and in 1838 made a deacon. A disagreement with Lapwai Nez Percé leaders in 1846 triggered his move to the beautiful Wallowa Mountains.

The chief's son was born in 1840 and named Hin-mah-too-yah-lat-kekt, which means Thunder Rolling Down From the Mountains, but he was also called Joseph. He proved to be wise beyond his years, becoming a gifted orator and diplomat. His younger brother, Olikut, distinguished himself as a hunter and warrior.

In 1863, the government tried to impose on the Wallowa band a treaty signed by some of the Nez Percé leaders but not by Old Chief Joseph. Angered, the aging chief destroyed his United States flag and Bible, then tried to negotiate a just agreement that would not deny his small band their Wallowa home. The old chief's health began to fail, but Joseph the Younger ably represented the band. When Old Chief Joseph died in 1871, Joseph the Younger was elected chief even though he was only 31. Chief Joseph skillfully countered government efforts to move the southerly bands for the next six years.

Though the nontreaty Nez Percé were not legally bound to the 1863 agreement, the Indian agent wanted them at Lapwai Reservation under his supervision. In addition, the governor of Oregon coveted their lands for white settlers. In May 1877, General O. O. Howard, under instructions from the Commissioner of Indian Affairs and General William T. Sherman, gave the nontreaty bands 30 days to move onto reservation lands.

Several chiefs wanted to resist, but Chief Joseph persuaded the other leaders to comply rather than risk war. Gathering as much of their livestock as possible, the Wallowa band hastily moved to a campsite near the Lapwai Reservation. But a small party of hot-blooded young braves from other Nez

Chief Joseph remained resolute in his dealings with U.S. officials who wanted to enforce the treaty of 1863.

THE NEZ PERCÉ

The Nez Percé were the largest group of Sahaptian-speaking Indians. When this Native American nation was first encountered by the French, some of them were seen with shell ornamentation in their pierced noses (*nez percé*). Captain William Clark of the Lewis and Clark Expedition stumbled upon a Nez Percé village in 1805, becoming the first American to have contact with this group. "They call themselves Cho pun-nish or Pierced Noses," Clark wrote in his journal, despite the fact that nose piercing is not a custom of the tribe.

The Nez Percé lived in what is now western Idaho, northeastern Oregon, and southeastern Washington. Though related by language and culture to those Indian nations native to the Columbia Plateau, they lived just far enough east to be influenced by the Plains Indians. At first, the Nez Percé centered themselves around small villages made up of A-framed communal lodges. The villages were located on rivers or streams filled with salmon, which became their main source of food. There was no leadership above the village level, and each village operated independently.

The ways of the Nez Percé changed dramatically after they acquired horses during the 18th century. Unlike other mounted Native Americans, the Nez Percé became expert horse breeders, specializing in fine Appaloosa ponies. The horse allowed them to hunt buffalo, which became their main source of food, and to trade with nations beyond the Rockies. The organization needed for such activities led to the formation of larger bands and the evolution of a tribal government. Like the Plains Indians, they became tepee dwellers. They also adopted war practices, war dances, and horse tactics from their Plains neighbors.

When the Nez Percé acquired firearms, they became unusually adept marksmen. They sometimes battled war parties

This photo of a Nez Percé tepee at the Yellowstone River was taken in 1871 by William Henry Jackson.

of other Indian nations in the traditional style of Plains Indians, but they enjoyed good relations with the white intruders who ventured into their magnificent homeland in the Pacific Northwest in the late 18th century.

The Nez Percé actually consisted of two groups, the Upper and Lower Nez Percé. Each occupied its own land, but they shared common hunting grounds. The U.S. government never fully realized the distinction between the two. When the Upper Nez Percé signed away the lands of both groups in an 1863 treaty, the stage was set for trouble between the whites and all the Nez Percé.

Percé bands went on a raid against offensive white settlers, putting the area into a panic.

General Howard sent for help from all outposts in the region. Captain David Perry led more than 100 troopers to protect settlers at Grangeville, only 15 miles from the camp of Chief Joseph. Adding several cowboy volunteers, Perry confidently rode toward the encampment on White Bird Creek. Perry deployed his men at dawn on June 17, 1877, but six Nez Percé rode out under a white flag. When this peace party was fired upon, Nez Percé marksmen opened fire on the soldiers. Both of the buglers fell, which rendered it impossible for Perry to readily communicate orders. The soldiers were routed, and the Nez Percé pressed their retreat for 18 miles. With 34 men killed and four wounded, Perry lost a third of his command.

Chief Joseph was not a warrior; he was responsible for the camp and stock herds during a battle or conflict. Since he had been the principal Nez Percé spokesman for years, however, General Howard assumed that Joseph was the primary leader. It was Olikut and

When Chief Joseph surrendered, he said, "...I am tired; my heart is sick and sad. From where the sun now stands, I will fight no more forever."

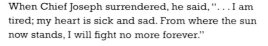

warriors from other bands who led the fighting in the ensuing Nez Percé War.

General Howard marched in pursuit of the Nez Percé with 500 men. The five non-treaty bands gathered for an exodus eastward through the mountains, hoping to find allies among the Crows. The Nez Percé mustered fewer than 200 warriors from 700 men, women, and children.

Although encumbered by infants and the elderly, the Nez Percé easily outmaneuvered Howard's column through rugged country. The warriors launched raids against the troopers. On July 11, 1877, Howard finally made contact with the Nez Percé camp at the South Fork of the Clearwater in Idaho Territory. Though the warriors were outnumbered three to one and faced artillery and Gatling guns, they outdueled the soldiers and then slipped away the next day.

After a difficult 11-day trek into Crow country, the Nez Percé found their way blocked by a timber barricade guarded by more than 200 soldiers and volunteers. Somehow, the Nez Percé clambered through where the whites claimed "a goat could not pass," and the barricade was derisively christened Fort Fizzle. The Crows wanted no part of a war against the army, so the Nez Percé found little help from them. Colonel John Gibbon intercepted the Nez Percé at Big Hole, Montana, on August 9. As soldiers charged into the camp, women and children were shot and clubbed. Joseph carried his infant daughter to safety. The warriors quickly counterattacked, enabling the noncombatants and wounded to retreat.

Continuing to outfox various pursuit columns, the tiring Nez Percé turned north toward Canada. Howard desperately sent orders to Colonel Nelson A. Miles at Fort Keough to try to block their path to the border; Miles mobilized eight companies within hours as Howard deliberately delayed his pursuit. Overestimating their safety, the Nez Percé camped at Bear Paw Mountain, a day's ride from the Canadian border. When Miles arrived, the Nez Percé women were taking down the camp. The soldiers hurtled into the camp, but they were repulsed by a counterattack.

The Nez Percé dug in and concentrated their fire on officers, taking a severe toll on army leaders. As a heavy snow fell on the second day, Miles called for a parley. When Chief Joseph came to negotiate, he was treacherously confined. The Nez Percé warriors countered by capturing an officer to exchange for Chief Joseph. When artillery was brought up, the Nez Percé pulled back to the cover of ravines.

By the time Howard arrived on the evening of October 4, Olikut and a majority of the warriors were dead. The next day Joseph surrendered. He delivered a bitter but moving oration that expressed the grief of his people, then turned over 431 Nez Percé, only 79 of whom were men.

Although Chief Joseph had not been a combat leader during the 1,600-mile campaign, abashed army officers and the press portrayed him as a military genius. As the starved and ragged Nez Percé were taken through Bismarck, admiring citizens turned out to cheer and hand out food. The captives were first taken to Kansas, then moved to Indian Territory in 1879. In the unfamiliar climate, large numbers of these mountain Indians sickened and died, including Chief Joseph's infant daughter. Joseph traveled to Washington, D.C., to make eloquent pleas with officials and the press on behalf of his people. Public sympathy finally resulted in the return of 268 surviving Nez Percé to the Northwest in 1885, although only 118 were permitted to rejoin their band on the Lapwai Reservation.

Chief Joseph and the others were placed on the Colville Reservation in Washington Territory, where he died suddenly on September 21, 1904. Prior to his death, he had traveled to Washington, D.C., to ask President Theodore Roosevelt to permit his return to the Wallowa Valley, but he was denied. Joseph reflected, "I have asked some of the great white chiefs where they get the authority to say to the Indian that he shall stay in one place. They cannot tell me."

This illustration from *Leslie's Illustrated Newspaper* depicts Colonel Nelson Miles's charge against the Nez Percé at Bear Paw Mountain.

QUANAH PARKER

1852?—1911

Kwahnah, meaning sweet odor, was the son of Comanche war chief Peta Nocona and Cynthia Ann Parker. Settlers on the Texas frontier came to know him as Quanah Parker, the most notable Comanche of his generation. As a youth, Kwahnah established himself as a gifted warrior, and his Khwahada band were the last Comanche to surrender to reservation life. On the reservation, Quanah Parker proved a fine peacetime leader.

Nine-year-old Cynthia Ann was abducted during an 1836 Comanche raid on Parker's Fort in central Texas. Called Nadua by the Comanche, she married Peta, and their first child, Kwahnah, was born around 1852, according to the best calculations. The couple had two other children, a son named Pecos and a daughter called Topsannah.

Kwahnah rode with the Khwahadas, who snubbed a peace council in 1867 and were singled out for fierce retribution.

Kwahnah grew into a tall, strong man with bold features. His eyes were bluish grey, but aside from his large physique, little else about his appearance indicated that he was half white. He became a splendid rider and was taught to handle the traditional Comanche weapons.

Texas Ranger Sul Ross led a raid on Peta's camp on December 17, 1860. The chief, his young sons, and his warriors were on a hunt, although Ross mistakenly thought Peta was among the dead. Nadua, fleeing with Topsannah, was almost shot down by Charles Goodnight, but the young Ranger held his fire when he saw her light-colored eyes.

The raiders realized that Nadua was Cynthia Ann Parker, and she and her daughter were taken to the Parker family. There she pined for her husband and sons. When Topsannah died of a childhood disease, Cynthia Ann became grief-stricken and refused to eat. She died at her brother's home in 1864.

During this period, Peta Nocona also died. His half-white sons faced a harsh existence as orphans. Kwahnah established himself in the only way possible to a Comanche male, overcompensating for his biracialism by excelling as a hunter and warrior. By the time Kwahnah was 15, he had slain his first victim in a raid, and he soon displayed qualities of leadership.

Now a ready participant in raiding parties, Kwahnah proved himself as a war leader. He left his father's band of Nawkohnees to ride with the implacably warlike Khwahadas. While raiding with a war party in north Texas, Chief Bear's Ear was killed by soldiers, and Kwahnah skillfully assumed command. Thereafter, he led his own war parties, distinguishing himself during the 1870s when the Llano Estacado hunting grounds in Comanche territory were invaded by soldiers and buffalo hunters.

In the fall of 1871, Colonel Ranald Mackenzie led a column into the Llano Estacado in search of the Khwahadas. Taking the offensive, the Khwahadas under Kwahnah raided Mackenzie's horse herd. The cavalrymen had camped at the mouth of Blanco Canyon, and their mounts were staked out with iron picket pins. Screaming warriors galloped into the herd, waving blankets and ringing bells. The cavalry horses plunged against their pins as the troopers rolled out of their blankets to form skirmish lines and tried to control the frightened beasts.

While the U.S. Army could not thwart Kwahnah, the vast number of buffalo hunters who wiped out his food supply did.

The Comanche dashed out of the camp with a number of stolen animals, then scattered in several directions. At dawn, Mackenzie sent several detachments in pursuit. Captain E. M. Heyl overtook about a dozen warriors herding some of the cavalry mounts. The Comanche abandoned their stolen horses to outdistance the soldiers. After rounding up the horses, Heyl sent them back to camp with a detail, then led the balance of his men into broken country after the warriors.

Suddenly Kwahnah launched a counterattack, which quickly sent Heyl and his troopers in retreat. Mackenzie's adjutant, Lieutenant Robert Carter, fought a rearguard action so courageously that he earned a Medal of Honor. When Private Sander Gregg's horse gave out on him, Carter reported that Kwahnah galloped forward and killed the recruit with a revolver bullet in the head.

However much they outmaneuvered Mackenzie's men, the Comanche were running out of time. Their world was disintegrating as the

CYNTHIA ANN PARKER

On May 19, 1836, a Comanche raid resulted in the annihilation of almost everyone at Parker's Fort in east-central Texas. The Comanche spared nine-year-old Cynthia Ann and her 11-year-old brother but took them as prisoners.

Cynthia Ann grew up with the Comanche and became content with the Native American way of life. She was called Nadua, and she darkened her hair with buffalo dung to look more like her adopted people. Nadua became the wife of Peta Nocona, a Comanche leader. She gave birth to two sons, Kwahnah and Pecos, and a daughter, Topsannah.

On December 17, 1860, Cynthia Ann and her daughter were "rescued" by a group of Texas Rangers and returned to her American kin. Although she longed to be with Peta and her two sons, her relatives would not allow her to leave, putting her under guard when she tried to escape.

Within three years, Topsannah died of a childhood disease. Cynthia Ann horrified her relatives by mourning like a Comanche, howling and slashing her arms and breasts with a knife. Grief-stricken, she refused to eat and died at her brother's home at the age of 37.

Cynthia Ann Parker and her daughter Topsannah lived unhappily among whites.

buffalo disappeared under the onslaught of hordes of hide hunters. The Comanche responded to the messianic promises of Eeshatai, who brought large numbers of Native Americans together for a ritual dance that lasted three days and nights. Eeshatai pledged magical protection from hunters' bullets as excited warrior societies planned a war of extermination against the hide hunters in Comanche lands.

On June 26, 1874, Kwahnah was prominent among 700 Comanche, Kiowa, Arapaho, and Cheyenne warriors who assaulted a buffalo hunters' encampment at Adobe Walls in the Texas Panhandle. Kwahnah led a dawn attack to the walls, but the professional hunters, forted up behind adobe and armed with powerful Sharps buffalo rifles, broke the charge with deadly fire.

The outnumbered defenders—28 men and a woman—fought back with desperate courage. One sharpshooter knocked a brave off his horse from a distance of nearly a mile. Four white men were killed during the battle, including two brothers who had been sleeping in a wagon outside the buildings.

The warriors were punished by the professional marksmen. Kwahnah's mount was shot out from under him. As he scrambled for cover, a slug caught him in the shoulder. By the time he was rescued, the warriors had given up the attack and turned on Eeshatai.

The Battle of Adobe Walls triggered the Red River War of 1874–1875. Small groups of hide hunters were attacked across the Panhandle. The army launched a massive convergence against the so-called Wild Tribes. In September 1874, Ranald Mackenzie and his crack 4th Cavalry discovered and penetrated

Kwahnah led a disastrous attack on a buffalo hunters' camp at Adobe Walls in Texas. The hunters fended the Indians off using their Sharps rifles with telescopic sights, which could kill a full-grown buffalo at 600 yards.

Palo Duro Canyon, the great refuge of the Llano Estacado and the last remaining source of buffalo. Routed from Palo Duro Canyon during the winter, Comanche and Kiowa were hounded by army columns onto their reservations in the southeastern corner of Indian Territory. Kwahnah and 400 diehard Kwahadas held out, stubbornly roaming the plains until June 2, 1875, when this last band of Comanche drove 1,500 horses onto the Fort Sill Reservation.

Although only 30, the ambitious Kwahnah immediately sought the approval of white officials as a means of solidifying his leadership position. He became extremely reticent about his exploits against Texas frontiersmen, realizing that information about his warrior days might arouse resentment. From this point, he was called Quanah Parker by Texans.

Early in his reservation career, Quanah sold grazing rights to the 3,000,000-acre reservation ranges, extracting lease fees for his people from Charles Goodnight, Burk Burnett, and other cattle barons. These tough businessmen taught him much about negotiation and subsidized his frequent lobbying trips to Washington. Shrewd and pragmatic,

Above: Quanah Parker (with one of his eight wives) became a prominent citizen and a voice for Native American concerns in Washington. **Right:** Comanche women celebrate at the Parker Monument.

Quanah dressed in business suits and successfully invested his personal earnings. In 1892, after exhausting every conceivable delay, an unhappy Quanah attempted to pacify his people after their reservation land was apportioned into 160-acre plots, then the surplus land was opened to white settlement.

Burk Burnett helped Quanah erect the Comanche White House, a rambling 12-room residence near Fort Sill. Quanah served as chief judge of the Court of Indian Offenses, deputy sheriff of Lawton, and president of the local school board he helped to create. "No like Indian school for my people," he stated pragmatically. "Indian boy go to Indian school, stay like Indian; go white school, he like white men. Me want white school so my children get educated like whites."

Quanah's prominence reached celebrity status, and he was in great demand for parades, including President Theodore Roosevelt's 1905 inauguration. During all of his interaction with whites, Quanah proudly retained much of his Comanche identity. He remained polygamous, rejected Christianity, and used peyote and mescal. Quanah often shed his business suits in favor of buckskins and never cut his flowing hair.

When Quanah died of pneumonia on February 2, 1911, his demise was presided over by a Comanche medicine man. He was buried beside Cynthia Ann. Quanah first became known as a Comanche warrior who courageously defended his homeland until reluctantly submitting to reservation existence. For the last 36 years of his life, Quanah's fame grew steadily as a romantic relic of the old days who used diplomatic skill and tenacity to guide his people to their best advantage.

THE COMANCHE

Like their neighbors the Kiowa, the Comanche were members of the Shoshonean language family. Sometime in the 17th century, the Shoshoni split into two divisions—the Shoshonis and the Comanche. The Shoshonis occupied what is now Montana and Wyoming, while the Comanche migrated south and east until they reached the southern plains around the end of the 17th century. By 1700, the Comanche dominated vast areas of prairie in Texas and Oklahoma and had already made contact with the northern Spanish frontier in New Mexico. The name Comanche derives from the Spanish phrase *camino ancho*, which means wide trail.

Prior to migrating south, the Comanche had lived subdued lives and survived by gathering wild plants for food and by hunting small game. After their migration and the acquistion of horses, their way of life changed. The Comanche turned to buffalo hunting as a primary source of food. The buffalo also provided hides for robes, coverings for their tepees, and even sinews for thread.

One of the first nations to acquire horses from the Spanish, the Comanche became the premier horsemen and warriors of the southern plains. They were expert breeders and trainers and athletic riders. They initiated the equestrian-based nomadic lifestyle that was characteristic of the Plains Indians. The Comanche nation was organized into 12 or more bands that lacked the lineages, military societies, clans, and tribal government of later Plains Indians such as the Sioux.

Among the most warlike of nations, the Comanche represented a hazard to travelers and frequently mounted raids deep into Mexico for slaves and live-

The Comanche were fierce warriors and expert riders but were nomadic and did not develop a high level of tribal organization.

stock. After 1790, they were sometimes accompanied by their allies, the Kiowa. Although other nations took prisoners from time to time, the Comanche were masters at kidnapping, especially when it came to Mexicans and Texans. The Comanche raided against the encroaching whites from the time of the California gold rush to 1875, when the depletion of the buffalo led to their acceptance of reservation life.

RED CLOUD

Red Cloud spent the first half of his lengthy life span as a free Oglala Sioux, a gifted warrior and hunter who reveled in the exhilarating life of the Indians of the northern plains. As a noted leader in his 40s, however, he recognized the impossibility of resisting the inexorable white advance. Submitting to reservation life for more then four decades, he was subjected to maddening injustice from whites and to endless criticism from fellow discontented Sioux.

Born in 1822 at the fork of Nebraska's Platte River, Red Cloud (a name probably not given until he became a warrior) was orphaned while very young. The boy grew up in the band of his maternal uncle, Chief Smoke, leader of the fierce Bad Faces clan. Taking up the warpath as a youth, he rode on raids against Crows and Pawnee. When he was 16, he claimed his first scalp while riding against the Pawnee. During a raid against a

Red Cloud led such intense assaults on the traffic along the Bozeman Trail that the U.S. government was never able to establish firm control of the area.

Crow camp, he killed a boy guarding the Crow pony herd and rode off with the horses. When the Crows pursued, Red Cloud boldly turned and killed the enemy chief. He earned even greater glory on another raid by killing four Pawnee braves. Red Cloud confirmed a growing reputation for cruelty during a fight against the Ute, when he dragged a drowning enemy out of a stream in order to scalp him.

By 1841, a dispute had arisen between Chief Smoke's Bad Faces and the Koyas of the noted Chief Bull Bear. The ambitious and brutal Red Cloud shot and probably killed Bull Bear near Fort Laramie. Although his reputation as a deadly warrior was still further enhanced, Red Cloud would never be trusted as chief of all Oglalas. The breach between the Bad Faces and Koyas was not healed for half a century; the Bad Faces allied with the Northern Cheyenne while the Koyas affiliated with the Southern Cheyenne. Red Cloud's ability as a fighting man remained unquestioned, as he continued his bloody career against traditional enemies of his people. Soon after assassinating Bull Bear, he caught a Pawnee arrow in his leg, a wound that would never cease to trouble him.

Red Cloud's first significant action against U.S. soldiers occurred spontaneously on August 19, 1854, near Fort Laramie. A Sioux brave killed a cow belonging to an emigrant, but Chief Conquering Bear's offer of a fine horse in compensation was ignored. Instead, a young officer named John L. Grattan led 30 men to Conquering Bear's camp, then belligerently opened fire. The chief was killed, but all Sioux warriors present, including Red Cloud and a number of Bad Faces, immediately swarmed the soldiers, who fled and were chased down and killed individually.

Red Cloud came to be widely acknowledged as the best war leader of the Oglala, a position he would solidify during the next few years with a bloody and successful campaign called Red Cloud's War. In the early 1860s, the Bozeman Trail cut through some of the richest hunting grounds of the Sioux and Cheyenne. The natives of the area, including Red Cloud's people, constantly harassed the intrusive whites along this trail, and in 1865 the federal government decided to establish and protect this dangerous route.

General Patrick Connor commanded the Powder River Expedition, directing three columns that were to shatter hostile resistance. Connor's column built Fort Connor (later renamed Fort Reno) to anchor the trail, then moved on to attack Arapaho, who had been peaceful until this unprovoked assault. Meanwhile, the other two columns, commanded by Colonel Nelson Cole and Lieutenant Colonel Samuel Walker, linked together and marched into Wyoming from the Black Hills toward a rendezvous with Connor.

In mid-August, Red Cloud and Chief Dull Knife of the Cheyenne learned of a large wagon train proceeding through the region, and they led about 500 braves against the intruders. The train, consisting of 80 wagons loaded with supplies for Virginia City, 73 civilians, and an escort of two infantry companies, circled up and held off the big war party. After a parley, Red Cloud and Dull Knife agreed to accept a wagon of supplies in exchange for safe passage, and during negotiations they heard for the first time about Connor's fort and expedition.

American Horse (left) participated in the skirmishes along the Bozeman Trail led by Red Cloud (right).

Red Cloud and other leaders rode to inspect the fort. Red Cloud decided that the fort's stockade and cannons rendered a direct attack too costly, so a series of raids was launched against travelers and soldiers. The hard-pressed Cole-Walker column ran out of supplies and staggered, battered and half-starved, into Fort Connor. General Connor was abruptly removed from command and the Powder River Expedition was terminated.

But the army soon returned in force, ordering Colonel Henry Carrington and his

THE BOZEMAN TRAIL

The rush started in Idaho and moved steadily eastward. Gold had been discovered in 1860, and a stream of prospectors poured across the land. Eventually, a creek-riddled gulch in southwestern Montana had become the focus of their activity. Thousands of miners wrested some ten million dollars from the ground, and Virginia City became the latest boomtown.

The diggers required a constant influx of supplies, and current overland trails to the area were arduous. In 1864, John M. Bozeman left Fort Laramie intending to find a more direct path to the gold. As later mapped out, the Bozeman Trail stretched from Julesburg in northeastern Colorado through Nebraska and Wyoming to Virginia City in Montana. For several years, it remained one of the main supply routes to Virginia City.

Bozeman's route ran through the coveted hunting grounds of the Sioux and Cheyenne along the Powder River east of the Bighorn Mountains. Use of the trail led to bitter conflict with the Oglala Sioux.

Cattlemen used the Bozeman Trail to drive beef north to the Montana goldfields.

18th Infantry to fortify and secure the Bozeman Trail. Carrington requested the Sioux leaders to negotiate with him at Fort Fetterman, and when Red Cloud finally arrived, he sullenly disdained to be introduced to the officers. Unable to secure acceptable terms, Red Cloud stormed out of the meeting, making angry threats to wage war with the intruders.

Carrington soon marched his regiment up the trail to Fort Connor. Red Cloud promptly launched a raiding party that stole the horses and mules brought to the post and then struck a civilian wagon train for good measure. Carrington detached one company to strengthen Fort Reno, then pushed on up the Bozeman and began construction of Fort Phil Kearny in July 1866. Two companies were sent to erect Fort C. F. Smith farther north on the Bighorn River, and Fort Phil Kearny was completed within four months.

Throughout the summer and fall, Carrington's command was constantly engaged against Sioux warriors under Red Cloud, who directed a deadly guerrilla war at the army and at travelers along the trail. By the end of the year, Carrington's force had faced the enemy in more than 50 skirmishes. Red Cloud's warriors had killed and mutilated 5 officers, 91 troopers, and 58 civilians and had stolen 306 head of oxen and cattle, 304 mules, and 161 horses from the vicinity of Carrington's fort. The garrison was virtually in a state of siege behind the elaborate fortifications of Fort Phil Kearny. The climactic battle occurred on December 21, 1866, a few miles north of the fort. After careful planning, a young warrior chief named Crazy Horse and a group of decoys enticed a pur-

suit column into an ambush, and Captain William Fetterman and all 80 of his men were slain. It was the worst loss the U.S. Army had suffered in the West up to that time.

Carrington was removed from command, but the military presence was maintained along the Bozeman Trail and hostilities continued in 1867. On August 1, warriors struck a hay-cutting party near Fort C. F. Smith, and the next day Red Cloud directed an attack against woodcutters near Fort Phil Kearny. At each battle site, large war parties swooped down on small bands of civilian employees and infantry escorts. The beleaguered soldiers had recently received new .50 caliber breech-loading Springfield rifles, though, and they fought for their lives with impressive firepower and courage. Each battle lasted for several hours, but the Oglala warriors finally withdrew after suffering heavy casualties.

In the end, Red Cloud's campaign proved effective. His warriors skillfully continued to strike civilians and soldiers at every opportunity. The War Department at last relented, pulling the garrison out of Fort C. F. Smith on July 29, 1868. The next morning, Red Cloud and a jubilant band of warriors rode in and burned the fort. A month later, Fort Phil Kearny also was abandoned, then burned, and within a few days the army marched out of Fort Reno. The Bozeman Trail was closed. Red Cloud had engineered the only successful Native American campaign against the U.S. government.

Red Cloud rode triumphantly into Fort Laramie in November and signed a treaty pledging never to fight again, but his triumph was short lived. After the government began to ignore the Fort Laramie treaty in 1870, Red Cloud traveled on a train to Washington, D.C., and met with President Grant. This trip, and his six other visits to the capital, revealed to him the true extent of his enemy's size and power. Red Cloud eventually brought his people onto reservations, and he helped to persuade his old ally, Crazy Horse, to yield to reservation life in 1877. He clung to power within his tribe by fighting political battles with government officials skillfully but with little success. For 40 years, he precariously remained his peoples' leader, but both he and they saw the steady erosion of the Oglala Sioux culture. Red Cloud died on December 10, 1909, a great victor in war but an ineffective victim of peace.

Top: In this 1868 Mathew Brady photograph of a peace council, Red Cloud appears at the far left. **Above:** Chief Red Cloud poses with his children in 1909. He became convinced of his enemy's power during several trips to Washington, D.C.

to New Mexico's Ojo Caliente Reservation to try to draw rations there. Agent John P. Clum regarded Geronimo as a renegade, and Clum had him arrested and shackled, along with seven of his braves.

Geronimo was moved to the San Carlos Reservation, then released a few months later by Clum's successor. Less than a year later, he broke away from San Carlos and headed for Mexico. During the Victorio War of the late 1870s, in which Victorio led an uprising of attrition against the whites, Geronimo operated with Juh in coordination with Victo-

Although Geronimo was not a chief, his personal magnetism drew many Apache warriors to follow him.

rio's Mimbres Apache. Late in 1879, Geronimo and Juh returned to San Carlos, but two years later they bolted the reservation once again to do battle in their own rebellion.

In the spring of 1882, Juh and Geronimo led 60 men back to San Carlos. At dawn on April 18, they audaciously broke Chief Loco and several hundred unarmed Mimbrenos off the reservation. Fighting their way back into Mexico, the renegades were attacked in camp by cavalrymen under a new agreement between the United States and Mexico. This so-called "hot pursuit" agreement permitted troops from either country to cross the border while chasing marauders. The Apache suffered numerous casualties, but they finally fought through to mountain hideaways in Mexico where they resumed their perpetual war against Mexicans.

During this period, Juh fell from his horse, either because of a heart attack or because he was drunk, and he drowned in a river. At six feet and 225 pounds, Juh was an imposing and cruel fighting man, but he was also a talented leader. His loss placed Geronimo in the forefront of the Chiricahuas who wanted to continue the life of mountain raiders.

The relentless effort of General George Crook was making that way of life increasingly more perilous. The Apache called the middle-aged general Gray Wolf because he operated like a cunning timber beast. Crook had been fighting Native Americans since the 1850s. He tried to think like a warrior so that he could understand their guerrilla warfare and methods of operation.

As Crook hounded the Apache in their Mexican lairs, one band after another headed north to the reservation. Geronimo agreed to parley with Gray Wolf in May 1881, but it was nearly a year before the vicious old warrior finally crossed the border, accompanied by nearly 100 diehard followers and 350 stolen cattle. San Carlos Reservation officials, however, confiscated his herd. "These were not white men's cattle," Geronimo resentfully complained, "for we had taken them from the Mexicans during our wars."

Geronimo located his reservation home on Turkey Creek, 17 miles southeast of Fort Apache. Although inclined toward stock-raising, the Apache were issued plows by the Indian Bureau and ordered to become farmers. While Geronimo's wives did the work on his farm, he remained peaceful for a year.

Geronimo and other leaders resented the bans on wife-beating, the drinking of *tizwin* (a weak beer brewed from corn), and other traditional practices. The wisdom of the prohibition against *tizwin* was verified in May 1885, when Geronimo and other Chiricahua leaders went on an all-night drinking spree. A few days later, Geronimo, perhaps fearful of repercussions and certainly restless for his old lifestyle, led four other chieftains, 38 braves, and 92 women and children in another outbreak. The renegades cut the telegraph wires, then headed for Mexico, pushing 120 miles before halting for their first camp.

The Apache scattered, with each of the five leaders taking a small band into a remote location. Crook coordinated the pursuit on the American side, while Mexican troops also rode to the chase. Thousands of soldiers tracked the fugitives relentlessly, yet Geronimo and a handful of followers remained elusive. Guided across the border by Apache scouts, one of Crook's detachments attacked Geronimo's camp on August 7, 1885, and captured one-third of the band's women and children. Six weeks later Geronimo slipped back into San Carlos, recovered a wife and child, then returned to northern Mexico with his family.

On January 10, 1886, Captain Emmett Crawford and a column of Apache scouts located Geronimo's *rancheria* near the Haros River in Sonora. Crawford routed the Apache with a dawn attack and seized most of their horses and camp gear. Geronimo sent a woman to arrange for a meeting with Crawford the next day, but dawn brought the approach of a Mexican column. The Mexicans apparently thought Crawford's scouts were hostile Chiricahuas and opened fire. Crawford was shot in the head, and four scouts were wounded, but the American party fired back, killing four and wounding five. Watching from concealment, Geronimo and his men enjoyed the unaccustomed role of spectators. Crawford never regained consciousness and died a week later.

Despite the efforts of two nations and thousands of troops, Geronimo remained at large until he chose to surrender.

When Mexican troops invaded his Sierra Madre sanctuary, Geronimo agreed to meet with Crook just below the border. Gray Wolf promised to try to persuade government officials to let the Apache return to their reservation after spending two years as prisoners in Florida. Crook hurried ahead to telegraph Washington about the surrender, only to receive the reply that Geronimo's terms were unacceptable.

Geronimo left the custody of Crook's scouts, however, and was on the loose in Mexico with a few followers. A bootlegger had provided the Apache with whiskey, and

APACHE

The most nomadic nation in the Southwest, the Apache became the last major Indian group to submit to American authority. The Apache called themselves the *Diné*, or the people. The word Apache derives from the Zuni word

This Apache camp in Arizona was quickly raised and could just as quickly be left behind.

for enemy, *apachu*. Along with their kinsmen, the Navajo, the Apache are members of the Athapaskan language family.

Some time in the distant past, while Europeans were still living in the Dark Ages, the Athapaskans migrated south from Canada to inhabit the parched lands of New Mexico, Arizona, and northern Mexico. In the vast lands of the

Southwest, the Athapaskans drifted apart. One group became the Navajo, who based their way of life on sheepherding and farming; the other became the Apache, who adopted a nomadic life.

The Apache way of life reflected the significance of mobility. They lived in hastily constructed thatch *wickiups* and did not rely on craftmaking like their counterparts, the Navajo. During the 18th century, raiding became a major source of meat and supplies for the Apache, although some of the Apache depended on farming and hunting small game for subsistence. Of the little farming that occurred by the Apache, it was the women who tended the crops and fields.

A characteristic of the Apache was their lack of tribal solidarity, which was indicated by the many subtribes, bands, and families. The Apache group was divided into six distinct subgroups: the Lipan, now extinct; the Western Apache; the Chiricahua; the Mescalero; the

Jicarilla; and the Kiowa-Apache. The Western Apache was further subdivided into 14 bands.

The Apache were fierce fighters, known for their guerrilla tactics. They fought with the Comanche to the north, the Navajo to the west, and the Spanish to the south. They were feared by the Pueblo Indian groups as well as by the Mexicans and Anglo-Americans. The U.S.'s post-Civil War policy of controlling all Native Americans included the Apache, who proved to be the most tenacious of the Indian guerrillas. Though most of the Apache were subdued during the 1880s, a few camps were never defeated, hunting and raiding in the mountains of Northern Sonora until 1930.

as Geronimo became drunk, his misgivings increased. "I feared treachery, and when we became suspicious, we turned back."

Crook was criticized by civilians, newspapers, and his superiors, which prompted the resignation of the army's finest strategist in the campaign against Native Americans. The capable and ambitious General Nelson Miles assumed command, throwing 5,000 troops into the field and establishing 30 heliograph stations to facilitate communications. Thousands of Mexican soldiers scoured Geronimo's old haunts, but the Apache somehow avoided contact. Only after Geronimo learned that the other Chiricahuas, including the families of those still at large, were about to be shipped to the East did he finally decide to surrender. Geronimo turned himself in to Miles in September 1886, and he shortly found himself aboard a train for Florida.

Geronimo was incarcerated at Fort Pickens, outside Pensacola, for the better part of two years. In May 1888, the Native Americans were moved to Mount Vernon Barracks, Alabama, an unhealthy site that decimated the Apache prisoners. Not until 1895 were they removed to a more favorable climate, Fort Sill in Oklahoma, where Geronimo spent the final 14 years of his life.

The old Indian warrior picked up a little English and learned to write his name. He became something of an entrepreneur, selling buttons from his coat for a quarter apiece, his hat for five dollars, and hawking bows and arrows that he made. For an extra 50 cents, the customer could purchase the old warrior's autograph. He proudly showed off his many battle wounds. He was a popular attraction at the Exposition in Omaha in 1898, the Pan-American Exposition in Buf-

falo in 1901, numerous Oklahoma celebrations, the St. Louis World's Fair in 1904, and Teddy Roosevelt's inaugural parade in 1905. Despite these extensive travels, he was never permitted to return to Arizona. As an old man, he remained a crack shot, and he enjoyed robust health into his 80s. He also continued to imbibe alcoholic beverages, and on a winter night in 1909, he drunkenly toppled from his horse and spent hours on the cold ground. Geronimo died of pneumonia on February 17, 1909, already a legend as the last renegade leader to surrender to the army.

Geronimo (front row, second from right) sits with other Apache captives on their way to Florida in 1886.

SOLDIERS AND CAVALRY

"**A**gain I repeat, this is a dangerous service." So said Lieutenant James H. Bradley, a veteran of the fierce combat around Fort Phil Kearney. Service in the frontier army indeed could be deadly. Moreover, soldiers suffered constant hardships along with isolation and low pay. "As regards myself," wrote Private Eddie Matthews, "can't say that I felt very rejoiced of a fight with the Indians; $13.00 a month is not an incentive to throw one's life away."

But any reluctance soldiers may have felt was overcome by dedicated and gifted leaders. General George Crook, who was deeply concerned about the welfare of his men, proved to be a superb field officer from the 1850s until the 1880s. Ranald Mackenzie became the best regimental commander of the Indian wars despite seven wounds. And George Armstrong Custer, a "boy general" during the Civil War, fought Indians with the same ferocity he employed against Confederates—until he was wiped out in the most controversial battle of the Indian wars.

Some of the key figures who developed and executed military policy in the West gather at Ft. Sanders in 1867.

SAM HOUSTON

1793—1863

Sam Houston endures as the human embodiment of the phoenix. He rose from the ashes of several ruined careers and a reputation as a drunk to become, in the words of Andrew

In 1835, Sam Houston went to New Orleans for money and volunteers; he returned to Texas with a company of fighters and more than $10,000.

Jackson, "enrolled as amongst the greatest chieftains." Samuel Houston was born in 1793 near Lexington, Virginia, the fifth of nine children of Major Samuel Houston, a career army officer and veteran of the Revolutionary War, and his wife, Elizabeth. After Houston's father died in 1806, his mother moved across the Alleghenies to a farm near Knoxville, Tennessee. Sam left home at age 16. He was curious about the Cherokee living along the Tennessee River and went to live with them, learning their language and customs. He was given the first of his two Cherokee names, Co-loh-neh, or the Raven.

After his sojourn among the Cherokee, Houston returned home. When army troops passed through Knoxville offering silver dollars for enlistees in 1813, the young adventurer joined the 7th U.S. Infantry and accompanied General Andrew Jackson's force to Alabama to wage war against the Creek nation.

At the Battle of Horseshoe Bend on the Tallapoosa River on March 27, 1814, Houston was among the first to scale a high stockade and fight hand-to-hand with the Red Stick band of the Creeks. He suffered wounds from arrows and gunshots in his leg, arm, and shoulder. The boldness of this young ensign came to the attention of General Jackson.

After the campaign, Houston completed a law course in Nashville and set up practice in nearby Lebanon. He was a frequent guest at the Hermitage, Jackson's estate in Nashville, and became a friend, ally, and protégé of the great soldier. With Jackson's endorsement, Houston was elected district attorney for the Nashville district and in 1823, at age 30, was elected to Congress. He served two terms as a Jacksonian Democrat, and after leaving office, he helped elect Old Hickory president. Jackson, in turn, showed his appreciation by putting Houston's name forward as governor of Tennessee.

Houston married 20-year-old Eliza Allen in 1829. Unfortunately, the marriage dissolved in three months for reasons unknown. Despondent, Houston resigned the governorship and drifted to Arkansas to live among his beloved Cherokee. On the Verdigris River near Fort Gibson, Arkansas, Houston set up a trading post called Wigwam Neosho. And he drank. So deep ran his whiskey addiction that the Cherokee called him Oo-tse-tee Ar-dee-tah-skee, or Big Drunk.

He still was respected enough by the Cherokee to become their counselor and public spokesman. He bid for a contract to supply food and trade goods to the Cherokee after learning that corrupt agents had been supplying them with inferior goods and pocketing enormous profits.

Through the influence of Jackson's secretary of war, John Eaton, and perhaps the President himself, Houston was awarded the contract. Ohio congressman William Stanbery questioned the arrangement, and on the floor of the House of Representatives, he accused Houston, Eaton, and Jackson of fraud. After Stanbery repeated his accusation, Houston met the

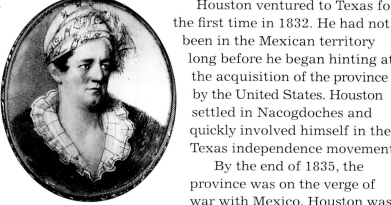

Sam Houston, here in Cherokee garb, wisely retreated from Santa Anna's army in 1836 until he could organize a tangible fighting force.

congressman on a Washington street and used his hickory cane to beat him senseless. Houston stood trial for contempt of Congress and was given a light reprimand.

Houston ventured to Texas for the first time in 1832. He had not been in the Mexican territory long before he began hinting at the acquisition of the province by the United States. Houston settled in Nacogdoches and quickly involved himself in the Texas independence movement.

By the end of 1835, the province was on the verge of war with Mexico. Houston was named Commander-in-Chief of the Texas army, and he appealed for volunteers in the newspapers. Land was offered to those who helped defeat the "usurper," President Antonio López de Santa Anna.

In a crude frame building in the village of Washington-on-the-Brazos, 59 Texas leaders declared Texas's independence and adopted a constitution on March 2, 1836. Houston began to plan his strategy to fight Santa Anna's 4,000-man army, which had surrounded the Alamo in San Antonio de Bexar.

Houston had earlier ordered the Alamo abandoned. However, Houston's order was countermanded by provisional governor Henry Smith, who dispatched Colonel William Travis to reinforce the mission. On March 6, Santa Anna attacked the Alamo, killing all 188 of its defenders. Three weeks later, while Houston was en route with his meager army to the Brazos River, Santa Anna defeated James Fannin's force at Goliad, executing Fannin and 350 men.

SAM HOUSTON AT
HORSE SHOE BEND

Sam Houston, major general of the Tennessee militia and commander of the outnumbered Texan victors at San Jacinto, first achieved military notoriety as a 21-year-old lieutenant at the Battle of Horse Shoe Bend.

During the War of 1812, Creek "Red Sticks" allied with the British and raided American settlers on the southwestern frontier. As General Andrew Jackson readied a column of Tennessee militia for a campaign against the Creeks, Sam Houston enlisted as a private on March 24, 1813, just three weeks after his 20th birthday. The towering young soldier was a natural leader. Within a month he was promoted to drill sergeant, and by December he was commissioned an ensign and placed in charge of a platoon.

Sam Houston charged over the barricade at Horse Shoe Bend even though he knew he'd face a barrage of arrows. One of them caught him in the thigh.

After a massacre of civilians at Fort Mims, Jackson retaliated against the Creeks at their village of Tohopeka, at Horse Shoe Bend of the Tallapoosa River, in what is today eastern Alabama. When Jackson's attack was repulsed in January 1814, other Creeks overconfidently moved to what they regarded as an impregnable stronghold. But two months later, Jackson again marched against Tohopeka, and his 3,000-man column included Sam Houston, now 21 and a lieutenant.

The Red Sticks had erected a zigzag log barricade across the entrance to their river peninsula. The Horse Shoe Bend peninsula comprised about 100 acres, and 1,000 warriors were positioned to protect this stronghold. On March 27, 1814, Jackson banged away at the barricade with a pair of six-pounders, then ordered an attack.

The first man over the barricade was 29-year-old Major Lemuel Montgomery, who was riddled with arrows. (When Alabama entered the Union five years later, the state capital was named after the slain officer.) The second man over was Lieutenant Houston, who caught a barbed arrow in the thigh. However, he fought off Red Sticks with his sword until other soldiers clambered over the barricade.

The arrow was ripped from Houston's leg. But even though General Jackson ordered him to stay out of the fighting, he soon limped back into the fray. Leading a charge against a Creek redoubt, Houston was shot in the right arm and shoulder. His arm was broken and the shoulder wound would trouble him for the rest of his life.

The battle raged on for hours, and about 800 warriors were killed. The power of the Red Sticks was broken, while Sam Houston had proved himself on the field of battle.

Before confronting Santa Anna's huge and well-provisioned force, Houston wanted to buy time to strengthen his puny army with volunteers. He conducted a zigzagging march through east and south Texas not only to fragment and confuse the Mexican army but also to enlist more troops. Everywhere he marched, he inspired enlistments to the cause by speaking of the Alamo and Goliad.

Houston shrewdly bided his time until April 21, 1836, six weeks after the Alamo's fall. He brought his army of 783 men to the juncture of Buffalo Bayou and the San Jacinto River to do battle with Santa Anna and his force of 1,400. At mid-morning, while the exhausted Mexican troops slept, Houston led his ragtag band through the prairie grass with shouts of "Remember the Alamo!" and "Remember Goliad!"

The 20-minute battle was little more than a slaughter. When the smoke cleared, 630 of the Mexican army lay dead, another 208 were wounded, and 730 were taken prisoner. Included among the prisoners was the self-styled Napoleon of the West, Santa Anna, who was dressed in a private's uniform. Houston, who took a painful ankle wound during the fighting, suffered the loss of nine men and 34 wounded. After signing a document declaring the independence of the province of Texas y Coahuila, Santa Anna was permitted to take the remnant of his army across the Rio Grande.

Houston was elected the first president of the new Republic of Texas. His platform included provisions of frugality in the administration of the new government and the immediate seeking of recognition of the Republic by the United States and then annexation into the Union. Recognition was granted in March 1837, but the annexation question languished for the next eight years. Whig opposition in Congress to Texas statehood was based on the belief that Jackson had promoted the revolution to add a new Democratic state to the Union. Opposition also centered around the provision in the Texas constitution that permitted slavery. As Houston's political career flourished amid the controversy, his personal life improved as well. In 1840, he married Margaret Moffette Lea of Alabama.

On December 29, 1845, President James K. Polk signed the act that admitted Texas into the Union. Houston served in Washington as the state's first senator, a post he held for 14 years. Among the issues that were dear to his heart were Indian affairs, antislavery, and the preservation of the Union. When he was elected governor of Texas in 1859, he continued to oppose the secession of southern states from the Union, making impassioned speeches that warned of the war it would create. When Texas voted to secede despite his warnings, he resisted joining the Confederacy and refused to swear an oath of loyalty to it. As a result, the Texas legislature declared the office of governor vacant, and Houston retired to his farm in Huntsville.

He died of pneumonia on July 26, 1863. Houston's final words were "Texas—Texas—Margaret!"

Commanding 783 men, Sam Houston routed Mexican troops at San Jacinto to secure Texas's independence.

GEORGE CROOK

1829–1890

"Indian warfare is, of all warfare, the most trying and the most thankless . . . " reflected General George Crook. "In it you are required to serve without the incentive of promotion or recognition, in truth, without favor or hope of reward."

George Crook engaged in Indian warfare during four different decades, and while most officers of the era found it almost impossible to move up in grade, Crook's abilities were so exceptional that he won promotion to major general. His final experience in the Indian Wars readily explains the bitterness of his tone, but the enormity of his overall success made his recognition a certainty. Crook achieved this success by understanding the Native Americans and by treating his longtime opponents with sympathy, respect, and dignity. "He never lied to us," summed up Chief Red Cloud. "His words gave the people hope."

George Crook learned guerrilla tactics in the 1850s while fighting the Yakima and others in the Northwest, and he employed those tactics in the Civil War.

Born on September 23, 1829, Crook was reared on an Ohio farm near Dayton. At age 18, he was admitted to West Point, where Phil Sheridan was his roommate. Graduating near the bottom of his class in 1852, he was commissioned a lieutenant of the 4th Infantry.

Crook served for eight years on the Pacific Coast, where he helped build military posts, escorted explorers' parties, and campaigned against Native Americans in the Rogue River War and the Yakima War. On June 10, 1857, First Lieutenant Crook led Company D of the 4th Infantry into an inconclusive clash against hostiles on the Pit River in California. The only casualty was Crook, who caught an arrow in the side. Surgeons extracted the shaft but were unable to remove the arrowhead, which remained with Crook throughout his life.

During these campaigns and skirmishes, Crook learned to fight frontier-style, emulating the guerrilla tactics of the Native Americans and subsisting off the land while in the field. He respected his opponents and regarded them as human, which was more than many military officers and soldiers did. With determination, he drilled his troops and instructed them in marksmanship.

Early in the Civil War, Crook obtained the colonelcy of the 36th Ohio Volunteer Infantry. After taking the novel step of intensively training his regiment of volunteers, Crook led them into combat in what is now West Virginia and employed his troops in a guerrilla campaign. In May 1862, he was granted a special commission as a major of regulars after a victory at Lewisburg, during which he was badly wounded. Three months later, Crook was promoted to brigadier general of volunteers. He then led his brigade at Antietam. In 1863, he was given command of the 2nd Cavalry Division. After heavy campaigning, he was promoted to command one of Sheridan's corps and placed in charge of West Virginia. During the final months of the war, Sheridan placed him at the head of one of his cavalry divisions, and Crook saw combat in the actions leading to Appomattox. By war's end, he had advanced to major general of volunteers. As his military career progressed, his personal life was enriched by his marriage to Mary Dailey on August 22, 1865.

Crook returned to the frontier late in 1866 as a lieutenant colonel of the 23rd Infantry in command of troops in the Northwest. Upon reaching Idaho Territory, he rode at the head of Company F of the 1st Cavalry in pursuit of Paiute raiders. Crook's actions against the Paiute indicated his skill in skirmishing with the Native Americans. Time after time, he managed to kill or capture sufficient numbers of the enemy to secure a victory while losing only a man or two.

On December 26, 1866, Crook encountered a war party at Owyhee Creek and soundly defeated them, slaying 30 Paiute and capturing seven. Only one trooper was killed and one wounded. Within two weeks, Crook and Company F cornered hostile Paiute at the Malheur River in Oregon. Crook directed the action so skillfully that there were no casualties on either side, but 30 Native Americans were forced to surrender. Three weeks later, at Stein's Mountain in Oregon, Crook led Company M of the 1st Cavalry against a large band of Paiute. One civilian employee was slain and three troopers were wounded, while Crook and his men killed 60 hostiles and rounded up 27 captives.

Crook continued to hound the Paiute throughout the spring and summer of 1867. His final clash with them occurred on March 14, 1868, at the picturesquely named Donner and Blitzen Creek. Although three of his men were wounded, 12 Paiute were killed and two were captured. Crook's innovative methods and unremitting pressure against the Paiute pacified the Northwest region within a year and a half. The Oregon Legislature expressed its gratitude, and Crook's superiors, recognizing a virtuoso performance, issued commendations.

By this time, Crook was known as an inveterate outdoorsman who tended to travel ahead of his column for solitary hunting and scouting forays. During his years in the West, he hunted animals of virtually every known species and caught almost every type of fish. He eventually became a taxidermist to preserve his trophies. Crook often made significant contributions to the mess supplies of his men with his hunting and fishing. When his men were on the march and saw smoke ahead, pack animals were sent forward to carry whatever game Crook had killed.

A fine hunter, George Crook learned how to supplement his troops' food supply with available resources from the surrounding countryside.

His personal probes also taught him a great deal about the plant life and terrain of the area in which he was stationed, information that he used in planning his campaigns. Crook almost always refused an escort, not wanting to overwork his men. He shunned uniforms, preferring to wear canvas clothes and a straw hat. Crook liked to ride a mule, with a rifle or shotgun balanced across his pommel for quick use. He never used liquor, tobacco, tea, coffee, or profanity. He was tall, lean, erect, and sported a forked beard.

Crook exacted loyalty, affection, and supreme effort from his men. He incessantly pumped his subordinates for information but never revealed his plans to them. He did not bother his officers with detailed instructions, expecting them to exercise initiative. Two keys to Crook's success against Native Americans were his use of mule pack trains, which provided far greater mobility than wagon trains, and the liberal employment of Native American scouts. Crook worked his native allies hard in the field, thus keeping his troopers fresh for combat. He also found it much easier to locate renegades with the use of Native American scouts. Native American allies could settle old scores with a vengeance, so the employment of native scouts reduced the potential number of hostiles.

In 1871, President Ulysses S. Grant ordered that Crook be placed in charge of the Department of Arizona, where the ferocious

The keys to General Crook's Arizona campaign were the Apache scouts he used. They alone had the skill to locate Apache renegades.

and resourceful Apache raided at will. The Southwest proved a more difficult region to secure against Native American hostilities. The warm weather foiled surprise winter campaigns, while the terrain was too treacherous for major assaults. Part of Crook's strategy involved moving rapidly with his patrols into the heart of Apache lands. To penetrate areas previously unknown to the army, he employed Apache scouts—a tactic that proved vital to his success. An old Southwestern proverb maintains that "It takes an Apache to catch an Apache." Crook took advantage of the group's warring factions to hire Apache scouts from one band to track those from another band. "An Indian in his mode of warfare is more than the equal of the white man," Crook wrote. "The only hope of success lies in using their own methods, and their own people." Crook was nicknamed Gray Wolf by the Apache, because he tracked them with the skill and tenacity of a cunning timber beast.

The following year, Crook learned of a plot by Native Americans to kill him the next time he visited Camp Date Creek. While conversing with Crook, the chief conspirator was supposed to roll and light a cigarette. The first puff was to be the signal to murder Crook and any other whites present. Crook's next visit to Camp Date Creek occurred when the camp's commandant died. Arriving on September 8, 1872, Crook strolled into the midst of the reservation Indians, accompanied by his aide, Lieutenant William J. Ross, and several packers, who were veteran frontiersmen bristling with revolvers and knives. As planned, the chief conspirator rolled a cigarette and puffed it, whereupon a brave beside him aimed a carbine at Crook and fired. Ross struck the warrior's arm, and the bullet went astray. A hand-to-hand melee ensued, and those Apache who did not flee were overwhelmed.

Crook's military tactics and sympathetic diplomacy placed most Apache on reservations by 1873. The Arizona Territorial Legislature commended Crook, and he was promoted to brigadier general to fill the vacancy of the recently slain E.R.S. Canby. Crook was advanced over numerous officers, and his

$13 A MONTH

Whether scouting the movements of Native Americans, escorting emigrants across the prairie, or participating in battle, thousands of U.S. military patrols crisscrossed the American West during the army's 100 years of service there. Permanent posts typically served as the headquarters for most army units, but smart commanders quickly learned the usefulness of patrols. The use of far-traveling squads of men—usually cavalry—proved to be the best means for policing the thousands of square miles of Indian territories that separated the forts.

A typical patrol of the late 1870s consisted of detachments of one to several companies of cavalry. Each company featured 50 to 100 mounted men. On patrol, each soldier was supplied for a journey of several days. His equipment consisted of a rifle, pistol, extra ammunition, canteen, tin cup, knife, shelter half, haversack, saddle bags, poncho, and a feed bag for his horse. His food while on the trail consisted of bacon, hardtack, and coffee.

For all his efforts, the enlisted man was paid $13 a month!

The members of Troop E of the 6th Cavalry, shown here in 1881, rode out of Fort Union, New Mexico Territory.

RANALD MACKENZIE

1840—1889

Ranald Slidell Mackenzie, the army's best Indian fighter, was born in New York City on July 27, 1840. His father, a naval commander who also authored several popular books, died when Ranald was eight, and his mother moved the family to Morristown, New Jersey. Ranald entered Williams College at age 15 to begin an unenthusiastic study of the law. In 1858, he secured an appointment to West Point, primarily to relieve his mother of the financial burden of his education.

To the surprise of his family, the frail young man demonstrated a keen aptitude for the military, graduating in 1862, the first in a class of 28. During the Civil War, Mackenzie distinguished himself at Second Bull Run, Chancellorsville, Gettysburg, Petersburg, and other battles. Wounded six times, he held the rank of major general of volunteers by the age of 24. Electing to remain in the regular army after the war, Mackenzie became a captain of engineers. Predictably, he found construction work tedious, and in 1867, he accepted the

After a raid in the Palo Duro Canyon in 1874, Ranald Mackenzie killed more than 1,000 horses belonging to the Comanche and Kiowa.

colonelcy of the 41st Infantry, an African-American regiment assigned to the Texas frontier. A strict disciplinarian whose men had threatened to shoot him during the Civil War, Colonel Mackenzie whipped his inexperienced soldiers into a top unit. Unfortunately for Mackenzie, his regiment did not see combat, and in December 1870, he accepted a transfer to the 4th Cavalry.

Mackenzie transformed his new regiment into the army's finest Indian-fighting outfit. His men found him solemn, strong-willed, modest, and dignified. He displayed great stamina and often worked far into the night, but he was impatient and frequently irritable, perhaps as a result of his several wounds. When he became nervous, he habitually snapped the stumps of two fingers that had been shot off his right hand during the Civil War at Petersburg. Native Americans dubbed him Bad Hand and Threefingers.

After a training period, the 4th was stationed at Fort Richardson. From there, Mackenzie led campaigns in 1871 and 1872 into Comanche and Kiowa territory. During the 1871 expedition, a great deal of information about the hitherto unexplored Staked Plains was compiled, although there was no decisive combat.

During a skirmish on October 15, 1871, at Blanco Canyon, Mackenzie spurred forward to the point of action, and a barbed arrow thudded into his thigh. Chagrined at having been wounded again, Mackenzie did not mention the injury in his official report. The wound remained troublesome, and a fortnight later, a surgeon informed the restless Mackenzie that amputation might become necessary unless he submitted to bed rest. Mackenzie angrily hurled his crutch at the doctor and sent him scurrying from the tent.

In the fall of 1872, Mackenzie returned to Comanche territory with 284 soldiers. Early in the summer, Texas newspapers had reported erroneously that Mackenzie and a number of troops had been massacred by Indians, but it was an alive and purposeful Bad Hand who struck a village of 262 lodges on the North Fork of the Red River on September 29. The warriors fought bitterly and launched two counterattacks, but the village was vanquished within half an hour. Two nights later, a band of warriors raided Mackenzie's camp and retrieved a number of horses, including Bad Hand's own mount and many other cavalry animals. Mackenzie would not forget this raid.

In 1873, Mackenzie and the 4th were transferred to Fort Clark to focus their attention on the Kickapoos from northern Mexico, who were raiding deep into Texas and escaping back across the Rio Grande. General Philip Sheridan and Secretary of War W. W. Belknap met with Mackenzie for two days in April, confidentially instructing him to violate the Mexican border and punish the invading raiders. Mackenzie ordered his men to grind their sabers to a razor edge, and then he put them through grueling daily drills and carbine practice.

A few weeks later, Mackenzie learned of a raid against a nearby ranch. He mounted a column of more than 400 men and started out. He did not tell them of their mission until they reached the Rio Grande. There, Mackenzie directed his troopers to stuff their saddlebags with rations and to fill their pockets with cartridges, after which the pack mules were cut loose. With Mackenzie in the lead, the command pushed into Mexico under cover of darkness.

Mackenzie drove his men through the night. Just after dawn on May 18, they set up to strike three Native American villages near Remolino, Mexico. All three villages were destroyed and prisoners were taken. Heading back to the border immediately, the soldiers had no rest, ate only whatever hardtack they had shoved into their packs, and rode at a trot or gallop through a second night. When the prisoners began to fall off their horses, Mackenzie ordered them tied to their mounts. With Mexican cavalry in pursuit, the exhausted soldiers reached the safety of the Rio Grande before dawn on May 19, having ridden 140 miles in 38 hours.

Following the Battle of Adobe Walls and other attacks by the Comanche and Kiowa on buffalo hunters in the Texas Panhandle, General Sheridan organized a campaign according to a plan Mackenzie had designed in 1872. Five columns totaling 46 companies and 3,000 men converged on the Panhandle in the fall of 1874. Mackenzie led a column that

THE DECLINE OF THE BUFFALO

When Lewis and Clark made their way to the Pacific Ocean and back again in 1804 through 1806, as many as 60 million buffalo roamed the Great Plains. By 1886, when scientists from the National Museum in Washington, D.C., went to the great West searching for buffalo to use in a new exhibit at the Smithsonian Institution, they hunted the Montana plains for eight weeks before they found the 25 specimens they needed.

The rapid demise of the buffalo was caused by the wholesale slaughter of them by both pleasure and market hunters as well as by the destruction of their native habitat. Shooting buffalo became the sport of the West, with railroad passengers often taking aim into large herds as they whisked by on trains. If these practices were not officially sanctioned by U.S. officials, particularly during the years following the Civil War, they were at least consciously overlooked.

Several nations of buffalo-hunting Plains Indians fought the white hunters and the military for their very survival. For example, the Kiowa and Comanche waged war against the hunters in Texas after witnessing the extensive slaughter of the buffalo in the early 1870s. The white hunters had previously killed the buffalo during the winters when their coats were long and shaggy. However, by 1870, a new tanning process had been developed that made short-hair hides usable as well. Between the new tanning process and the use of high-powered, telescopic Sharps rifles that could kill the animals from long distances, the rate of slaughter accelerated.

After destroying the herds in Kansas, the hunters moved to the Staked Plains of Texas, setting up a base with their skinners at Adobe Walls. Quanah Parker and his Comanche braves, along with their Kiowa allies, attacked the hunters at Adobe Walls on June 26, 1874, but the hunters held their own. The incident launched a series of skirmishes between the Comanche-Kiowa and the white settlers known as the Red River War, which quickly led to a massive offensive against the Comanche-Kiowa by the U.S. Army.

Probably the most important factor in the surrender of the Native American Plains nations was the wholesale slaughter of their most vital resource, the buffalo.

totalled over 600 men, including numerous scouts, eight companies of the 4th, and five infantry companies.

When scouts reported Indian signs nearby, Mackenzie recalled the night raid by Comanche and Kiowa in 1872, and he took every precaution. Guards were stationed every 15 feet around the camp, skirmishers were strategically placed, and every animal was hobbled, cross-sidelined, and tethered by a thick rope to its individual iron stake. When 250 warriors struck that night, they were repulsed by Mackenzie's men. They reappeared the next morning but withdrew, heading for their long-time refuge, Palo Duro Canyon.

Mackenzie knew about Palo Duro Canyon, perhaps as a result of torturing the location out of a *Comanchero* trader. As daylight broke on September 28, Mackenzie's men scrambled down the precipitous trail into the Palo Duro, where native camps stretched for three miles along the canyon floor. One troop raced for a huge horse herd, capturing over 1,400 ponies, while Mackenzie led two companies in a charge through the villages. Only three Native Americans were killed, but in their scramble for safety, everything was abandoned. Mackenzie ordered all lodges, equipment, and immense stores of food burned. After cutting out 350 of the best Indian ponies, the balance of the herd was shot. With Palo Duro Canyon now closed to them and their winter food supply destroyed, the Comanche and Kiowa were eventually forced onto reservations. The Battle of Palo Duro Canyon proved to be a major turning point in the Red River War. The 4th was transferred to Fort Sill to supervise the Comanche and Kiowa as they adapted to reservation life.

During the late 1870s, Mackenzie and the 4th were transferred around the Southwest to quell trouble at various reservations and hotpoints. Once, General Sherman ordered Mackenzie to Arizona, where Apache were conducting raids and Navajo were bellicose. Mackenzie skillfully placed six companies of the 4th in position to block any possible Apache and Navajo union. Sherman was so pleased that he appointed Colonel Mackenzie in command of all troops in the Department of Arizona, a move that understandably infuriated the two generals who were thereby technically subordinate to the colonel. Within five weeks, Colonel Mackenzie reported that the Apache had either surrendered or fled to Mexico.

On October 26, 1882, Mackenzie was promoted to brigadier general. His success was spoiled by the collapse of his health. By his early 40s, the once-slender officer had become overweight, and an earlier abstinence from alcohol had been replaced by habitual drinking. Overwork and the long-range effects of his multiple wounds led to a deterioration of his mental abilities. Following a lengthy medical leave, the 43-year-old bachelor announced his engagement to a San Antonio widow, but it became painfully obvious that he was unbalanced. In 1884, he was placed on the retired list. His sister cared for him until he died at the age of 48, on January 19, 1889, in New Brighton, New York.

Mackenzie was interred at West Point alongside other military greats. A brilliant and heroic general during the Civil War, he continued his selfless service during the Indian Wars and proved himself to be the army's most effective troubleshooter. His determined efforts were key to the army's success in subjugating the Indians of the southern plains.

NELSON A.
MILES

1839–1925

Nelson Appleton Miles was born on August 8, 1839, and raised on a Massachusetts farm. As a teenager, Miles worked as a clerk in Boston while spending his leisure hours in regular attendance at lectures, in night school,

Nelson Miles's rise through the ranks of the military came as much through his skillful politicking as it did through his abilities as a combat leader.

and in pursuit of a broad reading program. By 1860, he concluded that civil war was inevitable and that success in combat could provide the opportunity for the fame and position he craved. Miles began to study military volumes, and he joined a small group that employed a French veteran to provide them with drill instruction.

When hostilities erupted, Miles raised $3,500 to organize a volunteer company of infantry, but he was denied the captaincy by an ungrateful governor and resentfully accepted a lesser commission. The experience taught him a bitter lesson about the value of friends in high places. Throughout his career, Miles would shamelessly exploit every conceivable contact to promote his advancement.

During the Civil War, courage and a gift for utilizing terrain vaulted Miles to high rank. He experienced heavy combat duty and was wounded four times, while his exploits at Chancellorsville earned him a Medal of Honor. By the end of the war, he held the rank of major general of volunteers. In order to continue his military career, Miles had to accept a colonelcy in the regular army.

Marriage to Mary Sherman, niece of General William T. Sherman and of Ohio senator John Sherman, gave Miles invaluable contacts in his drive to the top of the frontier army. In 1869, Miles assumed command of the 5th Infantry at Fort Hays, Kansas. Combat against many of the Native Americans of the West was spearheaded by cavalry, however.

As the years passed, the ambitious Miles chafed at the exclusion of his regiment from campaigns that promised glory and promotion. At last, in 1874, he was assigned to lead a column in the Red River War in the Texas Panhandle. Miles finally received his initiation into Indian fighting, and he carried along a newspaper correspondent to insure personal publicity.

A tall, handsome officer, Miles repeatedly exhibited courage, boldness, and organizational skills while campaigning in the West. Unfortunately, he was also vain, pompous, and ruthless in his personal ambitions. He was loathe to give credit to other officers and was deeply jealous of West Point graduates. Yet for a decade and a half, he was an efficient and relentless Indian fighter who successfully employed infantry in wars otherwise dominated by cavalry.

In 1876, Miles was assigned to lead five companies of the 5th as part of the general pursuit of the Sioux after Custer's demise at the Little Bighorn. Overcoming temperatures of 60 degrees below zero, the 5th marched hundreds of miles and forced the surrender of nearly 2,000 Native Americans. The following year, when Chief Joseph was outmaneuvering the army, General O. O. Howard sent a dispatch asking Miles to intercept the Nez Percé in their flight toward Canada. After 12 hours of hurried preparations in the darkness, Miles eagerly readied his entire available force—five cavalry companies and five infantry troops, four of which were mounted on captured Indian ponies. Miles was a prominent figure in the remainder of the Nez Percé campaign, emerging as the only successful officer of the entire operation.

Displaying incessant and tactless self-promotion, Miles clashed increasingly with his superiors, even with his uncle by marriage, General William T. Sherman. His qualifications were undeniable, however, and when a vacancy occurred in 1880, he finally received his long-sought star. From 1881 to 1885, General Miles commanded the Department of the Columbia.

In 1886, Geronimo and a few renegade Apache escaped custody after having been corralled by General George Crook. Pressured into resigning, Crook was replaced by Miles, who placed guard details at water holes and mountain passes, organized a system of pursuit parties, and established a network of 30 heliograph stations. The elusive Apache were hounded relentlessly, and Geronimo and a handful of followers finally surrendered. Miles eagerly accepted total credit for the victory, ignoring years of effort by Crook and numerous junior officers. A public subscription for an engraved sword for Miles for his efforts at capturing Geronimo fell far short of the needed amount. Miles quietly paid the difference, then basked in the presentation ceremonies at Tucson.

When two vacancies occurred at the rank of major general, Miles launched a vigorous campaign to be awarded the rank. Though he exploited every possible connection, he was not given a second star. After his keenest rival, Major General George Crook, died in 1890, he made another determined effort at

Shown en route to Indian Territory after their capture by Miles, the Nez Percé had been promised that they could stay in the Northwest. Miles later helped them win the right to return to their homeland.

WOUNDED KNEE

While Christmas Day, 1890, was being celebrated by the American soldiers at the Pine Ridge Reservation, Minniconjou chief Big Foot lay seriously ill several miles away. Days before, his friend Sitting Bull had been killed by Sioux policemen on the Standing Rock Reservation. Big Foot and several of Sitting Bull's Hunkpapa followers, who had fled Standing Rock after their leader's murder, were on their way to Pine Ridge to seek the counsel of Chief Red Cloud.

On December 28, Big Foot's party sighted four companies from the 7th U.S. Cavalry, commanded by Major Samuel Whitside. Big Foot ordered that a white flag be raised. When Whitside entered the Sioux camp, the pneumonia-stricken Big Foot personally greeted the major. Although Whitside had orders to disarm Big Foot's band, scout John Shangreau persuaded him

to wait until the Sioux regrouped next to the army's encampment on nearby Wounded Knee Creek.

Once at Wounded Knee, Whitside again delayed disarming the Sioux due to the late hour. He ordered his men to assist the Indians in making camp and had rations issued to them. Then, he gave Big Foot a portable camp stove to put in his tent and sent the regimental surgeon to look after the sick chief.

In a grisly scene, a burial detail prepares a mass grave for the dead of Wounded Knee.

During the night, Colonel James W. Forsyth arrived in the army camp, relieved Major Whitside, and told him to prepare the Sioux for movement to a prison in Omaha. The next morning, the 7th Cavalry surrounded the tent village, awoke the Indians, and demanded that they disarm. A young Minniconjou named Black Coyote balked at turning over his newly purchased rifle. When several soldiers forcibly took the weapon,

someone fired a shot. The soldiers surrounding the Native American camp opened fire into the crowd. Within minutes, 146 Sioux men, women, and children lay dead in the fresh snow. Among the dead was Big Foot. Over two dozen soldiers were killed, and 39 were wounded.

Bad weather was imminent, so the soldiers left the dead Sioux where they lay. Later, when a burial detail returned, the corpses were frozen to the ground.

The survivors of Wounded Knee were taken to Pine Ridge, and after being exposed to the elements without shelter, they were finally taken in by members of the Episcopal mission. "We tried to run," exclaimed a survivor, "but they shot us like we were a buffalo. . . . soldiers must be mean to shoot women and children. Indian soldiers would not do that to white children."

the promotion. He even secured an interview with President Benjamin Harrison. Finally, Miles obtained the promotion he so coveted.

Assuming command of the Division of the Missouri, Miles was confronted by a problem with the Sioux, who were living a discontented existence on reservations. By the end of 1890, the religious frenzy of the Ghost Dance had spread with such fervor that the military feared an uprising. Tensions mounted after respected Sioux leader Sitting Bull was slain in an incident on December 15.

Miles established a command post at Rapid City, South Dakota, and tried to smother further resistance to authority. When 350 Sioux escaped the reservation, their movement was blocked by the 7th Cavalry at Wounded Knee Creek. The ensuing "battle" of Wounded Knee resulted in at least 200 Native American casualties, including numerous women and children among the 146 dead. Incensed at what he regarded as a blunder, Miles increased military pressure gradually while working through personal diplomacy to divide Sioux leadership. Further bloodshed was averted, and on January 15, 1891, the Sioux submitted to Miles's authority.

In 1895, Miles was appointed commanding general and moved his family to Washington, D.C. Two years later, he went to Europe as a military representative to Queen Victoria's Jubilee and as an observer of the Greco-Turkish War. During his European tour, he visited the German, French, Italian, Russian, and Austrian standing armies. After returning to the United States, he campaigned for a stronger American military force. Miles also published his *Personal Recollections* in 1897.

Upon the outbreak of the Spanish-American War in 1898, Miles vigorously pushed for naval action while the army prepared for combat in the tropics. He urged an assault on Puerto Rico, which lay along the sea route from Spain to Cuba. Miles opposed the hurried invasion of Cuba, and when he asked the

In the field, Miles proved himself to be a shrewd military strategist time and again.

president for permission to command the assault force, he was ignored. Shortly after Cuba surrendered, Miles landed in Puerto Rico with 3,500 men, conquering the defending troops in a skillfully executed 19-day campaign.

After the war, Miles continued to clash with the War Department and with Presidents McKinley and Roosevelt. In 1902, Roosevelt censured him after a public feud with Secretary of War Russell A. Alger. Miles was awarded the rank of lieutenant general, but he was denied a combat role in the Philippines.

When the United States entered World War I, the 77-year-old retiree eagerly volunteered for duty, but Miles's services were declined. Miles died on May 15, 1925, and was buried in Arlington National Cemetery.

GEORGE ARMSTRONG
CUSTER

1839—1876

Born on December 5, 1839, in New Rumley, Ohio, George Armstrong Custer was the son of the village blacksmith and the great-grandson of a Revolutionary War veteran. Impressed by his father's participation in a local militia unit, young Autie—as he was called—drilled near the men in a little uniform and with a toy musket. As a teenager, Autie attended an academy in Monroe, Michigan, where he lived with his married half-sister. There he met the lovely girl who later would become his devoted wife, Elizabeth "Libbie" Clift Bacon.

Custer became a rural schoolteacher at the ripe old age of 16, but the next year, he received an appointment to West Point, where he excelled at horsemanship. With each term, however, Cadet Custer piled up great numbers of demerits for slovenliness and tardiness. He was an inept pupil, graduating in 1861 as the last in a class of 34.

When the Civil War commenced, Custer proved audacious and fearless in combat. He saw action from First Bull Run to Gettysburg to Appomattox, with countless skirmishes between major engagements. By 1863, he was a captain in the 5th U.S. Cavalry, but because of his spectacular exploits, he was vaulted to brigadier general of the Michigan Volunteer Cavalry. The Boy General was the youngest United States officer ever to wear a star.

Above: Custer wears the uniform he designed for himself as a general in the volunteer army. **Right:** Clad in these showy buckskins, Custer set off for his fateful encounter with the Sioux nation.

General Custer designed for himself a uniform of blue velvet that was festooned with swirls of gold braid on the sleeves, silver stars on the collar, and a scarlet neckerchief. His thin, blond hair grew to shoulder length, inspiring his men to call him Old Curly. Despite his foppishness, he fought with distinction, leading victorious charges that earned him a second star, considerable publicity, and the admiration of such influential men as Generals Sheridan and Grant.

When the war ended, Phil Sheridan summoned Custer's unit to Texas for Reconstruction duty. His men grew disenchanted with Custer, considering him a martinet who cared nothing for the rank and file. Early in 1866, Major General of Volunteers Custer reverted to his regular army rank of captain, which entailed a salary reduction from $8,000 to $2,000 per year. He considered an offer of $16,000 to serve with the Mexican Army, but he turned it down when he could not obtain a year's leave of absence. Private business opportunities were also declined, and twice he refused an appointment as lieutenant colonel of the black 9th Cavalry because he wished "to be attached to an organization of *white* troops."

Custer's professional status was settled in late 1866 when General Sheridan secured for him the lieutenant colonelcy of the newly formed 7th Cavalry. In October 1866, Custer and his wife joined the regiment at Fort Riley, Kansas. Since the colonel was almost never present, Custer commanded the 7th in practice, if not in name.

The 7th's first campaign occurred in the spring and summer of 1867, when General Winfield Scott Hancock directed large-scale but ineffective efforts against the Cheyenne in Kansas. Custer was court-martialed for leaving his command without permission, using ambulances on personal business, ordering his officers to shoot deserters without trial, and abusing men and animals. One glaring example of foolishness occurred while Custer's column was on the march in Kansas. Custer was an avid hunter and had keenly anticipated pursuing his first buffalo. Early one morning, he spurred his big thoroughbred toward distant antelope, accompanied only by his bugler and a few greyhound hunting dogs. When he spotted a lone buffalo, he raced

Custer confers with his scouts on an 1870s mission to protect railroad workers as they pushed onto Indian lands in the northern plains.

after the beast for so great a distance that he was completely alone. When the buffalo finally turned to charge, Custer fired his pistol—into the brain of his horse! Afoot in Indian territory, with no idea of how far or in what direction his troops were, Custer trusted the instincts of two of his dogs. He trudged after them for miles, finally encountering the regiment and sending a detail after his gear.

Equally irresponsible was a forced march that Custer ordered, ostensibly to procure supplies from Fort Harker, but actually to provide him an opportunity to visit Libbie at Fort Riley. Custer drove his escort of 75 men night and day, covering 150 miles in 55 hours. When Indians jumped his rear guard and killed two men, Custer did not pause even to recover the bodies. When at last he allowed a rest halt at Fort Hays, he pushed on to Fort Harker with four men, taking just 12 hours to travel 60 more miles. He then took a train to Fort Riley, where he was soon in Libbie's arms—while most of his regiment remained in the field.

Custer's expedition snakes out of the Black Hills toward Fort Abraham Lincoln after the initial survey of the region in 1874.

Custer was convicted at a court-martial and suspended from duty for one year. General Sheridan persuaded the Custers to accept his quarters at Fort Leavenworth. In September 1868, Sheridan directed his protégé to resume duties with the 7th and join a fall campaign that resulted in Custer's brutal conquest of the Cheyenne chief Black Kettle at the Battle of the Washita.

Custer executed a forced march south from Camp Supply in Indian Territory, pushing through a snowstorm in order to be in position for a dawn attack on November 27. Deciding to launch the type of headlong charge that had won him victories and fame during the Civil War, Custer deployed his troopers into four squadrons to surround the quiet lodges. The regimental band was with Custer's detail and under orders to blast out the stirring tune "Garry Owen" when the assault commenced. Buglers with each column began to blow the charge, but all instruments froze up after just a few notes.

Black Kettle was killed as the troopers attacked the camp. Custer surged into hand-to-hand fighting astride a black stallion: He fired a revolver slug into the head of a warrior; he ruthlessly rode down another brave; then he positioned himself in the middle of the village and directed his command. Warriors fought desperately to defend their fleeing families. Over 100 Indians were slain, 53 women and children were captured, and 875 ponies were seized. Also seized were 1,100 buffalo robes, 4,000 arrows, 1,000 pounds of lead, and 500 pounds of gunpowder. Soldiers pulled down the lodges, piled up the confiscated food and domestic gear, burned these piles, and methodically shot the ponies. There were 19 dead and 14 wounded soldiers, but when the 7th marched away from the devastated village at midafternoon, Custer again had them strike up "Garry Owen."

By this time, Custer had molded the 7th into a crack regiment. Each troop rode the same color horse, and a training program—an unusual practice among frontier units—was instituted. The program featured daily target practice, and the best 40 marksmen were formed into an elite unit of sharpshooters exempt from menial duties.

Nevertheless, many of his officers and men continued to resent Custer's disregard for the safety and comfort of those under his command, particularly since he indulged himself luxuriously even while campaigning. Custer always maintained a large, well-appointed tent and was attended in the field by a female cook, while Libbie often accompanied her husband on campaigns. In the field and on the post, Custer was boisterous and highly energetic. When he received good news at home, he was given to hurling furniture across the room in exuberance.

In 1873, Custer led the 7th during the Yellowstone Expedition, which comprised 1,500 officers and men, over 2,300 horses and mules, and 275 wagons and ambulances. The force was out for three months and traveled over 900 miles. The 7th was assigned to protect Northern Pacific survey parties, but Custer frequently journeyed ahead of the expedition with two companies to break a trail through the rugged country.

While reconnoitering with his two troops on August 4, 1873, Custer and 90 cavalrymen of the 7th were jumped by 300 Sioux warriors near the mouth of Montana's Tongue River. Custer coolly dismounted his men and conducted a determined defense for three hours. Choosing his moment shrewdly, Custer finally ordered his troopers into the saddle and led a smashing charge that routed the superior force.

A week later, Custer took eight companies and set out in pursuit of a large band of warriors along the north bank of the Yellowstone River. When several hundred braves suddenly approached his column, Custer ordered the band to blare out "Garry Owen,"

THIS PHOTOGRAPH WAS MADE AT FORT LINCOLN, DAKOTA TERRITORY, 1874

then led a charge. The braves scattered in flight, and the cavalry pressed a close pursuit for nine miles before finally breaking off the chase. Custer's first mount was shot dead under him during the skirmish, but he soon set himself astride another horse and directed his troops to victory.

Custer sits with officers of the 7th and their wives at Fort Abraham Lincoln. Most of these men would die at the hands of Sioux warriors.

LIBBIE CUSTER

On February 9, 1864, a storybook wedding took place at the First Presbyterian Church in Monroe, Michigan. The bridegroom was 24-year-old George Armstrong Custer, the famous Boy General. The 21-year-old bride—Elizabeth Clift Bacon—was regarded as the prettiest girl in Monroe.

Libbie Bacon, who was born on April 8, 1842, in Monroe, was the only daughter of Judge Daniel Stanton Bacon. Judge Bacon provided his lovely, personable daughter with a solid education, training in the arts, and a stylish wardrobe.

Libbie first encountered George Custer when he spent two years at an academy in Monroe. As Custer strolled past Judge Bacon's house, Libbie was swinging on the gate of the white picket fence. "Hello, you Custer boy!" she said with a smile. She then ran into the house—and into 15-year-old George's heart.

Several years later, another chance encounter nearly derailed any future romance. From October 1861 until February 1862, Lieutenant Custer spent a sick leave in Monroe at the home of his half-sister. One day, he became drunk with some old schoolmates, and as he staggered to his sister's house, he passed the Bacon home. Libbie, a girl of strong religious convictions, observed the inebriated young officer with stern disapproval. Custer's sister apparently elicited a pledge from him to stop indulging in liquor or tobacco, and he kept his word.

At age 18, Libbie was formally introduced to Custer while she was a student at Boyd's Seminary. Subsequently, Custer courted Libbie, besieging her with letters.

Libbie Custer received many long letters from George; he once wrote an 80-page epic to his wife.

Custer's successes during the Civil War resulted in swift promotion to general. In September 1863, he returned to Monroe and proposed to Libbie. Despite Judge Bacon's reservations, Libbie accepted.

Following the wedding and a brief honeymoon, Libbie accompanied her husband to brigade headquarters. It was not customary for women to be at duty posts, but Libbie's presence noticeably improved behavior around headquarters, and other officers' wives began to join their husbands.

After the war, Libbie continued to live with George wherever he was stationed, and she often accompanied him on campaigns. When they were apart, he sent long letters to her. In 1867, Custer was court-martialed after leaving his regiment in the field to race 150 miles in 55 hours to see Libbie.

The 36-year-old Custer and more than 200 of his men were slain in 1876 at the Battle of the Little Bighorn. Libbie was only 34, but she remained a widow for the rest of her life. She promoted Custer's reputation through lectures and books, including *Boots and Saddles* (1885), *Tenting on the Plains* (1887), and *Following the Guidon* (1890). Libbie died in New York City on April 4, 1933.

In 1874, Custer commanded the Black Hills Expedition, reconnoitering the sacred Sioux land in violation of recent treaties. With 1,000 men and 110 vehicles, Custer explored the region, verifying reports of gold deposits and earning the name "Chief of Thieves" from the Sioux. The subsequent gold rush to the Black Hills triggered unrest with the Sioux, and a massive campaign was planned for 1876 in which Custer was to play a prominent part.

Frank statements Custer made while testifying against graft in the War Department resulted in orders to remain in Chicago while the 7th marched against the Sioux. Only a flurry of pleas by the 36-year-old officer allowed him to march at the head of his regiment, perhaps in hopes of scoring a spectacular success that would confound his opponents and generate political opportunities.

On June 25, 1876, Custer pushed the 7th to find a large Sioux-Cheyenne encampment reported by scouts to be on the Little Bighorn River. Leaving one company to guard the supply train, Custer sent two battalions of three companies each in search of the encampment. Clad in a blue flannel shirt and buckskin breeches and armed with a brace of English double-action revolvers and a Remington sporting rifle, Custer rode at the head of the remaining five companies. In the command of 215 men were his brothers, officers Boston and Tom (who had won two Medals of Honor during the Civil War); his brother-in-law Lieutenant James Calhoun; and his favorite nephew, 18-year-old Henry Reed.

First contact was made by the battalion of Major Marcus Reno. Hearing the gunfire, Custer hurried to attack the enormous village, which contained more than 10,000 Indians, including perhaps 3,000 warriors.

Custer's force was overwhelmed, with every man killed. Custer was found among the last group of soldiers to fall. According to ten Cheyenne and Sioux warriors who were the first to meet Custer's column, he rode in the lead and took a bullet in the chest, possibly the first soldier to get hit. As his stunned troops began to pull back, the stricken Custer was lifted into the saddle and carried along until the remnants of his command made the famous "last stand." Although it is impossible to refute Native American claims that he was knocked out of action early in the battle, it is equally impossible to refute the popular image of Custer going down fighting with the last of his troopers.

Only a courageous defense saved the rest of the regiment from destruction, and Medals of Honor were awarded to 24 soldiers who battled valiantly on July 25 and 26. Custer and his men were buried on the battlefield, but in 1877 the remains of Custer and nine other officers were removed for reinterment at West Point. Coyotes had burrowed into the shallow grave and torn apart Custer's body, and only a double handful of bones could be found to place inside his coffin.

Employing the aggressive tactics that had produced victory throughout his military career, Custer led the 7th Cavalry against an insurmountable force. Custer and his men fell courageously, against an equally fearless foe, and the tragedy at the Little Bighorn became the most famous battle of the Indian Wars. And thus, the flawed but fierce Custer became a legendary leader in the Indian-fighting army.

The Crow scout Curley warned Custer against riding on the hostile encampment and left the soldiers when Custer refused to heed his advice.

OUTLAWS

From their wild years as thieves and killers until the present day, western outlaws somehow have generated an irresistible appeal among the American public. Jesse James was regarded as a frontier Robin Hood, despite his surly disposition and readiness to shoot anyone who stood between him and ill-gotten gains. Although Billy the Kid was a killer and rustler, he also was a ladies' man and a popular *compañero.* John Wesley Hardin, a murderous psychotic, was nonetheless admired for his matchless skill with pistols. Killin' Jim Miller was the top man at his profession—the West's No. 1 assassin.

The Wild Bunch, led by Butch Cassidy and the Sundance Kid, caught the public's imagination. Butch had an engaging personality, and he and Sundance were the subjects of perhaps the most charming Western movie ever filmed. Although Butch and Sundance probably were shot dead by soldiers in South America, Butch may have escaped. Outlaw buffs openly hope that the affable Butch Cassidy was one desperado who lived to enjoy his booty.

The raucous atmosphere of the western saloon incited brawls and gunplay, which could turn a gunslinger into a bona fide outlaw.

JESSE AND FRANK
JAMES

In 1842, Robert and Zerelda James moved from Kentucky to a farm in Clay County, Missouri, where Reverend James assumed the pastorate of a nearby Baptist church. On January 10, 1843, their first child, Alexander Franklin, was born, followed by another son, Jesse Woodson, on September 5, 1847. Frank and Jesse lost their father, who succumbed to gold fever and journeyed to California, where he fell ill and died. Strong-willed Zerelda quickly remarried, but this marriage failed, reportedly because their new stepfather was mean to Frank and Jesse.

Legend elevated Jesse (top) and Frank (bottom) James to folk heroes, but sometimes they killed bystanders without regard.

Zerelda entered her third marriage in 1855, with docile, prosperous Dr. Reuben Samuel. The growing family remained on the old James farm, even acquiring a few slaves. They were sympathetic to the Confederacy when the Civil War erupted, resulting in their mistreatment by Unionists. Frank joined William Quantrill's infamous band of Missouri guerrillas, participating in the vicious raid on Lawrence, Kansas, on August 21, 1863. Jesse began to ride with the raiders the next year: He was one of 30 men led by Bloody Bill Anderson into Centralia, Missouri, on September 27, 1864. There, the guerrillas executed 25 unarmed Union soldiers in cold blood.

Jesse suffered severe wounds twice while riding with Quantrill, but he recovered to loot and raid until the end of the war. Jesse and Frank returned to the family farm after the war, but their wartime experiences had stimulated their natural inclination to grip revolvers instead of plows. On the morning of February 13, 1866, a dozen riders pulled off the first daylight bank robbery in United States history, looting the Clay County Savings Bank in Liberty, Missouri, of $57,000. As the gang galloped out of town whooping the rebel yell, they gunned down local college student George Wymore. It has long been assumed that the Jameses and Cole Younger, who was a former lieutenant of Quantrill's, were the ringleaders behind the Liberty job.

For the next decade, the James-Younger Gang robbed banks, stores, and stagecoaches. After 1873, they struck trains in Missouri and in surrounding states. Cole Younger and his brothers, Jim, Bob, and John, were stalwarts of the band, and Frank James was a frequent participant. Jesse, despite being younger than Frank and Cole Younger, became the leader of the gang. Ruthless, assertive, smart, and quick on the trigger, Jesse was a natural outlaw leader. Cole, who disliked Jesse, sometimes led his own holdups, but they were in addition to those he committed with the James-Younger Gang.

Because of their notoriety, the James-Younger Gang tended to get the blame for every robbery in the multistate region. Jesse sometimes published letters proclaiming his innocence, insisting he had alibis for the times when certain holdups had occurred.

Folklore tends to portray Frank and Jesse James as the Robin Hoods of the Wild West, preying on banks and railroads. They are painted as romantic figures who attacked institutions that heralded the modern, industrialist age at the expense of America's agrarian heritage. In other words, they supposedly struck back at the banks and railroads who had taken the land out from under small farmers and poor country folk. But the members of the James-Younger Gang were not folk heroes; they were violent men who robbed and occasionally killed.

One of their more violent robberies occurred on December 7, 1869, in Gallatin, Missouri. The James brothers nursed a grudge against the bank's proprietor, John W. Sheets, who was a former Civil War officer. Posing as customers, Jesse and Frank entered the bank and engaged in a minor transaction with Sheets. When Sheets began writing, one of the brothers shot him in the head and heart. As clerk William McDowell bolted for the door, he was wounded in the arm, but he shouted that Sheets had been killed. The robbers dashed outside with several hundred dollars. During the com-

motion, the brothers lost one of their mounts and rode out of Gallatin on one horse. They stole another from a farmer, then fled southwest toward Clay County.

Jesse (center) and Frank James (right) started killing as rebel irregulars in William Quantrill's gang during the Civil War.

A reward of $3,000 was offered for Frank and Jesse after the Gallatin murder and robbery. A week later, four bounty hunters surrounded the James family farm. As Deputy Sheriff John Thomason approached the farmhouse, Jesse and Frank surged out of the barn astride swift mounts. A wild exchange of gunfire ensued, followed by a running chase with Thomason leading the pursuit. At one point, Thomason reined in his horse, dismounted, and rested his gun across his saddle to fire at the fleeing brothers. The deputy's horse bolted unexpectedly and, riderless, pulled up beside the outlaws. One of the brothers shot the horse dead, and the Jameses outdistanced their pursuers.

Legends about Frank and Jesse James also stress their regard for the common folk, but on more than one occasion, innocent bystanders were harmed or killed during their robberies. In the fall of 1872, the gang attempted what they thought would be an easy heist. Three mounted gang members robbed the ticket seller at the Kansas City Fair. One of the thieves, perhaps Jesse, seized the tin cashbox and cleaned it out. As he was fighting off ticket seller Ben Wallace, the thief pulled a pistol and fired a wild shot, hitting a little girl in the leg. At that point, the robbers galloped away.

The James-Younger Gang branched out into train robbery on July 21, 1873, at Adair, Iowa. To stop their target, the outlaws pulled up a rail from the tracks, which sent the Chicago, Rock Island & Pacific train into a ditch, killing the engineer. The bandits looted the express

Jesse James (far left) was a natural leader and took the reins of the James-Younger Gang. Jesse had a deep hatred of the government and the Pinkertons that was intensified by the bombing of his mother's house.

car, then collected valuables in the passenger coaches before escaping.

Ruthlessness aside, the James brothers were not without a sense of humor. On January 31, 1874, five masked members of the James-Younger Gang barged into the depot at Gad's Hill, Missouri, and held everyone at gunpoint until a train pulled into the station. After robbing the passengers and express car of the train, the outlaws left a note detailing exactly what they had done, but they deliberately left the amount of stolen money blank. They explained, "We prefer this to be published in the newspapers rather than the grossly exaggerated accounts that usually appear after one of our jobs."

The governor of Missouri offered a $2,000 reward for each member of the gang, while the U.S. postal authorities kicked in another $5,000, and the governor of Arkansas added $2,000. The Pinkerton Detective Agency put one of its finest operatives, John W. Witcher, on the case, but within a month he was found dead. He had been shot in the stomach, head, and shoulder, and most of his face had been eaten away by wild hogs. Certain that Jesse and gang member Clell Miller had killed Witcher, the Pinkerton Agency launched a determined effort to crush the outlaws.

Gang members went underground, but on April 23, Jesse married his lifelong sweetheart, Zee Mimms. Such family functions as Jesse's marriage led the Pinkertons to discover that Jesse and Frank periodically slipped back to the old farm to visit their kin.

A posse of unidentified men, who were probably Pinkertons, surrounded the James farm one night in January 1875, erroneously thinking that the James brothers were inside. Hoping to flush the outlaws, the posse tossed

THE NORTHFIELD RAID

The James-Younger Gang arrived in Northfield, Minnesota, on September 7, 1876, to do some banking. Frank James, Jim Younger, and Bill Chadwell (alias Stiles) lingered at the edge of town to serve as rear guard. Cole Younger and Clell Miller stayed outside the First National Bank while Jesse James, Bob Younger, and Charlie Pitts entered. When a local citizen approached the bank, he was grabbed by Miller. Pulling away, the man ran down the street screaming, "Robbery! Robbery!" Frank, Jim, Chadwell, Cole, and Miller rode up and down the street shooting into the air to scare citizens and create confusion during the robbery.

Inside the bank, Jesse and the others had their hands full. When the cashier, Joseph L. Heywood, told the gang that a time lock controlled the opening of the safe, he was hit over the head by Pitts and then slashed in the throat. Employees Alonzo E. Bunker and Frank J. Wilcox were roughed up by Jesse and Bob. Ironically, the time lock was not in operation. The safe door was closed with the bolts in place, but the dial on the safe was not turned.

In the confusion, Bunker escaped out the back to warn others of the robbery in progress. Realizing that their plans had failed, the three bandits exited the bank. One of them turned and shot Heywood. A vicious street fight ensued. Townsman Nicholas Gustavson was slain, but so were outlaws Miller and Chadwell. Bob Younger was severely wounded and his horse was killed. One of his brothers picked him up under heavy fire and galloped out of town along with the other survivors.

The string of conquests experienced by the James-Younger Gang stopped after failing to rob this bank in Northfield, Minnesota. With the Youngers captured, the Jameses were on their own.

and Frank split with the gang. A couple of weeks later, Pitts was killed in a shoot-out with lawmen. Cole, Bob, and Jim Younger—who were all suffering from multiple

As posses combed the Minnesota countryside, Jesse reportedly tried to persuade Cole to abandon or finish off Bob. When Cole stiffly refused, Jesse wounds—surrendered. The James brothers made it back to Missouri, where they tried to disappear.

incendiary devices through the windows. An unexpected explosion killed the nine-year-old half-brother of Frank and Jesse and wounded their mother, resulting in the amputation of her hand. The incident aroused public anger against the Pinkertons, and there were efforts to secure amnesty for the James boys.

Jesse and Frank utilized this type of popular sympathy and support to avoid arrest. That sympathy and support began to wane during the mid-1870s because by that time they had become hardened criminals with no

Above: The myth of the Jameses as Robin Hoods was advanced by dime novels. **Right:** In later years, Frank appeared in a Wild West show with Cole Younger.

intention of giving up their outlaw way of life.

In 1876, the gang left their familiar Kansas-Missouri countryside to rob a bank at Mankato, Minnesota. The venture proved to be the downfall of the James-Younger Gang. In Mankato, they were frightened away by a group of rugged citizens, so the outlaws decided to shift their raid to nearby Northfield. On September 7, 1876, the gang failed in their attempt to rob the First National Bank there. Three gang members were killed while all three Younger brothers were captured, effectively destroying the James-Younger Gang.

The James brothers made it back to Missouri and then disappeared for a time. Using various aliases, Jesse and Zee lived in Texas, Kansas City, and Tennessee, where their son and daughter were born. On numerous occasions, Jesse was reported killed, but on July 15, 1881, he led his new gang onto a Chicago, Rock Island & Pacific train at Winston, Missouri, and cleaned it out.

Under the name of Thomas Howard, Jesse moved his family to St. Joseph to plan more robberies. However, with more than $50,000 in rewards posted for Jesse, living in anonymity grew more and more difficult.

Bob and Charles Ford joined his new gang with the intention of earning this fortune. On Monday morning, April 3, 1882, Jesse finished breakfast and entered his living room with the Ford brothers, perhaps to finalize plans for a bank holdup the next day. When Jesse stepped up on a chair to straighten a picture, Bob Ford recognized his chance. Bob drew a revolver and triggered a bullet into the back of Jesse's head. As Jesse fell dead, Zee rushed to his side. The Ford brothers headed for a telegraph office to claim their rewards, while townspeople swarmed to the house to view the infamous outlaw's remains.

Jesse was buried in the front yard of his mother's farm. For years afterward, his mother permitted tourists to visit the old James farm and her son's grave for 25 cents. Also included in the price was Mrs. Samuel's "performance." She cursed detectives, wept melodramatically over the persecution of her sons, and wished damnation upon the Ford brothers. Mrs. Samuel also sold pebbles from Jesse's grave for 25 cents each and regularly replenished her supply from a nearby creek. The Ford brothers were treated with contempt, and Charles committed suicide in 1884. Bob was shot and killed in 1892.

A few months after Jesse's death, on October 4, 1882, Frank surrendered himself to Missouri Governor Thomas T. Crittenden. Following a series of trials and legal moves, he was acquitted and released from custody. Frank lived a quiet, honest existence for 30 years. He worked as a race starter at county fairs, as a theater doorman, and as an attraction in traveling companies. In 1903, he became partners with Cole Younger in the James-Younger Wild West Show. Eventually, Frank returned to the old Missouri farm, where he died at the age of 72 on February 18, 1915.

There were rumors that Jesse was not the man murdered in 1882, and for decades impostors claimed to be the outlaw. Jesse did live on, however, as a romanticized legend in novels, in movies, and in the public imagination. Though he was a thief and murderer, even as esteemed a figure as Theodore Roosevelt wrote, "Jesse W. James is America's Robin Hood."

"I HAVE KILLED JESSE JAMES"

Bob Ford did not attain the success and fame he wanted after his murder of Jesse James in St. Joseph, Missouri, on April 3, 1882. Ford and his brother, Charles, had been members of Jesse's last outlaw gang.

Ford shot the notorious outlaw in the back while Jesse was straightening a picture on his living room wall. Immediately afterward, Ford telegraphed Missouri Governor Thomas T. Crittenden, stating "I have killed Jesse James." The local sheriff arrested Ford, and he was convicted of murder by a jury. After Governor Crittenden pardoned Ford, "the dirty little coward who shot Mr. Howard," as the folk song went, was forced by public opinion to leave Missouri. Charles Ford committed suicide in 1884.

After traveling with P. T. Barnum's sideshow, where he proudly narrated his epic version of the killing of Jesse James, Bob Ford moved to Colorado and opened a saloon in the mining town of Creed. He married one of the dancers and tried to start a new life. In June 1892, a former lawman named Edward (Red) O. Kelly strolled into Ford's saloon and accused Bob of telling lies about him. The two men scuffled, and Ford had Kelly thrown out of the bar. Kelly went across the street, picked up a shotgun, and went back to the saloon, where he shot Ford dead.

Bob Ford died the way he lived, amidst the violence and treachery of his times.

MILLER

1866—1909

The West's premier assassin was called Killin' Jim or Killer Miller—but never to his face. James B. Miller was born in Arkansas in 1866, but the family moved to Texas the following year. Within a few years, young Jim's parents died, and he was taken to Evant, Texas, to live with his grandparents. The boy's at-

Killin' Jim Miller (wearing white hat at table) enjoys a game of faro in Pecos, Texas.

traction to violence began early. His grandparents were murdered in their home when he was just eight years old, and Jim was arrested for the chilling crime but never prosecuted. Jim was sent to live with his sister and her husband, J. E. Coop, on their nearby farm. Jim clashed with Coop, and when he was 17, he shot his brother-in-law in the head while he slept on a porch. Convicted of murder and

sentenced to life in prison, Miller won release on a legal technicality.

Miller went to work as a cowboy on the ranch of Mannen Clements. When the hard-bitten gunman Clements was shot to death by Ballinger City Marshal Jim Townsend in 1887, Killin' Jim shotgunned Townsend out of the saddle from ambush. Four years later, Miller married Sallie Clements, Mannen's daughter, who brought him into the Methodist church with such outward enthusiasm that he became known as Deacon Jim.

Deacon Jim pinned on a badge as a deputy sheriff in Reeves County, then became town marshal of the county seat, Pecos. For a time he also served as a Texas Ranger. Prudently, Killin' Jim began wearing a steel breastplate under his clothing, a precaution that saved his life twice during a feud with Bud Frazer. While Frazer was sheriff of Reeves County, he arrested Marshal Miller for stealing a pair of mules. When Killin' Jim was free to walk the streets of Pecos once again, Frazer realized that he could be a target. On April 12, 1894, Sheriff Frazer shot Marshal Miller without warning. Hit in the right arm, Miller opened fire with his left hand but succeeded only in wounding an innocent bystander. Frazer then emptied his gun into Miller's chest, knocking him off his feet. However, Miller was saved because the bullets hit the breastplate.

The following December, Frazer, now an ex-sheriff, opened fire on Miller once again, striking him in the left leg and right arm. Miller again fought back with his left hand, and when two more bullets bounced off the breastplate, a demoralized Frazer turned and fled. Frazer left Texas for New Mexico. Two years later, he returned to the Pecos area to visit his mother and sister. Learning of Frazer's presence, Killer Miller found Frazer in a saloon and blew away most of his head with a shotgun. When cursed by the dead man's sister, he threatened to shoot her, too.

Miller won acquittal on grounds that "he had done no worse than Frazer." Three weeks after the trial, he ambushed and killed Joe Earp, who had testified against him, then galloped 100 miles to establish an alibi. When the district attorney who had prosecuted Miller died of food poisoning soon thereafter, it was widely speculated that Killin' Jim had slipped arsenic to him.

The Millers moved to Fort Worth, where Sallie opened a rooming house and Deacon Jim spoke regularly at prayer meetings. Between prayer meetings, however, Killin' Jim was increasingly busy as word spread that his services were available for $150 per victim. Miller was paid $500 to dispatch Lubbock lawyer James Jarrott. In 1904, he carried out a contract on Frank Fore in a Fort Worth hotel, and two years later he shotgunned Deputy U.S. Marshal Ben Collins in Emet, Oklahoma. Killin' Jim was also widely suspected in the 1908 murder of famed lawman Pat Garrett.

The following year, Miller was paid $2,000 to kill rancher A. A. Bobbitt in Ada, Oklahoma. After ambushing Bobbitt at his ranch, Miller hastened back to Fort Worth. Texas officials happily extradited him to Ada, where he was lynched, along with his three employers, on April 19, 1909.

The day of the gunslinger had ended. Delivered to a lynch mob by 20th-century authorities, the last—and perhaps the worst—of the notorious hired gunmen vanished from the West.

With chilling effectiveness, frontier justice finally catches up to Killin' Jim Miller and his coconspirators.

CHEROKEE BILL

1876–1896

The notorious outlaw known as Cherokee Bill was only 19 when he was sentenced to hang, but Judge Isaac Parker accurately described the vicious young killer as "a most ferocious monster."

The monster was born Crawford Goldsby at Fort Concho, Texas, in February of 1876. His multiracial father, a soldier, had met his part Cherokee, part white, part black mother while stationed at Fort Gibson in Indian Territory. In 1878, Sergeant Goldsby abandoned his family after being implicated in a shootout between soldiers and civilians. Crawford and his baby brother, Clarence, were brought to the Cherokee Nation by their mother. When Crawford was seven, he left home to attend the Indian school at Cherokee, Kansas. After three years, he was sent away to the famous Indian school in Carlisle, Pennsylvania.

He came home to Fort Gibson at the age of 12, but his mother had remarried, and Crawford disliked his new stepfather. He began carousing and drinking with rough companions. When he was 15, he moved to Nowata to live with his sister. He found that he disliked her husband, Mose Brown, and decided to leave Nowata. Returning to

Cherokee Bill became feared for his viciousness during his short life.

Graciously posing with the posse that will bring him in for murder, Cherokee Bill (center) shows the confidence he held that no hangman would ever put a rope around him.

Fort Gibson, he worked at a few odd jobs and continued to carouse.

Early in 1894, while at a dance near Fort Gibson, 18-year-old Crawford, who was now called Cherokee Bill, tangled with Jake Lewis, an African American in his 30s. A fistfight ensued, and Lewis pounded his younger opponent. Two days later, Cherokee Bill sought out Lewis, shot him twice, and galloped away. Lewis survived his wounds.

Cherokee Bill took up with a pair of criminal brothers named Bill and Jim Cook. On July 18, 1894, Bill and the Cooks stopped for supper at the Halfway House, an eating establishment operated by relatives of the Cook brothers. When an eight-man posse appeared, led by Sheriff Ellis Rattling Gourd, the three fugitives seized their Winchesters, and a furious fight erupted. Jim Cook was wounded seven times, and officer Sequoyah Houston was slain, apparently by Cherokee Bill. The posse retreated, allowing Cherokee Bill and Bill Cook a chance to escape.

Soon after this incident, Bill Cook organized the Cook Gang, and Cherokee Bill readily assisted in a succession of robberies and murders that terrorized the Cherokee and Creek Nations. Less than two weeks after the gunbattle with Sheriff Gourd, Cherokee Bill shot and killed J. M. Mitchell while looting the Lincoln County Bank of Chandler. In September 1894, following another disagreement with Mose Brown, he gunned down his brother-in-law. On November 8, while robbing a store in Lenapah, Cherokee Bill put a Winchester bullet in the brain of Ernest Melton. This was the murder for which he would hang.

Cherokee Bill was known to meet his sweetheart, Maggie Glass, at the cabin of Ike Rogers and his wife, who was Maggie's aunt. A mixture of Cherokee and African American, Rogers held a commission as a deputy U.S. marshal, but he was an ineffectual lawman. Cherokee Bill felt reasonably safe at his cabin, located five miles east of Nowata. Unbeknownst to Cherokee Bill, Rogers agreed to a plan to capture the outlaw for a one-third share of the reward money. On January 30, after a night-long sojourn with Maggie, Cherokee Bill was jumped by Rogers and Clint Scales. After a vicious struggle, Cherokee Bill was overpowered, then whisked by wagon to confinement at Fort Smith, Arkansas.

Convicted and sentenced to hang, Cherokee Bill engineered an escape attempt from Murderer's Row on July 26, 1895. With a revolver and ammunition that had been smuggled into his cell, he killed guard Lawrence Keating, then traded shots with other officers for 15 minutes. Another notorious inmate, Henry Starr, persuaded Cherokee Bill to give up his gun, and Judge Parker promptly issued a second murder charge.

On the day of his execution, March 17, 1896, Cherokee Bill was visited by his mother, brother, and sister, as thousands of sightseers crowded into Fort Smith. He gave away his personal possessions, then calmly faced the gallows and reportedly said, "Good-bye, all you chums down that way."

Before he was hung on St. Patrick's day, 1896, Cherokee Bill calmly accepted his fate, saying, "This is about as good a day to die as any.

A year after his brother was hanged, Clarence Goldsby shot Ike Rogers in the neck. When Rogers fell on his back, Clarence pumped two more slugs into his face. Clarence took his brother's gun from Rogers's corpse, eluded a posse, and disappeared. From somewhere "down that way" Cherokee Bill must have smiled.

JOHN WESLEY
HARDIN

1853—1895

The son of a Methodist preacher, John Wesley Hardin was named after the founder of his father's denomination. Hardin taught school in a one-room classroom, and he later became a lawyer. He conducted school, however, while hiding out from lawmen, and he studied for the bar while serving a prison term for murder. The preacher's kid was actually one of the most prolific killers of the last days of the Old West.

Hardin was born on May 26, 1853, in Bonham, Texas. His Methodist father selected the boy's name in the hope that he might become a minister. In order to supplement his income, Reverend Hardin taught school and practiced law, and when Wes was two, the family moved to southeastern Texas. While he was still a boy, Wes learned to handle guns in order to hunt game, then he refined his skill by using an effigy of Abraham Lincoln for target practice. Wes revealed his killer instinct at the tender age of 14 when he stabbed a boy in the chest and back during a knife fight. The boy recovered, but Wes moved on to more violent behavior the next year.

In November 1868, Wes visited an uncle's farm near Moscow in East Texas. During a

John Wesley Hardin claimed to have stared down Wild Bill Hickok in Abilene in 1871, though some historians dispute the story.

wrestling match between Wes, his cousin, and a former slave named Mage, Mage became angry, probably for good reason. The next day as Wes was riding home, Mage stepped into the road with a stick in his hand. Young Hardin, filled with the racist resentments prevalent in Texas during Reconstruction, hauled out his .44 and pumped three slugs into Mage.

Hardin hid out at the farm of a friend near Sumpter. Learning that three occupation soldiers were coming to arrest him for the murder of Mage, he armed himself with a shotgun and revolver, and he set an ambush at a nearby creek. When the troopers rode near, Hardin let loose with both barrels of the shotgun, killing two of his prey. The third soldier managed to shoot Wes in the left arm, but Hardin dropped the man with his .44. Hardin fled the area, and several ex-Confederate soldiers concealed the Union corpses.

Reverend Hardin took his deadly son to Navarro County, where there were numerous sympathetic relatives. A cave provided a secluded hideout. The nearby community of Pisgah Ridge offered employment as a teacher in a one-room school where bullies had run off a succession of schoolmarms. Hardin was only 16 and fuzzy-cheeked, but he commanded rapt attention from his pupils by wearing a pair of cap-and-ball revolvers at his waist. Professor Hardin gave up the classroom to work as a cowboy near Corsicana, Texas.

The number of gunfights in which two opponents face off in the street has been greatly exaggerated by western lore and literature, but John Wesley Hardin did engage in such a shoot-out in tiny Towash, Texas, on Christmas Day of 1869. He had been arguing over a card game with a gambler named Bradly, and late in the day, the two antagonists met on the street. Bradly missed Hardin with a pistol shot, but Wes gunned down his opponent with bullets to the head and chest.

On the run again, Hardin proved to be hot-tempered and quick on the trigger. Like a good street fighter who always threw the first punch, he did not hesitate to go for the opening shot as soon as he saw trouble brewing. There were other altercations, followed by fatal shootings.

While in Smiley in South Texas during September 1871, Hardin learned he was being hunted by two African-American state policemen, Green Parramore and John Lackey. The young gunfighter boldly approached the unsuspecting officers, who were eating crackers and cheese at the general store, and asked them if they knew Hardin. They replied that they had never seen Hardin, but that they intended to find and arrest him. "Well," snapped Wes, drawing a revolver, "you see him now!" Wes shot Parramore dead and wounded Lackey in the mouth. Lackey bolted out of the store, thus surviving his encounter with Hardin.

The young killer took time away from gambling and fighting to marry Jane Bowen in 1872, and they eventually became the parents of two daughters and a son. Marriage did little to settle him down.

Hardin was eventually arrested, but he was rescued from jail by Mannen Clements. He then joined his Clements cousins in the violent Sutton-Taylor feud, a personal conflict that had been going on between the Suttons and the Taylors since they had lived in South Carolina in the 1840s. The Clements sided with the Taylors. Each family recruited gangs of about 200 "regulators" to protect their interests. In a Cuero saloon in April 1873, Hardin killed J. B. Morgan, who worked as a deputy for DeWitt County Sheriff Jack Helm. Helm was a leader of the Sutton Regulators. In July 1873, Hardin and Jim Taylor encountered Helm in Albuquerque, Texas. Wes blasted Helm in the chest with a load of buckshot, and Taylor emptied his revolver into the fallen man's head.

The next year, Wes celebrated his 21st birthday by winning heavily at horse racing in Comanche, Texas. Afterward, he quarreled in a saloon with Deputy Sheriff Charles Webb, and the two men pulled their pistols and fired. Hardin was struck in the side, but Webb took a bullet in the head. Webb jerked his trigger as he was hit, and two of Hardin's companions pumped slugs into the officer as he went down. An enraged mob chased Hardin and his party out of town. Hardin escaped, but his brother, Joe, and two others were lynched in Comanche. Eventually, five more cousins and friends of Hardin died as retribution for Webb's death.

Posing as J. H. Swain, Jr., Hardin traveled with his family by steamboat to Florida. For three years he tried to remain anonymous by working for a living. He traded in cattle and horses, operated a saloon, and ran a logging business. It worked until 1877 when he was spotted by Texas Ranger John Armstrong on a train at a depot in Pensacola. Unable to get to his gun, which got caught in his suspenders, Hardin was jumped by several lawmen. Armstrong clubbed him senseless with his long-barreled .45, and the fugitive was whisked back to Texas.

Tried for the murder of Deputy Webb, Hardin was sentenced to 25 years in the penitentiary at Huntsville. While in prison, he joined

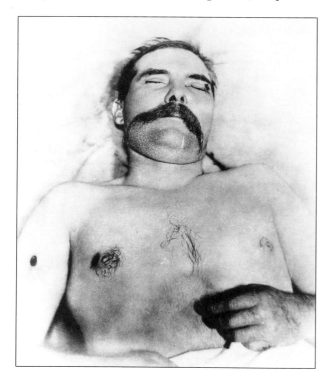

John Wesley Hardin was shot through the back of the head. Note the bullet hole through his left eye.

a debating society, became superintendent of the Sunday school, and studied for the bar. He maintained an extensive correspondence with his wife, and his letters were sometimes surprisingly poignant for having come from the pen of a seemingly cold-hearted killer. Jane Hardin worked ceaselessly for his release,

but she died a year before Hardin was granted a full pardon in 1894.

For a time, he lived with his children in Gonzales, Texas, where he opened a law office. He moved his legal practice to Junction and married teenager Callie Lewis. Callie left him on their honeymoon. He gravitated to El Paso, a notorious border town that was one of the last gunfighter haunts. Drinking and carousing with a hard crowd, he kept company with a married woman, a former prostitute known as Beulah McRose. Beulah left Hardin, but that did not stop him from trying to protect her. After she was arrested by John Selman, Jr., Hardin ran into John Selman, Sr., and threatened to kill him and his son.

A 53-year-old gunfighter who understood the menace in Hardin's threats, Selman was determined to face the trouble. The elder Selman charged into the Acme Saloon on the evening of August 19, 1895, and opened fire on Hardin's back. A slug crashed into the outlaw's head and emerged from his left eye. Selman fired again but missed Hardin as he fell. He then walked over to Hardin's prostrate form and deliberately pumped two more slugs into his victim. John Selman, Jr., ran into the saloon, clutched his father's arm, and shouted, "Don't shoot him anymore, he's dead."

He was indeed dead, at the age of 42. Not long after Hardin's death, a manuscript was discovered titled *The Life of John Wesley Hardin, As Written by Himself*. The autobiography, which ends abruptly in the 1880s, describes more than two dozen killings, though other sources attribute over 40 shooting deaths to Hardin. While these numbers are unreliable, there is no question that from 1868 through 1874, young Wes Hardin was one of the most lethal shootists in frontier history.

HARDIN GOES TO JAIL

John Wesley Hardin spent 15 years in the Huntsville prison in Texas on a second-degree murder charge stemming from the killing of Deputy Sheriff Charles Webb. While serving his time, Hardin proved to be surprisingly industrious and hard working. Much has been made of the fact that he spent the latter years of his term engaged in a variety of intellectual pursuits; he studied, among other things, theology, algebra, and law from his prison cell.

When he first arrived at Huntsville, however, Hardin devoted his energies to some less-admirable activities. He aggressively worked at stirring up other inmates and inciting unrest in the prison, and he also made repeated attempts at escape during the first ten years of his sentence. In one incident, Hardin led a group of prisoners in a revolt and nearly captured the prison armory. After an overnight standoff, the inmates were subdued when additional forces arrived to back up the prison guards.

For his rebellious actions, Hardin repeatedly received severe beatings and was kept in solitary confinement for long periods and restricted to subsistence rations. Through it all, his spirit proved to be remarkably resilient. Many prisoners and guards alike came to respect and admire his tenacity and provided him with food, blankets, and other items against prison orders during his punishments.

The following excerpt from his autobiography *The Life of John Wesley Hardin* details his ongoing efforts to escape from a jail in Austin, Texas, where he was held during his unsuccessful appeal of the trial.

"The rangers took me back to Austin to await the result of my appeal. Judge White affirmed the decision of the lower court and they took me back to Comanche in the latter part of September, 1878, where I received my sentence of twenty-five years with hard labor.

"While I was in that Austin jail I had done everything in my power to escape. The cells were made of good material and in fact the jail was a good one, with one set of cages on top of the other, separated by sheet iron. I soon got so I could make a key that would unlock my cell door and put me in the runaround. I made a key to unlock that and now all I had to do was to climb to the window and saw one of the bars. I could then easily escape.

"But some 'trusties' found out the scheme and gave it away to the jailor, who placed a guard inside the jail day and night. Thus it became impossible for me to do the work in the window though I had the key to the cell and the runaround.

"There were from 60 to 90 prisoners in that jail all the time and at least 50 of these stood ready to inform on me at any time. [That] was the trouble [in] getting out...."

from Territorial Governor Lew Wallace. Apprehensive over the formalities of his approaching trial, the Kid left Lincoln, thus violating the terms of his amnesty agreement. The Kid formed a gang of rustlers, which included Dave Rudabaugh, Charlie Bowdre, and Tom O'Folliard.

Boldly refusing to leave Lincoln County, the Kid rustled livestock and accepted shelter from numerous friends and sweethearts. In November 1880, the Kid was nearly caught by a posse when he was trapped in a ranch house near White Oaks with two other outlaws. After darkness fell, he shot his way free.

By this time, Sheriff Pat Garrett was leading a relentless manhunt. On the night of December 19, 1880, the Kid led five other fugitives into Fort Sumner for food and recreation, but Garrett and his posse opened fire. Tom O'Folliard was mortally wounded, but the others escaped. The Kid and his men were trailed through the snow to a hideout at Stinking Springs. After Charlie Bowdre was killed, the Kid, who was surrounded and outgunned, finally surrendered to Garrett.

Tried, convicted, and sentenced in Mesilla, the Kid was incarcerated in Lincoln to await hanging. On April 28, 1881, he procured a revolver, which may have been planted in an outhouse, and killed guard J. W. Bell. Bob Olinger, a guard who had bullied the Kid and threatened him with his shotgun, came running to see what the problem was. He was met

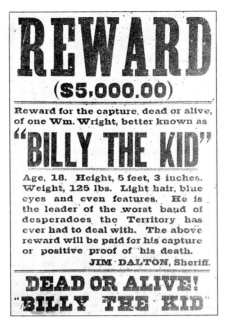

REWARD
($5,000.00)

Reward for the capture, dead or alive, of one Wm. Wright, better known as

"BILLY THE KID"

Age, 18. Height, 5 feet, 3 inches. Weight, 125 lbs. Light hair, blue eyes and even features. He is the leader of the worst band of desperadoes the Territory has ever had to deal with. The above reward will be paid for his capture or positive proof of his death.
JIM DALTON, Sheriff.

DEAD OR ALIVE!
"BILLY THE KID"

This reward poster attests to the Kid's diminutive stature as well as his ominous reputation.

by the Kid, who was brandishing Olinger's shotgun. "Hello, Bob," the Kid sneered. The ominous greeting was punctuated with the roar of both barrels blasting into Olinger. The Kid tossed the shotgun into the dust beside his tormentor's body, reportedly shouting, "You won't follow me any more with that gun." Once again he escaped, and once again he brazenly hid out in the nearby countryside.

On the night of July 14, 1881, Garrett led two deputies into Fort Sumner, then ventured alone into the darkened bedroom of Pete Maxwell to ask the whereabouts of the Kid. That evening, the Kid had come in to visit a sweetheart. About midnight, he slipped his double-action .41 into the waistband of his pants, picked up a butcher knife, and walked in his stocking feet to Maxwell's quarters. Intending to ask for the key to the meat house so he could cut a steak, he passed the two deputies and peered at the dim form sitting on Maxwell's bed. He asked, *"Quien es? "Quien es?"* As a reply, Garrett triggered a bullet into the Kid's heart. He was buried the next day in the Fort Sumner cemetery between confederates Tom O'Folliard and Charlie Bowdre.

In a four-year span, he fought in at least 16 shoot-outs, he killed four men himself, and he helped to kill five others. Who was Billy the Kid? He was a bold and deadly gunfighter who earned his ostentatious reputation.

THE LINCOLN COUNTY WAR

Although the name Billy the Kid is closely associated with the Lincoln County War, the troubles in that remote New Mexico county during the late 1870s and early 1880s went far deeper than the youthful Kid. Like most range wars in the West, this one had its origins in pure greed. On one side of the war was a powerful Lincoln merchant named Lawrence G. Murphy and on the other were several cattlemen, including John Chisum.

Murphy, an Irishman who had migrated to the United States as a teenager, owned L. G. Murphy & Company, a general store that he opened in the county seat of Lincoln in 1874. Early on, Murphy became an ally of the Republican leadership of the territory, which helped him corner lucrative government contracts to provide beef and other supplies to army posts and Indian reservations. Murphy's associates included James Riley and James Dolan, a hothead who did not hesitate to use a gun.

Murphy was resisted by Chisum, a cattle baron who wanted to monopolize the government-owned public range for his own purposes. The situation was further complicated in 1875 when John Tunstall, a well-to-do Englishman, went into the cattle business with Alexander McSween, a lawyer. Tunstall and McSween, who also wanted to secure government contracts for beef, became allies of Chisum. They opened a store in direct competition with Murphy and his associates, and they also started a bank.

After Murphy sold his interest of L. G. Murphy & Company to his partners, sales lagged, and Riley and Dolan found many of their customers switching their allegiances to Tunstall and McSween. Accusations and threats were hurled from both sides, and each mounted a force of men and associates for protection.

When some of Dolan's men murdered Tunstall, the war was triggered. Billy the Kid, who was employed by the Englishman, swore revenge. Tunstall's foreman headed a force called the Regulators, who were loyal to McSween. Over the next several months, members of both sides were killed in cold blood. The violence between the two factions climaxed in mid-July of 1878 when McSween's house was burned down and he was shot dead. By that time, Murphy had drunk himself to death. With Murphy, Tunstall, and McSween all dead, the Lincoln County War soon ended.

James Riley and James Dolan bought out Lawrence Murphy's interest in this store and other Lincoln, New Mexico, enterprises just before the start of the Lincoln County War.

THE DALTON
BROTHERS

On October 5, 1892, Bob, Emmett, and Grat Dalton achieved a lifelong ambition. They staged the most spectacular bank holdup in western history. The Dalton gang simultaneously hit two banks in Coffeyville, Kansas, and in the bloodbath that followed, a dozen men were shot, including all three Dalton brothers and their two confederates.

The outlaw trio was born in Cass County, Missouri: Grattan was born in 1865, Bob in 1868, and Emmett in 1871. All the Dalton children—ten sons and five daughters—were reared by Lewis and Adeleine Dalton on a succession of farms, including an Oklahoma homestead near the Kansas bordertown of Coffeyville. Post-Civil War Kansas and the Indian Territories were awash in the violence that was a legacy of the border conflicts and the influence of the James-Younger Gang. The Daltons were distant relatives of the Youngers, and they claimed an even more distant kinship to the Jameses. Most of the children grew up to be law-abiding, but four of them claimed that outlawry was in their blood.

An older brother, Frank Dalton, was killed by whiskey runners while serving as a deputy

Bob Dalton and sweetheart Eugenia Moore had this photo taken at a studio in Indian Territory in 1889.

Emmett Dalton, in 1910, had long since abandoned his violent outlaw life.

U.S. marshal under Judge Isaac Parker. Seeking revenge, Grat, Bob, and Emmett promptly sought lawmen badges themselves. Grat was appointed to take Frank's place as a deputy U.S. marshal. Bob joined Grat as a member of his regular posse and then later became a deputy marshal. Emmett, who worked on a ranch for a while, served as a posse member for his two brothers. The Dalton brothers proved to be able lawmen because they had nerves of steel and they could shoot fast and straight. Unfortunately, they tended to break the law as much as they protected it. They rustled herds of horses and cattle and sold them in Kansas. When Judge Parker found out about the Daltons' sideline, he revoked their appointments and issued warrants for their arrest.

By this time, the brothers had fled to Oklahoma, where they visited their mother and siblings. Lewis Dalton had died in 1889. Bob and Grat wanted to move their brothers to California to join a couple of other brothers, Littleton and Bill. They had plans to become train and bank robbers, but Charles and Henry Dalton refused, declaring they wanted no part of being outlaws. In the end, Charles, Henry, and Emmett stayed in Oklahoma to take care of their mother, while Bob and Grat left for California. Emmett wanted desperately to go to California, but Grat thought him too young for the life of a train and bank robber.

Grat rode west to join Littleton and Bill, and Bob followed. Grat, Bill, and Bob attempted to rob a Southern Pacific train in February 1891 near Alila, California. While Bill kept the passengers subdued by firing over their heads, Bob and Grat forced the engineer to take them to the express car. The engineer tried to slip away but was killed by a shot to the stomach. When Grat and Bob reached the express car, the guard refused to open the door. When he fired down on the Daltons through a small hole in the door, the brothers gave up and rode away.

Bill and Grat were apprehended, but Bob eluded capture and returned to Oklahoma. Grat was quickly tried and sentenced to 20 years in prison. On April 1, he made a spectacular escape and returned to Oklahoma, where Bob had already organized a band of outlaws.

Members of the gang included Bob, Emmett, and Grat, Bill Doolin, Bitter Creek Newcomb, Dick Broadwell, Charley Pierce, Bill Powers, and "Black Faced" Charley Bryant. Bob's sweetheart, Eugenia Moore, who was also known as Flo Quick, was the gang's advance agent until she died of cancer. Emmett also had a sweetheart, whose name was Julia Johnson. He realized that his outlaw life would make it difficult for a wife and family, so he bid Julia farewell, telling her he

was sure he was headed for Boot Hill. Emmett later reflected, "What had I to offer Julia, a man with a price on his head and no clear way to extricate myself from the compounding results of crime? I rode away. An outlaw has no business having a girl, no business thinking of marriage."

For a year and a half, the Daltons terrorized the region, pulling train holdups in such Oklahoma whistle stops as Wharton, Lelietta, Red Rock, and Adair. The gang was blamed for a number of other area robberies as well. After they had a number of robberies under their belts, they planned their most daring job—the looting of two banks in Coffeyville.

On the way into Coffeyville, Bill Doolin's horse pulled up lame, leaving the three Daltons, Dick Broadwell, and Bill Powers to ride into town. They had planned to hitch their horses in front of the banks, but a repair party had removed the hitch rails, and the gang tied their animals to a fence in a nearby alley. Bob and Emmett proceeded to the First National Bank, while Grat led Powers and Broadwell across the street to the Condon Bank.

The Daltons were recognized by a citizen who quietly spread the word that bank robbers were among them. As Bob and Emmett dumped $21,000 into a grain sack, townspeople began shouting orders and arming themselves in nearby hardware stores. The brothers emerged from the bank with hostages in front of them, but gunfire forced them back inside, and they fled through a rear door toward their horses.

Their way was blocked by a pistol-wielding man named Lucius Baldwin. Bob dropped him with a fatal Winchester slug to the chest. As the brothers sprinted down the street, Bob spotted George Cubine and Charles Brown, bootmakers who were old acquaintances since boyhood. But old acquaintances were forgotten that day because Cubine held a Winchester. Bob dropped him with one shot, then he shot Brown dead when the old man angrily picked up the rifle. Filled with the lust of battle, Bob then shot bank cashier Thomas G. Ayers through the left cheek.

Inside the Condon Bank, cashier Charley Ball bluffed Grat, Powers, and Broadwell with a story about a time lock on the vault. When a bullet crashed through a window and hit Broadwell in the arm, Grat quickly scooped $1,500 into his bag, then led his men around the corner toward the alley. City Marshal Charles T. Connelly was on their heels, firing rapidly, but Grat killed him with one shot.

Suddenly, livery stable owner John J. Kloehr stepped into "Death Alley" and triggered a rifle bullet into Bob's chest. Grat whirled toward Kloehr, but the livery man coolly shot him in the neck. When Grat collapsed, Powers jumped onto his horse, only to be shot out of the saddle. When Broadwell also clambered aboard a mount, he, too, met a deadly fusillade. Emmett tried to pick up Bob, but Kloehr shot him in the hip, and barber Carey Seaman blasted a load of buckshot into Emmett's back and shoulders.

Seven townspeople were wounded, including three fatally, but among the wounded outlaws, only buckshot-riddled Emmett stayed alive. While Emmett was carried to a hotel bed, souvenir hunters snipped locks of hair

The Condon Bank in Coffeyville shows obvious signs of the Daltons' infamous failed raid.

Dead or dying, Bob (left) and Grat (right) Dalton are propped up for display on the streets of Coffeyville.

from Bob's head. The outlaws were propped up to be photographed alongside the victorious townspeople, and Grat's arms were pumped up and down to make blood spurt from his neck.

Having escaped the massacre, Bill Doolin formed a gang of "Oklahombres," but he was killed by a posse in 1896. Embittered by the treatment of his brothers' corpses, Bill Dalton turned outlaw. He served as Doolin's lieutenant, then organized his own gang. Following an 1894 bank robbery, he was slain by lawmen. Nursed back to health by his mother and sweetheart, Emmett was sentenced to life in prison, but he was pardoned in 1907. He finally married the long-suffering Julia. He began a successful career as a building contractor, real estate agent, and, after moving to Los Angeles, a movie consultant. Until his death in 1937, the last of the outlaw Daltons worked as a vigorous anti-crime crusader.

EMMETT DALTON ON OUTLAWRY

Once pardoned from prison in 1907, Emmett Dalton "went straight." He turned to honest labor to make a living, including working as a building contractor and a real estate agent. After he moved to Hollywood, he parlayed his colorful background as an authentic Wild West outlaw into a brief career as a technical adviser for Hollywood westerns. He even appeared in a couple of silent films himself. In 1909, he returned to Coffeyville to act as the adviser on a short film about the Daltons' famous raid.

Emmett also used his former career to try to keep others on the straight and narrow. He spent much of his time crusading against crime by describing the tragic and violent deaths of his brothers, Bob, Grat, and Bill. He declared that anyone who thought he could beat the law was "the biggest fool on earth," and he pointed to his brothers as examples.

He detailed his exploits as an outlaw in numerous lectures and writings, including *When the Daltons Rode,* published in 1931.

"One thing I must say to the credit of the old-fashioned badman. He seldom shot his victim in the back. He had a certain pride at arms, a code of craft, a certain *punctilio* in his deadly dealings. His reputation didn't hang on potting someone in the rear or on the run—which requires no guts at all. When he came a-smokin' it was in the face of his challenger. . . . In this respect the Western gunplay was more like the older duello. It was entirely unlike the savage behavior of the modern city gangster or mountain feudist who places his victim 'on a spot' without a chance, to be mowed down in the dark with machine guns or rifles spitting from ambush."

Laid off along with a host of other cowboys during the severe winter of 1886–1887, Harry stole a horse, saddle, and six-gun from the VVV Ranch near Sundance, Wyoming, on February 27, 1887. Returning to Miles City, young Longabaugh was arrested on April 8 by Sheriff James Ryan. Sheriff Ryan made a lengthy detour by train because of business in St. Paul, Minnesota. When Ryan went to the lavatory, Longabaugh picked the locks on his handcuffs and leg irons, then jumped off the speeding train.

Incredibly, the youthful fugitive went back to Miles City, where he was arrested two months later. This time, handcuffed and shackled, he was driven in a buckboard directly to Sundance, where he pled guilty to horse theft. Sentenced to 18 months of hard labor, he was permitted to serve his term in the county jail at Sundance rather than at the Wyoming Territorial Prison because he was still a minor. Now called the Sundance Kid, he was released in February 1889, trying his luck first in Deadwood, South Dakota, then at the Colorado home of his cousins.

After heading north, the Sundance Kid tried crime again on September 29, 1892, helping to rob a Great Northern train near Malta, Montana. The take was minuscule, and Sundance's two henchmen were taken into custody two days after the holdup. Sundance was arrested, too, at the depot in Malta, but he escaped and headed for the outlaw hideout at Hole-in-the-Wall near Kaycee, Wyoming. During the next few years, he appeared occasionally in Montana and Canada, and he briefly worked with a band of horse rustlers who operated in northeastern Montana. Sundance also acquired a lover, Etta Place, a comely brunette of obscure background who

was reputed to have worked as a schoolmarm. By 1897, Sundance and Etta had found refuge under a tent in Robber's Roost.

For the next few years, members of the Wild Bunch committed numerous holdups, concentrating so frequently on railroad express cars that they sometimes were called the Train Robbers' Syndicate. Key members of the gang included Butch and Sundance, Harvey Logan and his brother Lonnie, Ben "The Tall Texan" Kilpatrick, Elzy Lay, "Deaf" Charley Hanks, Will Carver, and "Flatnose" George Currie. Between robberies, Butch rendezvoused with Mary Boyd and other sweethearts. He also liked to lead fellow gang members on roisterous vacations to such retreats as Denver, San Antonio, and Fort Worth.

Usually operating in small groups, members of the Wild Bunch avoided arrest by moving along the Outlaw Trail, which ran from Hole-in-the-Wall to Brown's Park to Robber's Roost. A few weeks after Butch engineered the Castle Gate payroll robbery in April 1897, Sundance led "Flatnose" George Currie, Lonnie Logan, 15-year-old George Putney, and a drunken Tom O'Day against the Butte County Bank in Belle Fourche, South Dakota. The holdup was abbreviated when O'Day, who had neglected to tie up his mount, spooked his horse and fellow thieves by foolishly triggering a shot into the air. Bolting out of the bank with only $97, the four men with horses galloped out of town with a huge posse in pursuit, while O'Day ducked into an outhouse. O'Day was captured in this dubious hideout and incarcerated in Deadwood.

The other outlaws split up, but after a couple of months in Hole-in-the-Wall, Sundance, young Putney, and Harvey Logan rode north to Montana. In camp near Lavina on September 24, 1897, the fugitive trio was jumped by a posse. The three outlaws were jailed with O'Day in Deadwood, but on October 31, the four desperadoes overpowered a deputy and rode to freedom on horses that had been staked out by an accomplice. The following summer, Sundance, Harvey Logan, and Currie pulled a couple of jobs, then scurried back to Brown's Park.

In 1899, Cassidy planned the most ambitious Wild Bunch robbery to date, involving Sundance, Harvey and Lonnie Logan, "Flatnose" George Currie, Ben Kilpatrick, and Will Carver. Two hours past midnight on June 2, two gang members boarded a Union Pacific train between Wilcox and Medicine Bow,

Wyoming. At gunpoint, the engineer was forced to advance his train across a bridge, which was then blown up while the passenger cars were uncoupled. The train and express car steamed forward two miles to a rendezvous with the rest of the gang, who blew open the express car door. The safes were blown open with charges that demolished the car, and the bandits gathered $30,000 in loot.

After rewards totaling $18,000 put such accomplished detectives as Charles Siringo and Joe LeFors on his trail, Cassidy discreetly inquired about the possibilities of amnesty. The Union Pacific agreed not to prosecute him if he never robbed a U.P. train again. U.P. officials even offered him a job as an express guard. Amnesty didn't work out, however.

The Wild Bunch dynamited this Union Pacific express car outside Wilcox, Wyoming, and made off with $30,000.

THE HOLE-IN-THE-WALL GANG

The hideout for outlaws called Hole-in-the-Wall existed among the jagged outcroppings along the eastern face of the Rocky Mountains in central Wyoming. Attractive primarily because of its isolation, the surrounding area contained only a few scattered homesteads whose inhabitants seemed willing to tolerate the presence of outlaws as long as it caused them no loss or inconvenience.

The gang that frequented the place was a loose-knit group of robbers and bandits who hid there when their trails were hot.

Although the chain of command among the members of the Hole-in-the-Wall gang was somewhat relaxed, it was Butch Cassidy who was the real leader, assisted by Harvey Logan, known

Harvey Logan killed himself on June 8, 1904, to avoid capture after a train robbery.

throughout the country as Kid Curry.

Among the other notorious members of the Wild Bunch were Tom O'Day, O. C. Hanks, Elzy Lay, Will Roberts, Harry Longabaugh (known as the Sundance Kid), Bob Lee, Dave Atkins, and Peg Leg Elliott. The Bunch's files took up considerable space in the Pinkerton Agency's cabinets.

Historian James D. Horan has called Harvey Logan, alias Kid Curry, the "tiger" of the Wild Bunch. Logan, who was born in Kentucky but raised in Missouri, was part Cherokee. When he was 19, Logan killed his first man, thus commencing his career as an outlaw. Over the next few years, he became proficient at bank robberies and killing. In the late

1890s, Logan hooked up with Butch Cassidy at Hole-in-the-Wall, and for the next few years, traveled all over the country plying his trade as a bank and train robber.

In December 1901, in far-away Knoxville, Tennessee, Logan was captured by city police after he wounded two officers. William Pinkerton warned Knoxville officials to watch out for Logan. "He has not one single redeeming feature," the head of the Pinkertons wrote. After spending nearly one and a half years in jail, Logan outwitted a guard and escaped on June 27, 1903. He had become such a noted inmate in the Knoxville prison that when he died in Colorado in 1904, the Pinkertons sent a man from Knoxville to identify the body.

When U.P. officials were late—delayed by a storm—for a meeting at a remote rendezvous point, Cassidy became skittish and disappeared. The outlaw leader left an angry note for his attorney, Douglas Preston, who was accompanying the U.P. men: "Damn you Preston you have double crossed me. I waited all day but you did not show up. Tell the U.P. to go to hell and you can go with them." Cassidy and three accomplices robbed another U.P. train in Wyoming after midnight on August 29, 1900, riding away with more than $55,000. In December 1900, while carousing in Hell's Half Acre in Fort Worth, Butch, Sundance, Kilpatrick, Carver, and Harvey Logan donned three-piece suits and derbies and posed for a studio photograph. Perhaps the most famous outlaw photo ever shot, the likeness aided detectives in their pursuit of Wild Bunch fugitives.

Butch and Sundance continued their vacation in San Antonio, visiting Fanny Porter's sporting house and other favorite haunts. Sundance journeyed to New Orleans, accompanied by Etta Place. The couple visited Sundance's relatives in Pennsylvania, toured Niagara Falls, then met Cassidy in New York City and spent three weeks vacationing in America's largest city. On February 20, 1901, under the aliases James Ryan and Mr. and Mrs. Harry Place, Butch, Sundance, and Etta boarded a steamer for Argentina.

The trio homesteaded a ranch at Cholila, near the border of Chile. After a couple of years, Sundance returned with Etta to the United States. She may have had an appendectomy at a Denver hospital, or an abortion, or she might even have borne a child. Etta went back to South America for a time, then returned north for an obscure end in the United States.

By 1904, Butch and Sundance knew that Pinkerton detectives had investigated their activities in South America. Fearing that American detectives or Argentine officials might ferret them out for the reward money, Butch and Sundance abandoned the Cholila ranch and pulled at least four robberies. They went on the run throughout Argentina, Chile, and Bolivia.

The Union Pacific employed posses such as this one to ride down the Hole-in-the-Wall Gang and other train bandits.

After what turned out to be their final holdup, Butch and Sundance rode mules into the remote Bolivian village of San Vicente on November 6, 1908. Arriving early in the evening, they were confronted by an armed posse consisting of two soldiers and a police inspector, who were led by a captain. A shoot-out erupted between the officers and the bandits. Cassidy fatally wounded soldier Victor Torres, but he was shot in the arm. Sundance took several bullets in the same limb. Everyone ducked for cover, whereupon Cassidy apparently shot Sundance in the head, then committed suicide.

Rumors persisted that Cassidy escaped the Bolivian gun battle and returned to the West, where he occasionally saw relatives, searched for caches of stolen loot, and lived under an assumed identity until 1937. Less persistent rumors suggested that Sundance, too, slipped back to the United States to live a quiet life. Perhaps no one wanted to believe that the last of the great Wild West outlaws were truly gone.

GHOST TOWNS
OF THE
WILD WEST

Tombstone, Arizona . . . Deadwood, South Dakota . . . Lincoln, New Mexico . . . Bodie, California . . . Cripple Creek, Colorado . . . Tascosa, Texas. The wild frontier towns of the Last West attracted dreamers, schemers, and adventurers from near and far. These were places where vice and violence were plentiful.

Tombstone's O.K. Corral was the site of the West's most notorious gunfight, and the Corral is still there along with the Bird Cage Theatre, The Crystal Palace saloon, the Tombstone Epitaph, and Boot Hill. Another famous Boot Hill is at Tascosa, where ten shoot-outs occurred during the 1880s. Lincoln remains almost unchanged since the days of Billy the Kid. These and other old haunts are windows to our past, surviving today as ghost towns of the Wild West.

Visitors to Tombstone, Arizona, often check out The Crystal Palace saloon, a booming bar and gambling house back in the 1880s.

days, but in November, Frank Bryant returned and found gold just east of the log cabin his party had built a few months earlier. When news of the strike spread, thousands of claims were staked out along Whitewood, Deadwood, Gold Run, Blacktail, and other area creeks.

A tent city quickly went up along Deadwood Gulch. The first building to go up was V. C. Gardner's grocery store. Throughout 1876, one structure after another was erected on the floor of the narrow gulch. Eventually, there were more saloons and dance halls than stores. By the time the Grand Central Hotel was finished, a telegraph line had been strung to the outside world and upward of 20,000 men surged into the area.

Prospectors panned for gold and ran sluice boxes along Deadwood Creek and other nearby streams. The muddy main street was filled with men and horses, mule- and ox-drawn wagons, and huge piles of lumber for the frenzy of construction projects. The Chinese laundries, restaurants, and import shops in the lower end of the gulch soon came to be known as Chinatown.

Wild Bill Hickok was the most famous of a stream of frontier notables who gravitated to the West's newest boomtown. Wild Bill and two

Right: Mathew Brady portrait of George Armstrong Custer. **Far right:** During the 1874 Black Hills Expedition, Custer's 1,000-man column enjoyed baseball games, community sings, hunting, and fishing. An avid hunter, Custer (center) fulfilled his dream of bagging a grizzly bear.

Deadwood's busy Main Street in 1876. The frontier town was less than a year old when this photo was taken, its rapid growth fueled by the discovery of gold in the surrounding hills.

During its heyday, Deadwood's Main Street was routinely jammed with "bull trains" and tall freight wagons; teamsters could barely keep up with the demand for supplies.

friends set up a tent, the most common accommodation, and Hickok was soon invited to make Number 10 Saloon his gambling headquarters. Wyatt and Morgan Earp turned up, as did

the Number 10 Saloon when Wild Bill Hickok was murdered by Jack McCall. The killer, who owed Hickok $110 and who may have been hired to assassinate the famous gunfighter, caught Wild

CALDWELL
KANSAS

Caldwell was a trail town of such unrestrained violence that it proved fatal for more law officers than any other Kansas community.

In 1880, George Flatt, at one time an effective city marshal, was killed in an ambush as he lurched drunkenly down Main Street during a midnight spree. A few months later, assistant marshal Frank Hunt was shot to death in Caldwell's infamous Red Light Saloon. In 1881, mayor and former marshal Mike Meagher was killed during a street fight. The following year, city marshal George Brown was gunned down when he tried to arrest a pair of trouble-making Texans.

What manner of town was this to sport such a casualty rate among its chief representatives of law and order? Dubbed the "Border Queen" because its southern limits coincided with the line between Kansas and Oklahoma, Caldwell also benefited from its position astride the fabled Chisholm Trail. By the

Mural of Caldwell, the "Border Queen," painted on a Main Street building.

Caldwell seems so peaceful today that it's hard to imagine it as the wild frontier town it once was.

Right: Caldwell's *Weekly Advance* press room in the early 1900s. Twenty years earlier, Caldwell boasted three newspapers: the *Commercial,* the *Journal,* and the *Post.* **Below:** Group photo of Caldwell's volunteer firemen in the 1890s.

THE WARPATH OF
HENRY BROWN

Born in Missouri in 1857, Henry Newton Brown headed west at the age of 17, learning the cowboy's trade and spending a season hunting buffalo. In 1876, a quarrel in a Texas Panhandle cattle camp led to gunplay, and Henry pumped three slugs into his unlucky adversary.

Subsequently, he gravitated to turbulent New Mexico, where he became a participant in the bloody Lincoln County War. Brown was indicted for murder (unsuccessfully), and he fought in numerous shootouts, including the climactic five-day battle in Lincoln. Afterward, he teamed up with Billy the Kid and various other fugitives, who formed a band of horse and cattle thieves.

In 1878, Billy the Kid, Brown, and three other rustlers moved a herd of stolen horses to the Tascosa area of the Texas

Bank robbers John Wesley, Henry Brown (wearing the light-colored hat and bandanna), William Smith, and Ben Wheeler are assembled in front of the Medicine Lodge jail shortly after their capture. All four men would be dead by morning, victims of vigilante justice.

Panhandle. Brown stayed, working as a stock detective and as a cowboy, although he was fired because, as he once put it, he was "always on the warpath." Next, Brown pinned on a deputy sheriff's badge, but was discharged again because he was found to be too violent. By 1882, he had become city marshal of

lawless Caldwell, which welcomed the kind of service that Brown was willing to provide. The aggressive gunfighter quickly tamed the Border Queen, and grateful citizens presented the marshal with a magnificent engraved Winchester, raising his pay to $125 per month.

But just one month after marrying a local lass,

Marshal Brown returned to his wicked ways, leading his deputy and two other gunmen in robbing a bank 70 miles to the west in Medicine Lodge. The bank president and a cashier were killed, but the outlaw marshal and his gang were captured. Brown was shot that night, trying to escape. The others were lynched.

TASCOSA
TEXAS

ascosa sprang up beside the Canadian River in the Texas Panhandle in the mid-1870s, just as the buffalo herds and the Comanches and Kiowas were disappearing from the landscape. Great cattle ranches such as the LS, the LIT, the Frying Pan, and the three-million-acre XIT developed in the vicinity, and for nearly two decades Tascosa proudly proclaimed itself the "Cowboy Capital of the Panhandle."

Indeed, the West's only cowboy strike occurred in Tascosa in 1883, this while herds in the region were owned by such legendary cattle barons as Charles Goodnight, John Chisum, and George Littlefield.

Tascosa's Boot Hill included victims from one of the deadliest saloon fights in frontier history. Billy the Kid, Pat Garrett, Henry Brown, and Temple Houston were among the lethal gunfighters who rode the town's dusty streets, and when the cowboys, gunmen, gam-

Tascosa's frame school was built at the north end of town. Later renovated as a private residence, it is one of only two buildings that remain from the era when Tascosa was known as the "Cowboy Capital of the Panhandle."

The only two-story building in Tascosa was the stone courthouse, built in 1884. After the dying town lost its position as the seat of Oldham County, the abandoned courthouse was purchased by Julian Bivins, who added a porch to what became his ranch headquarters (visible in background).

CRIPPLE CREEK
COLORADO

Since its first gold discovery in 1858, the state of Colorado has produced nearly a billion dollars' worth of the precious metal—approximately three percent of the world's supply. Half of that bounty came from the legendary Cripple Creek District.

Gold was discovered in the district in 1890, and during the next decade at least two dozen large-scale mines were put into operation. By the turn of the century, annual production exceeded $18 million.

The town of Cripple Creek, for which the district was named, traces its origins to 1885, when a pair of Denver real estate men, Julian Meyers and Horace Bennett, bought considerable land around what would become the town site, initially intending it as a cattle range and fishing location. When gold was discovered nearby, they decided to create a town instead, which they platted in 1891, naming

Cripple Creek today. At the turn of the century, the valley was jammed with buildings, and the population reached 25,000.

Almost all of the buildings in Cripple Creek are a century old. Commercial structures housed almost every type of business, including more than 70 saloons. Above these ground-floor enterprises were the offices of some 60 doctors and 90 lawyers.

exchange was housed in a three-story masonry structure on one prominent corner. Across the street was the city's grandest building, the five-story, 150-room National Hotel, featuring a plush penthouse suite.

The Grand Opera House, located on Meyers Avenue, boasted two balconies and the finest performers and troupes of the day. Also on Meyers Avenue were most of the more than 70 saloons that served Cripple Creek, including the Bon Ton and Crapper Jack's, and an astonishing variety of brothels. The Old Homestead, just across the street from the opera house, was considered the finest.

The quality of brothels declined as Meyers Avenue stretched eastward toward Poverty Gulch, where the cheapest women could be obtained. When Cripple Creek first boomed, prostitutes openly plied their trade all over town, much to the annoyance of women shoppers and sedate businessmen. Marshal Hi Wilson soon confined such activities to Meyers Avenue, but when hatchet-carrying temperance crusader Carry Nation visited Cripple Creek, she called it "a foul cesspool."

In 1914, a journalist by the name of Julian Street published an article about Cripple Creek in *Collier's,* focusing primarily on the red-light activities of Meyers Avenue. Cripple Creek civic leaders angrily demanded a retraction, and when the magazine refused to comply, the name of Meyers Avenue was officially changed to Julian Street.

With 475 mines, the Cripple Creek District was an inevitable target of the aggressive labor organizers of the era. In 1894, the Western Federation of Miners staged a violent strike that lasted 130 days and cost the district $3 million in lost production and wages, but which won for union members a three-dollar, eight-hour workday.

In 1903 and 1904, there was an even worse labor war that wracked the district with murders and sabotage of property. When the depot at Independence was dynamited, the public finally became outraged. Soldiers arrived and arrested large numbers of agitators, but deep bitterness lingered.

By this time, gold production had begun a steady decline, and flooding had become an expensive problem in the mines. As Cripple Creek's population departed, most of the magnificent buildings were abandoned, and many—such as the National Hotel—were razed to avoid annual taxes. But two of the smaller hotels have survived, along with a number of commercial structures and churches, the high school and hospital, and even the Old Homestead itself.

Today, Cripple Creek is a lively tourist town. In 1991, when gambling was legalized, many of the old buildings were remodeled as casinos, although most true ghost town buffs would find the pre-casino Cripple Creek far more appealing.

Above left and right:
Rediscovered by tourists,
Bennett Avenue, Cripple Creek's
main business street, is thriving
again. **Left:** The Imperial
Hotel's century-old bar after a
recent restoration.

THE NAMING OF CRIPPLE CREEK

In 1871, Levi Welty and his family moved from their ranch near Colorado Springs to the high country west of Pikes Peak. The Weltys centered their new ranch around a winding creek, and Levi and his sons George, Frank, and Alonzo began building a protective shack over the spring that fed it.

As the men toiled, a log rolled onto Frank, injuring him slightly and causing Levi to accidentally discharge his shotgun and nick himself in the hand. The commotion caused a calf to panic and break a leg, and Alonzo, who was chopping wood, cut his foot badly enough to lay him up for weeks.

Several months later, while repairing the roof over the spring house, George fell to the ground and injured his back. At about that time, the Weltys killed a bear and sent a hired hand to take some of the meat to a neighbor. The bear meat spooked the hired hand's horse, which fell on him and put him in bed for three months.

On another occasion, Levi saw a buffalo calf in his cattle herd. He dismounted and drew his revolver to shoot the calf for meat, but accidentally shot himself in the left hand, permanently paralyzing his second finger.

As the accident toll mounted, the Weltys, who apparently were not without a sense of humor, began calling their stream Cripple Creek.

During Cripple Creek's heyday, as many as 475 gold mines were operating in the district. Today, the countryside is dotted with abandoned mine buildings.

CENTRAL CITY

COLORADO

"Go West, young man, go West." Throughout the 1850s, Horace Greeley, respected editor of the *New York Tribune,* preached his famous theme to adventurous Americans. Among the multitudes who heeded Greeley's advice was John H. Gregory, who left Georgia in 1858 with the intention of working his way to the California gold fields.

Along the way, Gregory gravitated to Cherry Creek in the Colorado Territory, where gold had just been discovered at the future site of Denver. Heeding the speculation of veteran prospectors who suspected the source was in the mountains to the west, Gregory braved frigid winter conditions and altitudes of 8,500 feet, finally locating gold in a precipitous canyon in May of 1859.

Prospectors rushed to "Gregory Gulch" by the thousands, and even Greeley himself appeared, in the midst of a long-planned trip to California. The 48-year-old Greeley rode a mule into Gregory Gulch,

Contemporary overview of Central City. During its heyday, the town was known as "the richest square mile on Earth."

Looking down Central City's picturesque Main Street, which dead-ends at historic Eureka Street. Beyond the well-preserved commercial district, private residences climb the slopes of the surrounding hillsides.

In 1874, a fire started in the house of a Chinese resident who was burning incense, and within several hours most of Central City had been leveled. But the boomtown quickly rebuilt in brick and stone. Cornishmen who had emigrated to find employment in the mines lent their skills as masons to the reconstruction, and much of their fine masonry work may still be admired. The Cornishmen added a unique flavor to Central City, singing songs of their homeland as they marched to and from work.

Perhaps the most impressive structure to rise from the ashes was the Central City Opera House, which showcased Sarah Bernhardt, Edwin Booth, Lotta Crabtree, and other notables of the stage.

Although the initial success of the Opera House lasted only a few years, the magnificent old theater was responsible for an annual revival during Central City's most somnolent period.

By the early 20th century, the mines were depleted and Central City was a shadow of its former self. But in the summer of 1932, during the heart of the Great Depression, the Opera House was reopened for a two-week run of *Camille,* starring Lillian Gish. The summer theater festival became a popular annual event.

A devastating blaze on May 21, 1874, destroyed most of Central City. One of the few structures left standing was the stone Wells Fargo office (foreground). Despite the massive destruction, the boomtown was quickly rebuilt.

The Opera House featured such giants of the American stage as Edwin Booth and Sarah Bernhardt.

The Central City Opera House, built at a cost of $25,000, opened in March of 1878. The balcony was reserved for miners, who often tromped to performances straight from the mines.

THE REMARKABLE
TELLER HOUSE

For more than a decade, Central City lacked a first-class hotel. In December of 1868, two prosperous citizens pledged $3,000 toward building one, triggering a community-wide drive to raise $10,000.

The amount had not quite been reached by 1871, when Henry M. Teller, president of the Colorado Central Railroad that would soon reach nearby Black Hawk, offered $30,000 if the populace would provide $25,000. Within three days the money had been pledged, and ground was broken in July of 1871.

A year later the Teller House opened with an eight-course banquet and a grand ball that lasted until dawn. Visitors admired the hotel's ornate parlors, a dining room that could accommodate nearly 200, an enormous cooking range that looked like a

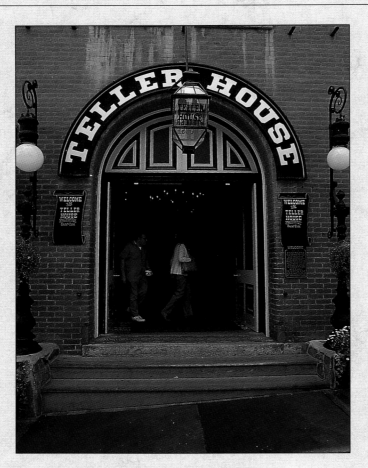

Central City's historic Teller House hotel and casino.

narrow-gauge locomotive, a reading room, and a splendid barroom with billiard tables.

One observer approved of the lack of transoms: "Guests may therefore lie down to peaceful slumbers undisturbed by apprehensions of getting their heads blown off or valuables lifted by burglars."

For its first New Year's dinner, the Teller House promised "the most elaborate bill of fare" ever offered by a Western hotel, and it may very well have succeeded. The menu included an incredible array of fish, beef, veal, mutton, pork, turkey, mallard duck, mountain grouse, prairie chicken, wild turkey, antelope, venison, buffalo, and Rocky Mountain black bear, with a full complement of vegetables, relishes, and other side dishes, plus pastries, puddings, ice cream, and a pyramid of cakes.

H.A.W. Tabor was only one of many mining millionaires to stay in the Teller House. Governor John Evans spent $20,000 to furnish the front suite that he claimed as his own; other distinguished guests included poet Walt Whitman and President Ulysses S. Grant. Their rooms may be visited today by any history-minded tourist who wants to step inside this superbly preserved relic.

Top photo: Lobby of the Teller House in 1901. The cases along the right wall displayed a fine collection of minerals and and other geological specimens. Adjoining the lobby were a library, barber shop, billiard room, and bar. **Bottom photo:** One of the hotel's parlor rooms.

VIRGINIA CITY

MONTANA

After gold began to flow from a Montana mining camp called Bannack City in 1862, hundreds of prospectors swarmed to the site. Others, like Bill Fairweather, ventured into the neighboring mountains.

Fairweather led five other miners into Alder Gulch, a tributary of the Gallatin River. In May of 1862, the men discovered paydirt, and after panning gold for a couple of days, they left to buy supplies at Bannack, 70 miles away.

Although intending to keep their strike secret, the information leaked out, and when Fairweather and his partners returned to their claim, they were accompanied by a horde of other prospectors.

The camp that sprang up was called Varina by Confederate sympathizers, in honor of the wife of Jefferson Davis. Unionists objected to the name, but a compromise was reached, and the name was changed to Virginia City (which caused considerable confusion with Easterners unfamiliar with the geography of the West, since

Virginia City sprang up quickly in Montana's gold-rich Alder Gulch.

Looking south at Virginia City. The center of town is dominated by the impressive Madison County courthouse, begun in 1875. To the left is St. Paul's Episcopal Church, a stone building erected in 1902 to replace the 1868 frame structure.

Virginia City, Nevada, had been settled four years earlier).

Within a year, Virginia City's population was up to 4,000, with thousands more in Nevada City and other nearby boomtowns. During that period, $10 million worth of gold dust and nuggets was found in Alder Gulch, and $20 million more was mined during the next four years.

In May of 1864, the United States Congress, responding to petitions circulated among the mining camps, created the Territory of Montana. The following December the territorial legislature, meeting in Bannack, selected Virginia City as the territorial capital, convening there the following February.

The capital city's population rollicked in scores of saloons, gambling halls, bawdy houses, billiard parlors, opium dens, and various other centers of masculine amusement. From the earliest days of the Alder Gulch rush, there was a degree of criminal activity unusual even for a frontier mining town. Murder, robbery, and claim jumping were so rampant that in December of 1863, a vigilance committee pledged itself "to the laudible purpos of arresting thieves & murderers & recovering stollen property...." [sic].

By this time there had been more than 100 murders in the vicinity, and the vigilantes responded by lynching nearly 30 criminals. On January 14, 1864, the vicious killer Boone Helm and

Below: The stone Creighton block still stands on the south side of Wallace Street, Virginia City's main thoroughfare.

Left: Chinese general store, on the north side of Wallace Street, around the turn of the century. **Below:** Content Corner was built for Soloman P. Content on the south side of Wallace Street at the intersection of Jackson. When completed in September of 1864, it was Virginia City's most impressive business structure, and for a time the upstairs housed offices of the territorial government. Robert Vickers bought the building in 1883 and in 1895 extensively remodeled the front, altering the pointed gothic window arches and installing plate glass for merchandise displays.

four other desperadoes were hanged in an unfinished building. Ropes were dropped over the ceiling rafters, and the badmen were hoisted up to strangle to death.

Another famous Virginia City execution was carried out the following March. Jack Slade had established a notorious reputation before coming to Virginia City, where he tried to start a ranch. But Slade was plagued by alcoholism, and after a particularly troublesome saloon quarrel he was dragged outside and hanged from a beam. "My God! My God!" cried Slade. "Must I die like this? Oh, my poor wife!"

His poor wife sealed the corpse inside a tin coffin filled with raw alcohol, traveling as far as Salt Lake City before the cargo became so odorous that it had to be buried in a Mormon Cemetery—more than four months after the lynching.

A somewhat more tranquil Virginia City soon boasted Methodist, Episcopal, and Catholic churches, as well as a Masonic Lodge. Most of the principal buildings lined mile-long Wallace Street, a 75-foot-wide, east-west thoroughfare that paralleled Daylight Creek.

The town had a handsome courthouse and several good hotels, but the proposed capitol building was never erected. It was just as well; gold production soon slowed in Alder Gulch, and in 1875, the territorial capital was moved to a more promising mining town, Helena.

Even though the population declined, Virginia City maintained itself as an outfitting point for tourists heading to Yellowstone National Park and as a business center for area ranches. Today, tourists still flock to Virginia City to enjoy its lively Old West atmosphere.

Left: Thompson Hickman Memorial Library and Museum on Wallace Street.
Below Left: William H. "Bill" Fairweather led the prospecting company that discovered gold in Alder Gulch. He died in 1875 at the age of 39 and was buried in Virginia City's new cemetery on a hill overlooking Alder Gulch.
Below: The Fairweather Inn originally was the Anaconda Hotel. It boasted a restaurant, a barroom with billiard tables, a bowling alley in the basement, and a rear entrance for ladies of the night. Remodeled in the 1930s, the old hotel became the Fairweather Inn a decade later.

BANNACK
MONTANA

John White and several partners found gold along Montana's Grasshopper Creek on July 28, 1862. Soon, hundreds of Idaho prospectors hurried up the Mullan Road, a military highway, to get in on the strike. From a population of 400 in the fall of 1862, Bannack boomed to 800 the following spring, then to 3,000 by midsummer, with another 2,000 scattered around nearby diggings.

The notorious Henry Plummer was an early arrival in Bannack, and it wasn't long before he organized fellow criminals into a band of "Road Agents" or "Innocents" (the latter because one of their secret greetings was "I am innocent"). The Road Agents identified themselves by secret handshakes and neckerchief knots, and they were known to mark stagecoaches with code symbols indicating they were to be robbed.

A promontory three miles north of Bannack was the site of so many holdups that it was dubbed Road Agents' Rock. No one knows for certain how many solitary travelers and miners were killed at the

The road into the town of Bannack is a road into the past. No automobiles are allowed into this State Historic Park.

The building with the bell tower is the Masonic Lodge and school. The two-story structure in the center is the Montana Hotel, built in 1867. To the right of the hotel is a log residence that once served as a miners' rooming house and bar.

LINCOLN
NEW MEXICO

Mexican-American settlers in the 1850s established a pioneer community they named La Placita del Rio Bonito ("The Little Town by the Pretty River"). They erected a round stone *torreon* (tower) as a refuge from attack by Apache raiders, and additional protection was available from Fort Stanton, established 10 miles to the west in 1855.

As the town developed, flat-roofed adobes were built on either side of the only street, which ran roughly a mile east to west, parallel to the Rio Bonito.

The community was called "Rio Bonito" or "La Placita" until 1869, when it was renamed Lincoln and made the county seat. Lincoln County covered 27,000 square miles and was the largest county in the United States. Comprising the entire southeastern quarter of loosely governed New Mexico, Lincoln County was inadequately policed by a sheriff and a handful of deputies, making frontier outlawry and violence almost inevitable.

A reenactment of a Western shootout staged during Billy the Kid Days.

The adobe buildings of Lincoln date from the town's violent frontier days during the 1870s and 1880s.

Looking north on C Street late in the 19th century. Nevada's first skyscraper, the six-story International Hotel, is just right of center. The magnificent hotel was built in 1877 for $200,000, with another $50,000 thrown in for furnishings and the first elevator in the West. The hotel burned in 1912.

boisterous heyday the "Queen of the Comstock" was the world's wealthiest city. More than $400 million in bullion was mined from the depths of the California, Belcher, Gould & Curry, Ophir, and other mines that honeycombed the rock beneath Virginia City.

Forty-niners had found gold traces in Gold Canyon and Six-Mile Canyon, adjacent to what would be named Mt. Davidson, but pressed on to California for more promising claims. By 1859, however, prospectors were panning profitably at a ramshackle camp they called Gold Hill.

At the north end of Six-Mile Canyon, deposits were found that contained more silver than gold. Ore from the Comstock Lode (named after loud-mouthed mine owner Henry Comstock) likewise contained impressive amounts of gold and silver. Mining companies quickly moved in, and dozens of large-scale operations introduced industrialization—and pollution—to the area.

James Fennimore, a prospector from Virginia known as "Old Virginny Finney," drunkenly dropped his whiskey bottle, and as he watched the precious liquor ooze across the rocks, he

Left: Reenactment in 1933 of an ore car being hauled to the elevator of the Consolidated Virginia Mine. **Below:** A sign overlooking Gold Canyon explains the significance of the site, which ultimately produced even more silver than gold. **Bottom of page:** Abandoned mine at Gold Canyon.

··· THIS IS ···
GOLD CANYON

"Gold Was" Discovered at the Mouth of this Canyon Dayton, Nev. in 1849. Yet it Took Ten Years for Prospectors To Work Their Way Up the Canyon to Uncover the Fabulous Silver Lode at Virginia City. By 1863 this Ravine, From Dayton to Virginia, A Distance of Seven Miles Was A Continuous City of Mines, Mills, Stores, Homes, Restaurants, Offices, Saloons and Fandango Houses. An Endless Stream of Traffic Passed Here Headed for Virginia City. For A Fine Souvenir of Virginia City Get Your Copy of the Territorial Enterprise, Nevada's First Newspaper. *HOME OF MARK TWAIN MUSEUM*

sadly pronounced, "I christen this ground Virginia." Thus named, Virginia City quickly reached boomtown proportions.

The first thoroughfare, A Street, was laid out north and south part of the way up the east side of 7,900-foot Mt. Davidson. Within a year there were several thousand inhabitants and hundreds of buildings.

Built on the side of a mountain, Virginia City "had a slant to it like a roof," according to Mark Twain. B Street was on the slope below A Street; C Street, still further down the slope, became the main thoroughfare; and D Street, just below, was the home of hundreds of prostitutes.

The town plat went all the way down to P Street, although the lower streets were never developed. The Victorian mansions of wealthy mine owners and merchants were perched above A Street, on Howard and Stewart Streets. When precipitous cross streets were formed, frequent wagon wrecks and runaways occurred, especially during icy winter months.

By 1864, narrow business lots in choice locations were selling for as much as $20,000. More than 25,000 people bustled through the streets of Virginia City and adjoining Gold Hill. Two-story brick commercial buildings abounded by 1865, along with imposing residences, fine churches and schools, two theatres, and three daily newspapers.

On October 26, 1875, fire broke out in a rooming house and destroyed 33 blocks, but Virginia City was rebuilt even more lavishly than before. The most impressive structures were the Storey County Courthouse, Piper's Opera House, St. Mary's in the Mountains Catholic Church, and the six-story International Hotel.

Surrounding the community were enormous mine and mill buildings, and as the years passed, the barren landscape began to be dotted by huge mounds of tailings. Indeed, beneath Virginia City was an "underground city" with about 30 miles of tunnels and drifts; the Gould & Curry Mine, for example, employed 500 miners to work five miles of tunnel.

Underground conditions were extremely hot (130 degrees Fahrenheit in some shafts) and dangerous, causing miners to unionize and secure an 8-hour workday and above-average wages. As many as 10,000 miners worked the Comstock Lode. It is estimated that more than 300 were killed in accidents, while another 600 were maimed or crippled.

The biggest year was 1876, when $38.5 million worth of bullion was hoisted out of the mines. The ensuing decline in production accompanied a drop in silver prices, caused largely by government policies that began in 1878.

By the turn of the century, Virginia City was a mere shadow of its early days, and by mid-century the population stood at less than 500. But many of the grand old structures still stand, and from May through October, C Street teems with tourists.

Far left: St. Mary's in the Mountains. The Catholic priest and nuns assigned here cared for Virginia City's poor and needy. After the fire of 1875, the church was magnificently rebuilt with generous donations from wealthy citizens. **Left:** The Nevada State Fireman's Museum is appropriately housed in an 1864 firehouse. **Below left and right:** Piper's Opera House on B Street faced the rear of the International Hotel.

BODIE
CALIFORNIA

Bodie was one of the most lawless mining camps on the frontier, for a time averaging six murders a week; today, it survives as what many consider California's finest ghost town.

Despite destructive blazes in 1892 and 1932, more than 150 weathered structures await the adventurer willing to journey 13 miles along a gravel road to a remote valley on the eastern slope of the Sierra Nevada. The only residents today are state park employees, but the deserted old town once rocked with raucous music, bawdy laughter—and gunfire.

California's original gold strike was on the western slope of the Sierra Nevada mountain range, but in the fall of 1859, prospector Bill Bodey and three partners found paydirt at the site that would eventually bear an altered spelling of his name.

The four men agreed to come back the following spring, but

Overview of Bodie. Miners' hall is at left. Structure just above center of photo, at the end of the street, was the town's Methodist Church.

The two-story building with the false front was the Odd Fellows Lodge, built in 1878. The Bodie Athletic Club also met there.

View of Bodie from the Standard Mine. Despite fires in 1892 and 1932—and more than a century of severe winter weather—at least 150 structures still survive.

Bodey returned within weeks with a miner named Taylor. They built a log cabin and began to work the diggings, until Bodey was caught in a blizzard and froze to death. During the spring thaw, Taylor buried Bodey where he found the body, although the remains were reinterred in the Bodie cemetery two decades later. A year after Bodey's death, Taylor was killed and scalped by a Paiute war party.

For a decade and a half, Bodie was a small mining camp with only a couple of dozen cabins.

All of that changed in 1876, when a cave-in at the Bunker Hill Mine revealed a rich gold vein. By the next year, 2,000 people had rushed to Bodie.

Another discovery in 1878 produced ore that assayed at $1,000 per ton, boosting the population past 10,000. Soon, Bodie's main street was a mile long, with three newspapers—the *Daily Free Press,* the *Free Union,* and the *Weekly Standard*—recording the boomtown's activities.

The residents of Bodie led a hard existence, especially during the bitter winters. (Mark Twain

A three-legged race on Bodie's main street during a Fourth of July celebration. Races between volunteer fire companies also were favorite holiday events.

the man the bare et being the same I thought it might be him after all . . . If it is him you will know it by his having six toes on his left foot . . . Find out all you kin about him without him knowing what it is for, that is if the bare did not eat him all up. If it did I don't see as you kin do anything and you needn't to trouble . . ."

The situation in Bodie began to change after 1881, when mining production dropped rapidly and people began leaving town. Water in the shafts became a serious problem, and soon only six mines were in operation.

Bodie experienced a partial revival in the 1890s with the advent of a cyanide process of extracting gold from mine tailings, but it only forestalled the inevitable. Mining came to a complete halt before World War II. By that time, Bodie was abandoned, but the isolation helped protect the buildings of what is today considered a truly superb ghost town.

The sun hitting the rooftops of Bodie's historic buildings creates a beautiful array of textures. Maintained in a state of arrested decay, the old mining town became a California state park in 1964.

BEST
TOWN NAMES

Baby Head, Texas. Located in Llano County, this town was named for Baby Head Creek and Baby Head Mountain. The creek and mountain were named in the 1850s, when settlers found the head of a white baby placed on a pole atop the mountain by Comanche raiders.

Big Bug, Arizona. In 1862, prospector Theodore Boggs discovered pay dirt at his Big Bug Claim along Big Bug Creek, named for the large, shiny brown beetles that live in the area.

Bumble Bee, Arizona. Shortly before the Civil War, a small cavalry outpost was established where a scout reported Apache to be as thick as bumblebees. Another story has soldiers mistaking the sounds of a distant pow-wow for a swarm of bees. In a third version, prospec-

Cripple Creek, Colorado, during its bustling heyday in the 1890s

tors found bumblebees and honey near the creek they were working.

Bitter Creek, Texas. Settled in the 1880s near Sweetwater, Bitter Creek was named for the nearby alkali stream.

Bridal Veil, Oregon. A steamboat passenger on the Columbia River remarked that a waterfall on the river looked like a bride's veil, and the name was adopted when a settlement was organized.

Contention City, Arizona. An ore-milling town, Contention City took its name from the Contention Mill. The "Contention" was between miner Hank Williams and businessman Dick Gird over land claims.

Copperopolis, California. Copper deposits were discovered in 1858, and soon the largest copper mine in the U.S. was located at Copperopolis.

Cripple Creek, Colorado. The area's first settler started a ranch near a

stream, and when a series of accidents occurred, he grumbled, "Well, this here is sure one hell of a cripple creek." Another story maintains that cattle wading into the small stream were often lamed by sharp rocks.

Crowheart, Wyoming. In 1866, Chief Washakie of the Shoshones challenged a Crow chief to a duel in which the victor would cut the heart out of his fallen foe. The fight took place atop a mesa later named Crowheart Butte—because Washakie won. When a town was settled a couple of miles away, it was dubbed Crowheart.

Cut and Shoot, Texas. The wilderness community was filled with feudists ready to use their knives or guns.

Deadwood, South Dakota. When prospectors arrived in the narrow gulch they found it littered with deadwood, giving the rowdy mining town its name.

Gunlock, Utah. In 1857, an expert hunter and gunsmith known as "Gunlock Bill" Hamblin settled at a favorite campsite in Utah along the Santa Clara River. When other pioneer families arrived, they named their community Gunlock.

Medicine Bow, Wyoming. The Wyoming town was named after the Medicine Bow River, which was located in the center of a vast buffalo hunting range. There were no hardwoods in the region, but Indians learned that a tough, supple shrub along the river was suitable for making bows. The shrub, commonly called buffalo berry, was "good medicine" for the bow, and the river became known as the Medicine Bow.

Residents of Medicine Bow, Wyoming, gather together at the Virginian Bar.

Rough and Ready, California. A band of Forty-niners from Wisconsin, led by Captain A. A. Townsend, who had served under General Zachary Taylor ("Old Rough and Ready") during the Mexican War, named themselves the Rough and Ready Company and named their settlement Rough and Ready in honor of Taylor, who by this time was President of the United States.

Show Low, Arizona. Arizona pioneers Marion Clark and Croydon Cooley played a game of seven-up, with a mountain townsite at stake. "If you can show low," declared Clark, "you win." "Show low it is!" exulted Cooley at the turn of the card, which named his town. When the site was laid out, Show Low's main street was named Deuce of Clubs.

Silverbell, Arizona. Silverbell was dubbed after a silver-haired dance hall owner named Bell; or because Spaniards had found a chunk of silver large enough to fashion a bell; or

because of the nickname of a desert flower.

Sod Town, Oklahoma. Founded in the Oklahoma panhandle, Sod Town was so named because all of the early structures were prairie-style sod buildings.

Ten Sleep, Wyoming. Indians named the site beside the Nowood River because it was "ten sleeps" from Fort Laramie.

Tombstone, Arizona. When prospector Ed Schieffelin told soldiers at Fort Huachuca that he was venturing into nearby Apache country in search of something useful, they assured him, "All you'll find is your tombstone." But he found silver, and a town found its name.

Total Wreck, Arizona. After making a silver strike, John Dillon observed that the hillside looked like a total wreck, which labeled the subsequent community.

GREATEST SHOOT-OUTS

he Gunfight at the O.K. Corral. The Newton General Massacre. Tascosa's Big Fight. The Battle of Lincoln. These and other furious shoot-outs provided a lethal arena for western gunfighters. From brawling to duels to knife fights, violence was a feature of every frontier. And in the Last West, men armed with revolvers, Winchesters, and shotguns clashed in spectacular explosions of gunplay.

Tombstone's O.K. Corral showcased western legends Wyatt Earp and Doc Holliday, but the Big Fight in Tascosa produced more fatalities. The ferocious Lincoln County War climaxed in the five-day Battle of Lincoln. Although the Sam Bass Gang was destroyed by Texas Rangers in a firefight in Round Rock, three Oklahoma lawmen were slain by Bill Doolin's Oklahombres in the Battle of Ingalls. Buckshot Roberts single-handedly shot it out with Billy the Kid and a dozen other gunmen at Blazer's Mill. And while such large-scale shoot-outs highlighted western violence, never was there a greater display of deadly courage than the *mano-a-mano* faceoff between two combatants with revolvers and knives in the main street of Medicine Lodge, Kansas.

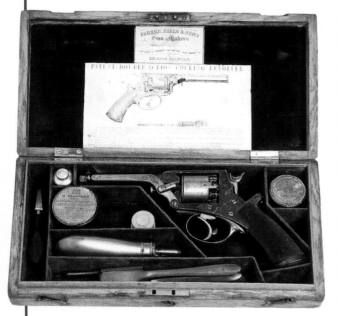

The famed Gunfight at the O. K. Corral lasted less than a minute, but the tale has been retold countless times for more than a hundred years.

THE BATTLE OF
LINCOLN

In 1878, the nation's largest county, Lincoln County, New Mexico, was wracked by murders, ambushes, and ongoing fights. The Lincoln County War came to a bloody climax during a five-day battle along the single street of the little county seat.

During the night of July 14–15, Billy the Kid and more than 40 fellow Regulators slipped into Lincoln for a showdown. Almost an equal number of their adversaries, the Seven Rivers Gang, slept in and around the House, a two-story building that dominated the west end of town.

Billy the Kid and 13 other gunmen quietly barricaded themselves inside the U-shaped, 12-room store and home of Alexander McSween, who was a major supporter of the Regulators. McSween's house was to be headquarters for the Regulators, and the remaining gunmen positioned themselves in buildings from which they could protect the rambling adobe structure.

Early the next morning, Regulators opened fire upon the startled Seven Rivers men, but they scrambled for cover and there was little other action during the first day. Throughout the following day, Seven Rivers

Sheriff William Brady and John Henry Tunstall. Brady dispatched the posse that murdered Tunstall. Tunstall was killed at the age of 24, an event that triggered the bloody Lincoln County War.

riflemen sniped at the McSween building from a tall hill behind the House, but at the end of two days of fighting, the only casualties were a horse and a mule.

On the third day, the Regulators succeeded in wounding a deputy, and on the fourth day, they hit the commander of nearby Fort Stanton. Colonel N.A.M. Dudley sent out a large detail of troopers with a howitzer and a Gatling gun. The military camped at the east end of town and declared their intention of staying out of the fight, but their imposing presence, coupled with the widespread knowledge that Colonel Dudley sympathized with the Seven Rivers faction, demoralized many of the Regulators.

By the fifth day, July 19, over half of the McSween force had slipped across the Rio Bonito, just north of Lincoln, and vanished into the rugged countryside, abandoning their allies inside McSween's house as well as a few other stalwart Regulators stationed elsewhere. The rear portion of the west wing of McSween's adobe was set afire by Jack Long and a confederate. Long then scrambled for cover inside an outhouse. As Regulator riflemen riddled the privy, Long descend-

The old McSween-Tunstall Store in 1954, still doing business three quarters of a century after the Lincoln County War. Today the building is operated as part of historic Lincoln.

ed into the pit, where he was pinned down all day. Long later described his sojourn in the pit as "gruesome," but added that it "beat dying all hollow."

The blaze fed on rafters, flooring, and window framing. Mrs. McSween and two other women were permitted to leave the slowly burning adobe, but by nightfall only the three rear rooms of the east end remained standing. Billy the Kid and his *compañeros* refused to surrender, and the Seven Rivers men crept close for the inevitable breakout.

Tom O'Folliard and Harvey Morris were the first to burst outside, but enemy riflemen immediately appeared from behind the low adobe wall that enclosed the rear of Mc-Sween's yard. Morris was shot to death, and O'Folliard was hit in the shoulder when he stooped to help his fallen comrade. O'Folliard managed to scramble to safety down the nearby riverbank as more Regulators bolted out of the house.

Three Mexican gunmen were riddled with bullets. Alexander McSween refused the weapons offered him and marched boldly toward his enemies—armed only with a Bible clutched to his chest. The Seven Rivers men cut him down with a blast of rifle fire.

Billy the Kid darted unscathed through the hail of lead. The Kid and some other McSween men shot their way past their besiegers and scattered into the darkness.

The victorious Seven Rivers men drank and danced by the light of McSween's burning house. Two fiddlers provided music, and a number of soldiers joined the triumphant celebration. Billy the Kid and the other surviving Regulators would form a band of rustlers and become outlaws, but the Lincoln County War was over.

TASCOSA'S
BIG FIGHT

Tascosa, the "Cowboy Capital of the Texas Panhandle" was the scene of at least ten shoot-outs during the 1880s, but its most spectacular explosion of violence was an 1886 gun battle known as "The Big Fight."

Ed King, John Lang, Fred Chilton, and Frank Valley, cowboys for the vast LS Ranch, attended a *baile* (dance) at Casimero Romero's plaza a short distance east of Tascosa. At two in the morning, they rode into town, and King, an abrasive man with a number of enemies, dismounted in Tascosa's main intersection to meet sporting lady Sally Emory. Ed and Sally strolled arm in arm in the bright moonlight toward her house, while the other boys continued west in search of recreation at a saloon down the street.

As the lovers passed the Jenkins and Dunn Saloon on the southeast corner of the intersection, several men on the porch exchanged words with King. A gunshot rang out, and King collapsed, dead when he hit the ground. Lem Woodruff, a cowboy who had been trying to win Sally's affections, ran out of the saloon and fired a Winchester slug into the fallen King's throat. "Boys, they've killed Ed," shouted John Lang at his companions. "Come on."

Brandishing their revolvers, Lang, Chilton, and Valley sprinted toward King's corpse. The angry trio slipped into the rear of the Jenkins and Dunn Saloon, and moments later a barrage of gunfire erupted inside the darkened building. With Woodruff were the Catfish Kid, Charley and Tom Emory, and Louis Bousman, among others, and these men blazed back at their attackers.

Woodruff bought two bullets low in the abdomen, and Charley Emory was hit in the leg. The wounded Woodruff staggered away, still clutching his Winchester. Valley pursued Woodruff but was stopped in his tracks by a slug in the left eye.

Jesse Sheets, owner of the North Star Restaurant next door, was awakened by the gunfire. When he unwisely appeared in the saloon doorway in his night clothes, he was gunned down by Chilton. As Sheets dropped with a hole in his forehead, two bullets ripped toward Chilton's gun flash. Both rounds tore into Chilton's chest. He handed his revolver to Lang and died.

Lang now retreated outside, exchanging furious fire with the men in the saloon. Sheriff Jim East hurried to the scene, and his deputy shot at the Catfish Kid, who escaped into the night.

Woodruff and Emory survived their wounds, but the following afternoon a mass funeral was held for the three LS men and Jesse Sheets, who left a widow and five children. Four coffins were built, the bodies were clad in new black suits, and the entire populace of Tascosa, along with numerous area cowboys, formed a half-mile procession to Boot Hill.

THE NEWTON GENERAL
MASSACRE

Newton, Kansas, was the terminus of the Chisholm Trail for just one year before the railroad was extended farther south to Wichita. But during that year Newton was a wolfhowl of a town, and one of the bloodiest shoot-outs in western history erupted there.

Mike McCluskie was foreman of a railroad construction crew. Known for his two-fisted ability to keep his men in line, he moonlighted as a policeman in rowdy Newton. On August 11, 1871, he was forced to kill a hard-drinking Texas gambler named William Bailey.

McCluskie left town the next day, hoping that Bailey's numerous Texas friends would cool off in time. After a week in exile, he returned to Newton, defying the sinister threats of Texas cowboys such as Hugh Anderson, still bitter over Bailey's death. McCluskie hit town on Saturday, August 19, and spent the evening in Perry Tuttle's Dance Hall. An hour or so after midnight, McCluskie was sitting at a faro table when Anderson approached him with a drawn pistol.

"You are a cowardly son of a bitch!" announced Anderson. "I will blow the top of your head off." Anderson then pumped lead into McCluskie's neck, leg, and torso. Other cowboys drew guns, and the firing became general. A drover named Jim Martin was struck in the throat, and two railroad men— brakeman Patrick Lee and a shoveler named

The Main Street of Newton, years after the Newton General Massacre of 1871. During Newton's single wild season as the railhead of the Chisholm Trail, Main Street looked more ramshackle.

Hicke—were shot in the stomach and leg, respectively.

As Martin staggered outside to die, Jim Riley, a young friend of McCluskie, locked the door behind him and emptied his gun at the Texas cowboys. When the smoke cleared, the blood-spattered room revealed a squad of punctured cowhands: Anderson had been hit twice in the leg; Billy Garrett had been fatally wounded in the chest and shoulder; Henry Kearnes was dying from a chest wound; an unnamed cowboy had suffered a leg wound; and Jim Wilkerson's nose had been grazed.

McCluskie was carried to his hotel room, where he died the next morning. Hugh Anderson recovered but was stalked by McCluskie's brother. Their eventual meeting was one of the West's most violent duels and served as a belated epilogue to the Newton General Massacre.

THE SAM BASS GANG IN
ROUND ROCK

In 1877 and 1878, Sam Bass led various desperadoes in robbing at least seven stagecoaches and five trains. There were persistent manhunts, and two of his men were killed by officers, but in July 1878, he decided to rob a bank in Round Rock, about 20 miles north of Austin, Texas.

Eluding several posses, Bass reached Round Rock with Seaborn Barnes, Frank Jackson, and Jim Murphy. On Friday afternoon, Bass decided to check out the town one more time.

Murphy had betrayed Bass, however, informing Texas Rangers of the robbery plan in exchange for leniency. Knowing that Round Rock was swarming with lawmen, Murphy dropped behind his companions, muttering something about buying corn for the horses.

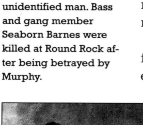

Sam Bass (center), Jim Murphy (left), and an unidentified man. Bass and gang member Seaborn Barnes were killed at Round Rock after being betrayed by Murphy.

Bass, Barnes, and Jackson tied their horses in an alley, then went into the Koppel store adjacent to the bank to buy tobacco for Bass. There they were approached by deputy sheriffs A. W. Grimes and Morris Moore, who had noticed bulges in the strangers' coats. Grimes grabbed the back of Barnes's shoulder and asked him if he was armed.

In reply, Barnes pulled his gun and whirled around, and all three outlaws opened fire. Grimes was killed on the spot, Moore collapsed with a chest wound, and Bass was shot in the hand.

Bass led a sprint for the horses, and several Texas Rangers and local citizens opened fire. Ranger Private Dick Ware emerged from a barbershop, bib around his neck and lather on his face, and shot Barnes to death.

Jackson and Bass vaulted into their saddles and spurred away, but a bullet ripped into Sam on the right side of his spine, exiting to the left of his navel. Bass clung desperately to the saddle horn, but after another 200 yards he fell off his horse. Coolly firing his six-gun, Jackson braved a hail of lead to help Bass into the saddle, and the two fugitives galloped into the approaching darkness.

The fleeing outlaws reached their camp, picked up two rifles, then headed into a thicket. But Bass could go no farther, and he insisted that Jackson escape while he could. Frank tied Sam's horse nearby, then rode into permanent anonymity.

Binding his wounds with strips of his shirt, Bass suffered through the night. A posse found him sitting against a tree the next morning. He was taken into Round Rock, where he clung to life until Sunday, July 21, 1878—his 27th birthday.

THE LAST
GUNFIGHT

At the age of 70, Jim Roberts still wore a badge in the Arizona town of Clarkdale. Roberts was a veteran gunfighter, but Clarkdale was a quiet mining community by 1928. The septuagenarian had no reason to believe he would ever again have to use the old single-action .45 in his worn holster.

Born in Missouri in 1858, Roberts headed west at the age of 18. When he reached Arizona, he began a small cattle ranch in Pleasant Valley, where he became friends with the Tewksburys. When the Pleasant Valley War exploded in 1887, Roberts fought alongside the Tewksburys against the Grahams. Roberts was perhaps the best fighting man on either side, but he was cleared of legal charges when hostilities ended.

His ranch had been burned at the start of the feud, so he became a peace officer in Jerome, a rowdy mining town where he again had to resort to his gun. During his long service in Jerome, he held a variety of commissions: deputy sheriff, constable, and town marshal.

Eventually Roberts moved to nearby Clarkdale, where he spent the rest of his life as a special officer for the United Verde Copper Company, with the additional authority of a deputy sheriff's commission. The venerable officer was making his morning rounds on June 21, 1928, when two Oklahoma criminals, Earl Nelson and Willard Forrester, drove up to the Bank of Arizona.

Nelson and Forrester quickly bagged $40,000, then darted to their getaway car. Forrester climbed behind the wheel, while one of the two robbers fired a shot at Roberts. The old gunfighter palmed his single-action Colt and coolly shot the driver in the head.

Forrester slumped dead at the wheel, and the car careened into a school building. Nelson emerged, took one look down the barrel of Roberts's Colt, and quickly surrendered.

Before Jim Roberts died of a heart attack in 1934, he was the last survivor of the Pleasant Valley War. His final shoot-out was the last gunfight involving a western shootist, and it gives an idea of how the old gunfighters might have fared against their better-armed twentieth-century counterparts.

Jim Roberts (1858–1934). At the age of 70, Roberts dueled modern bank robbers with his old, single-action Colt.

BEST EPITAPHS

Death and dying developed a unique style in the West, or at least in the popular image we have of the West. Clear evidence of this lies along with the remains of countless outlaws, lawmen, cowpokes, and others on the grave markers that dot the various Boot Hills and other bone orchards of the Old West.

Shoot 'em up
Jake.
Run for sheriff in 1872
Run from sheriff in 1876
Buried in 1876.

Jack Wagner
Shot
Ed Masterson
April 9, 1878
Shot by
Bat Masterson
April 9, 1878
Buried on
Boot Hill
April 11, 1878

Sophia Wife of
Gearhart
Spencer
& Spratt

1850–1931
She was Faithful to her 3
Soldier Boy Husbands
And is waiting the Reward
for Faithful service

Edward Hurley
Shot January 1, 1873
He drank too much and
Loved unwisely

Alice Chambers
Died Sunday May 5, 1878.
A full-fledged member
Of the group referred to as soiled doves.
She was a favorite of many.
Her last words were
"Circumstances led me to this end."

Mac McDermott
Died February 1873
McDermott shot Casey's friend
So Casey shot McDermott.
Eye for an eye and tooth for a tooth.
The frontier code.

Jack Reynolds
Died September 1872.
A tracklayer put six balls
Through his head before

you could say scat
And forever quieted a
Notorious and
contemptible desperado.

George Hoyt
Shot July 26, 1878
One night he took a pot shot at
Wyatt Earp.
Buried on Boot Hill August 21, 1878.
"Let his faults, if any,
Be hidden in the grave."

HERE
LIES
Lester Moore
FOUR SLUGS
FROM A .44
NO LES
NO MORE

"Lame Johnny" was a horse thief with a mouth big enough to hold a cantaloupe. He was hanged and then buried with an amusing epitaph:

Lame Johnny
Stranger, pass gently over this sod.
If he opens his mouth, you're gone,
by God!

Here lies
Johnny Yeast
Pardon me
For not rising

Paul Lennis Swank
Here under the dung of
the cows and sheep,
Lies an old highclimber fast asleep.
His trees all topped
and his lines all hung,
They say the old rascal
died full of rum.

Of course, the great majority of western grave markers featured only a name, perhaps death and birth dates, and possibly a traditional sentiment. Doc Holliday's grave marker in Glenwood Springs, Colorado, proclaims, "HE DIED IN BED."

Russell J. Larsen
Two things I love most,
good horses and beautiful
women, and when I die I hope
they tan this old hide of mine
and make it into a ladies riding
saddle, so I can rest in peace
between the two things I love
most.

Billy the Kid is buried alongside two members of his rustling gang, Charlie Bowdre and Tom O'Folliard, at the old Fort Sumner post cemetery in New Mexico. The three graves are marked by a single stone that reads, "PALS."

The West's most notorious woman, Belle Starr, is buried on private property in Oklahoma. The original stone was destroyed by souvenir hunters, but the landowner provided an inscribed headstone featuring a star, a bell, and a horse. Her epitaph reads:

Shed not for her the bitter tear.
Nor give the heart to vain regret.
It's but the casket that lies here.
The gem that filled it sparkles yet.

Wild Bill Hickok's burial at Deadwood's Mount Moriah Cemetery was arranged by a friend, Colorado Charlie Utter. Colorado Charlie placed the following sentiment on the marker:

Pard We Will
meet Again
in the happy
hunting ground
to part no more.

THE BEST-KEPT GRAVE IN THE WEST

The notorious Jesse James was murdered by Bob Ford on April 3, 1882. The 34-year-old outlaw was buried in the front yard of his mother's farm. At that site in 1875, the iron-willed woman had lost a hand in an explosion caused by a posse led by Pinkerton agents.

As the legend goes, Jesse's mother, Zerelda James Samuel, allowed visitors to tour the home place and Jesse's well-attended grave for 25 cents apiece. Somewhat melodramatically, she wept bitterly at the persecution of Jesse and Frank, cursed detectives, and wished damnation upon Bob Ford. Zerelda also sold pebbles from Jesse's grave for a quarter each and regularly replenished her supply from a nearby creek.

Mrs. Zerelda Samuel,
mother of Jesse James

MOST DARING HOLDUPS

"**S**tick 'em up!" These or similar words were shouted out in banks, trains, and stagecoaches all over the West. Rising above the common lot of holdup men and rustlers were Black Bart, Jesse and Frank James, the Younger brothers, the Dalton brothers, and Butch Cassidy and the Sundance Kid. Such men attained a legendary, mythical level of notoriety in part because of the spectacular nature of their nefarious exploits.

The James-Younger Gang pulled off the first daylight bank robbery in the United States in 1866. A decade later, these same hard-bitten outlaws struck a bank at Northfield, Minnesota. But the Northfield citizens fought back, triggering a vicious gun battle followed by a two-week manhunt that destroyed the gang. In 1884, another bank robbery, in Medicine Lodge, Kansas, was engineered by the gunslinging city marshal and deputy of a neighboring town. The bank president and cashier were slain, but another angry citizenry pursued and lynched the entire gang. Black Bart boldly robbed dozens of stagecoaches—alone and on foot!—while the West's final stage holdup was pulled off by a *female* bandit.

Shots blasted through the windows of the Condon Bank during the Dalton Gang's robbery in Coffeyville, Kansas.

FIRST DAYLIGHT BANK
ROBBERY

Until February 13, 1866, no bank in the United States had ever suffered an armed daylight holdup. But the James-Younger Gang opened a new chapter in American outlawry with an assault against the Clay County Savings Association on the courthouse square in Liberty, Missouri.

At mid-morning, a dozen armed men rode into town. Jesse James missed this raid because he was still recuperating from a lung wound. But his older brother Frank and the redoubtable Cole Younger led ten other thieves into Liberty. Three of the riders positioned themselves at strategic points around the square, while the rest of the gang reined up in front of the bank.

Two men dismounted and entered the bank, stopping first at the store to warm themselves. Proceeding into the bank, they met Greenup Bird and his son, clerk William Bird. One of the men handed a $10 bill to William and asked for change. Then he pulled a revolver and added, "I'd like all the money in the bank." The robbers hurried around the counter. Pointing a six-gun at

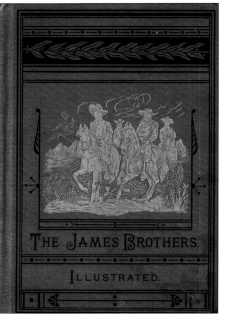

The James Brothers, published only a few years after Jesse's 1882 murder, was just one of numerous books about the notorious outlaws.

Greenup, one hardcase warned, "Make a noise and we'll shoot you down."

The other bandit produced a grain sack, struck William on the head with his gun barrel, and shoved him toward the open vault. William began to dump gold and silver coins into the sack. "Damn you," snarled the robber, "be quick."

Greenup was forced to produce a tin box containing currency, bonds, and bank notes. This valuable paper was added to the grain sack, which now bulged with loot exceeding $57,000. Greenup and William Bird were locked in the vault. "Stay in there," quipped one of the thieves. "You know all Birds should be caged!"

After the outlaws remounted with the grain sack, the gang thundered out of town, whooping the Rebel yell and firing indiscriminately. A 19-year-old student named George Wymore was shot down and killed.

The James-Younger Gang, usually led by Jesse, went on to rob other banks, and throughout the West, thieves eagerly practiced this new form of outlawry.

BLACK BART AT
COPPEROPOLIS

One of the West's legendary outlaws was a California stagecoach robber who sometimes left verse at holdup sites with the signature "Black Bart, The Po-8." Black Bart's real name was Charles E. Boles, and he was born in New York in 1830.

Attracted to the West by the gold rush, Boles eventually decided that the only gold he could find was inside Wells, Fargo, & Co. strongboxes. On July 26, 1875, he prepared a robbery attempt at a steep grade near Copperopolis. He tied down several sticks in the bush along the road to give the appearance of rifle barrels, presumably held by concealed gunmen. Then, he donned a linen duster and a flour sack mask with eyeholes and wrapped cloth around his shoes to blur footprints. Finally, he perched a derby hat atop his mask, checked his double-barreled shotgun, and waited for the scheduled stagecoach.

When the team driven by John Shine labored up the grade, the masked bandit stepped into the road. "Please throw down the box," requested the robber politely. He turned toward the "riflemen" backing him up. "If he dares to shoot, give him a solid volley, boys."

Assuming he was surrounded, Shine hastily dropped the strongbox to the ground. The bandit cracked the box with a small ax and began shoving bags of gold coins into his duster pockets. A panicky female passenger tossed her purse out the stagecoach window.

"Madam, I do not wish your money," stated the bandit as he handed back her purse. "In that respect, I honor only the good office of Wells, Fargo."

The stagecoach departed, and the masked bandit disappeared. Shine quickly returned to pick up his empty box, then recognized the ruse of the fake rifle barrels. In the meantime, the highwayman rapidly hiked cross-country with $300 of Wells, Fargo, & Co. money.

During the next seven years, Black Bart staged nearly 30 robberies, always with the same pattern and the same attire. Black Bart, The Po-8 left his first verse after the third holdup, and the gentleman bandit quickly captured the public's imagination. Between robberies, he resided at a San Francisco hotel, nattily dressed in a derby hat and business suit and sporting a diamond ring and stickpin, a gold watch and chain, and a walking cane.

Wells, Fargo finally captured Black Bart, and he served four years in San Quentin, then disappeared. His loot totaled only $18,000, and he never shot anyone or robbed a passenger. But his one-man campaign of banditry against the West's most prestigious express company assured him a special place in the rogue's gallery of American outlaws.

"Black Bart, The Po-8" was dapper Charles E. Boles, who robbed 27 Wells, Fargo, & Co. stagecoaches.

THE DALTONS IN
COFFEYVILLE

After a year and a half of holding up trains, the Dalton Gang planned their most daring job: the simultaneous robbery of two banks in Coffeyville, Kansas. The large Dalton family had once lived near Coffeyville, and their father and their brother Frank, who had been killed while serving as a deputy U.S. marshal, were buried there. The Dalton brothers felt that by looting two banks at once, they would earn a special niche in the annals of western outlawry.

On the morning of October 5, 1892, six members of the gang—Bob, Grat, and Emmett Dalton, Dick Broadwell, Bill Powers, and Bill Doolin—rode toward Coffeyville. But on the way into town Doolin's

The Condon Bank still stands in downtown Coffeyville. Grat Dalton led Bill Powers and Dick Broadwell into the Condon Bank, while Bob and Emmett Dalton robbed the First National Bank, across the street to the left.

horse pulled up lame, and Bill was unable to participate. At about 9:30 A.M., the rest of the gang reached Coffeyville.

They had planned to hitch their horses in front of the banks, but a repair party had removed the hitch rails, and the gang tied their mounts to a fence in a nearby alley. Emmett and Bob walked to the First National Bank, while the other three bandits crossed the square to the Condon Bank (which still stands today, complete with bullet holes).

The Daltons were recognized by a citizen named Aleck McKenna, who quietly began to spread the alarm. Inside the First National Bank, Bob and Emmett held guns on teller W. H. Shepherd, cashier Thomas G. Ayres, and customers C. L. Hollinsworth, J. H. Brewer, and A. W. Knott, who was a deputy sheriff. While Bob and Emmett scooped $21,000 into a towsack, townspeople were shouting warnings and arming themselves in nearby hardware stores.

When Bob and Emmett emerged from the bank, they were pushing Shepherd, Ayres, and Knott before them. But gunfire forced them back inside the building, and they fled through the back door toward their horses. A young man named Lucious Baldwin waved a pistol and tried to block their path, but Bob fired a Winchester slug into his left breast, inflicting a fatal wound.

As the two brothers raced past Rammel's drugstore, Bob spotted George Cubine and

Charles Brown, bootmakers who had known the Daltons during their boyhood. Cubine held a Winchester, and Bob killed him with one shot. When Brown angrily grabbed the rifle, Bob shot the old man dead. Ayres had dashed from the bank into Isham's Hardware Store, and as he emerged from the building, Bob dropped him with a bullet in the left cheek. Emmett caught a bullet in the right arm, but he still clutched the grain sack and managed to climb into the saddle.

Inside the Condon Bank, vice president Charles Carpenter, bookkeeper T. C. Babb, and cashier Charley Ball were confronted with drawn guns and harsh orders to open the safe. Thinking quickly, Ball lied that the safe had a time-lock that would not open until 9:45, a three-minute wait. Grat announced that he would wait. When a citizen fired a bullet into the bank and hit Broadwell in the arm, Grat changed his mind. He scooped $1,500 in loose bills into his bag and led Powers and Broadwell around the corner toward "Death Alley." City Marshal Charles T. Connelly ran toward the bandits firing rapidly, but Grat killed him with one shot, then turned toward his horse.

At this point, livery stable owner John J. Kloehr stepped out five feet from the outlaws. Bob whirled toward him, but Kloehr fired a rifle bullet into his chest. Bob staggered back, sat down in the street, rolled over, and died. Grat turned his gun toward Kloehr, but the livery stable owner coolly pumped a slug into the outlaw's neck.

Powers jumped onto Grat's horse, but a slug ripped into his heart, and he pitched to the ground. Broadwell climbed into the saddle and spurred his mount, but he was met by a deadly fusillade that ended his life. Emmett tried to lean over and pick up Bob, but Kloehr shot him in the hip, and barber Carey Seaman blasted a load of 18 buckshot into him. Emmett was carried to a hotel, where he was nursed back to health by his mother and his sweetheart before being tried and sent to prison.

Seven townspeople had been shot—three fatally—and four of the outlaws were dead, including three of the four Dalton brothers. Curious citizens pumped Grat's arms up and down to watch the blood spurt out of his neck wound, and his corpse was lifted onto a board to be photographed with the triumphant survivors.

The bodies of the Dalton Gang after the shoot-out, propped up against the wall of a livery stable owned by John J. Kloehr, who had shot three of the Dalton brothers. Only Emmett (inset) survived his wounds.

THE WILD BUNCH AT
WILCOX

Members of the Wild Bunch, on vacation in Fort Worth, December 1900. From left, seated: Harry Longabaugh—the Sundance Kid; Ben Kilpatrick—The Tall Texan; Butch Cassidy. Standing: Will "News" Carver and Harvey Logan.

The last notable band of western outlaws was the Wild Bunch, led by Butch Cassidy during the gang's turn-of-the-century heyday. Cassidy's most stalwart confederates were the Sundance Kid, Harvey Logan, Elzy Lay, Flat Nose George Curry, and Ben "The Tall Texan" Kilpatrick.

Perhaps the most spectacular Wild Bunch holdup took place about two hours past midnight on June 2, 1899. Using a red lantern, the gang halted the Union Pacific's Overland Limited a mile west of Wilcox, Wyoming. The engineer was ordered to pull the train across a nearby bridge, then stop.

When express messenger E. C. Woodcock refused to open the door, the gang used dynamite to demolish the express car. Woodcock was knocked unconscious, and the bridge was damaged. The safe had to be dynamited, and so much money was destroyed that the gang netted only about $8,000.

The outlaws rode north, past Medicine Bow, about 15 miles from the robbery site. Hundreds of men helped form posses, and the gang scattered.

On June 5, the Sundance Kid, Harvey Logan, and Flat Nose George Curry sat down to supper in a camp near the Red Fork of the Powder River. They were jumped by a posse led by Sheriff Joe Hazen, but Logan pumped a rifle bullet into the sheriff's stomach. Hazen died several hours later, while the outlaw trio escaped on foot after swimming the turbulent, rain-swollen Powder River.

Soon there were at least 300 men riding in posses across the countryside, hoping to collect some $18,000 in posted rewards. The outlaws stopped at their Hole-in-the-Wall hideout, but pressure from the manhunters sent them toward wild Jackson Hole country. Railroad detective F. M. Hans estimated that the robbers traveled 1,500 miles as they successfully eluded pursuit.

THE LAST STAGECOACH
ROBBERY

The West's final stagecoach holdup occurred in 1899, when there were few stage lines left to rob. Since western states led the movement to give women the right to vote, to serve on juries, and to obtain divorces, it seems fitting that the last stagecoach robbery was committed by a female bandit.

Pearl Taylor was born in or around 1871 and placed in a Toronto boarding school. At age 16, Pearl eloped with a man named Hart, who was a wife-beater. She left him, but he periodically reappeared in her life.

Pearl wandered to Trinidad, Colorado, worked for a time as a housemaid back East, and turned up in Arizona in 1892 with another scapegrace. Dan Bandman, a dance hall musician and tinhorn gambler, taught Pearl to smoke, drink, and take opium. Pearl bore him a son and a daughter, but soon sent the babies to her mother.

Morose, she ineptly attempted suicide a few times, then found employment as a cook for Arizona miners in Mammoth and in Globe, where she encountered a shiftless prospector who called himself Joe Boot. On May 29, 1899, Pearl donned men's clothing and helped Joe hold up a stagecoach near Globe.

Mounted on their horses, the bandits met the stagecoach at a bend in the road. Joe brandished a Colt .45, Pearl held a .38, and the stage driver pulled to a stop. Pearl dismounted and ordered the three passengers to "pile out." She took $390 from one man, $36, along with a dime and two nickels, from another, and $5 from the third passenger, as well as two revolvers found in the stagecoach. Returning a dollar each to the victims, Pearl remounted and rode off with Joe.

Within a few days, a posse captured the outlaw couple while they were sleeping in a pasture. During her trial, Pearl appeared at her best and charmed the all-male jury. Joe was found guilty—and Pearl was acquitted. But the irate judge ordered her retried for theft of the revolvers, and she was sentenced to five years in Yuma Territorial Prison. Joe was given a 35-year term, but he escaped soon afterward.

At Yuma, Pearl was sensationalized by yellow journalists and eagerly photographed by Sunday visitors to the prison. She was paroled on December 19, 1902, and briefly appeared with a traveling troupe as "the Arizona Bandit." In 1904, she ran into trouble with Kansas City police. She then returned to Arizona and married a rancher named Calvin Bywater. Pearl Bywater lived quietly on the little spread until her death on December 30, 1955.

Pearl Hart helped Joe Boot conduct the West's last stagecoach holdup. Pearl posed for this photo—with empty guns—while she was an inmate at Yuma Territorial Prison.

VOICES OF THE WEST

"With 80 men I could ride through the Sioux nation."
Captain William J. Fetterman, who had his chance—and the Sioux killed him and all of his men

"The Comanches fought without giving or asking quarter until there was not one left to bend a bow."
Captain Earl Van Dorn

Adna Romanza Chaffee

"If any man is killed, I will make him a corporal!"
Captain Adna R. Chaffee

"When you see Apache 'sign,' be keerful; 'n' when

you don't see nary sign, be more keerful."
Joe Felmer, Arizona scout

"Here goes for a brevet or a coffin!"
Major Joel H. Elliott, on his way to a coffin at the Battle of the Washita

"As regards myself, can't say that I felt very rejoiced at the prospects of a fight with the Indians. $13.00 a month is not an incentive to throw one's life away."
Private Eddie Matthews, 8th Cavalry

"I have often been asked why we exposed ourselves to such danger. My answer has always been that there was a charm in the life of a free mountaineer from which one cannot free himself, after he once has fallen under its spell."
Bill Hamilton, mountain man

"Again I repeat, this is a dangerous service."
Lieutenant James Bradley

"Indian warfare is, of all warfare, the most trying and the most thankless.... In it you are required to serve without the incentive of promotion or recognition, in truth, without favor or hope of reward."
General George Crook

"They make you take off your hat and put on a coat, but the grub is strictly A-No. 1."
Cowboy, reporting on the cuisine and decorum of a Harvey House

"The Mexicans are upon us—give 'em Hell!"
William Barrett Travis, Commander of the Alamo

"They don't walk. They plod."
Trail emigrant, commenting on the steady but slow pace of oxen

"[T]he white man never lived who loved an Indian, and . . . no true Indian ever lived that did not hate the white man. . . . God Almighty made [me] an

The food at the Harvey Houses, a chain of restaurants in the West, was second to none.

Sitting Bull

"Indian and did not make me an agency Indian, either, and [I do] not intend to be one."

Sitting Bull

"We have again to repeat the hackneyed phrase, 'the stage has been robbed!'"

Black Hills newspaper, on yet another stagecoach holdup

"I've labored long and hard for bread
   for honor and for riches
   But on my corns too long you've tread
   You fine haired Sons of Bitches."

Poem left by Black Bart after his third stagecoach robbery

"Don't shoot again, I am killed."

Billy Claiborne, after being shot by Buckskin Frank Leslie in Tombstone

"We are rough men and used to rough ways."

Bob Younger, wounded after the Northfield raid, on behalf of his wounded brothers Cole and Jim

"Good-bye, Emmett. Don't surrender; die game."

Bob Dalton's dying words to his brother after their gang's disastrous attempt to rob two banks in Coffeyville, Kansas

"May God continue the unity of our Country as this Railroad unites the two great Oceans of the world."

Prayer engraved on the famous Golden Spike, which completed the first transcontinental railroad

"By God, I'm for battle—no peace."

General William S. Harney

"With my cavalry and combined artillery...I wanted no other occupation in life than to ward off the savage and kill off his food until there should no longer be an Indian frontier in our beautiful country."

General John M. Schofield

"WANTED—YOUNG, SKINNY, WIRY FELLOWS not over 18. Must be expert riders, willing to risk death daily. Orphans preferred. Wages $25.00 per week."

Ad for Pony Express riders

San Francisco turns out to celebrate the arrival of the first Pony Express rider to bring a mochila to the West Coast, on April 14, 1860.

GREATEST BATTLES

The Alamo...San Jacinto...The Fetterman Massacre...Adobe Walls...Glorieta Pass...The Little Bighorn. These battles were among the most epic struggles of a strife-torn West. For three centuries, warriors fought for control of North American frontiers. The combatants included Spanish *conquistadores*, Mexican *soldados*, Native American warriors, Anglo pioneers, and U.S. cavalrymen.

One of the most famous battles in world history took place in San Antonio at a crumbling old mission called the Alamo. Fewer than 200 sharpshooting Texans fought to the death rather than submit to thousands of Mexican soldiers, who themselves battled with astounding heroism while suffering horrific casualties. A few weeks later, an undermanned army of Texans, lusting for vengeance, assaulted a Mexican camp at San Jacinto and won independence for Texas.

In 1864, at Adobe Walls in the Texas Panhandle, General Kit Carson and a few hundred soldiers displayed combat skills and courage of the highest order in fighting off 3,000 warriors. A dozen years later, at the Little Bighorn, George Armstrong Custer also led several hundred soldiers against 3,000 warriors—who scored the most memorable Native American victory of the Indian wars.

General George Custer (*center, two guns blazing*) and his 7th Cavalry attacked Sitting Bull's camp on June 25, 1876, but the cavalry—outnumbered ten to one—was annihilated by the Native American warriors.

DEEDS OF THE
HEROIC WARRIORS

More than 400 Congressional Medals of Honor were issued to soldiers during the Indian wars. But many Native American warriors also performed deeds of incredible daring and self-sacrifice.

In 1870, a patrol commanded by Lieutenant Howard B. Cushing encountered a pair of Apache braves in central Arizona. The two warriors fled on foot, and several troopers went in pursuit. Although armed only with a single-shot rifle, one of the braves made a stand. He fired a shot that killed the blacksmith of Company K and then sprinted to the attack, swinging his rifle like a club. He knocked Corporal Costello senseless and struck both Sergeant Harrington and Private Wolf on the head, but a mortal wound to his body finally brought him down.

An Indian pictograph of the Battle of the Little Bighorn.

In 1853, at the Texas Indian Agency at Clear Fork Crossing, several Wichitas were unexpectedly arrested and sent toward Fort Belknap under guard. Among the prisoners were a chieftain named Koweaka, his wife, and their seven-year-old son. As the group camped overnight, Koweaka sat in a lodge with his family and solemnly removed his moccasins in a gesture equivalent to a death chant, since the moccasins no longer would be needed. Holding her child in her arms, Koweaka's wife nodded her assent, and the chief then stabbed his wife and son in the heart, covered their bodies, and readied his weapons. At midnight, a brave rushed the sentry but was shot down. Koweaka reached the sentry, however, and stabbed him to death before being killed by a soldier. The suicidal distraction proved successful, allowing most of the Wichitas to escape.

In 1860, a large 2nd Cavalry patrol led by

Major G. H. Thomas was returning to Camp Cooper, Texas, when they came upon 13 Comanche braves breaking camp beside the Salt Fork of the Brazos. A running fight lasted for three miles, with the Indians holding a half-mile lead. An old warrior dropped off to cover the retreat of his comrades. When the soldiers galloped into range, the old brave expertly began to fire iron-tipped dogwood shafts from his bow. Thomas was struck twice, and the patrol pulled up. Using an interpreter, Thomas called on the Comanche to surrender, but the brave shouted defiance. The old warrior was shot more than 20 times, but he fired arrows into three troopers, one of whom died. When the soldiers closed in for the kill, the dying Comanche wounded two more men with lance thrusts before collapsing.

As the Battle of the Washita raged in Oklahoma in 1868, Major Joel Elliott and 17 men were cut off from the main body of the 7th Cavalry. The embattled troopers were holding the Indians at bay until an Arapaho warrior boldly rushed into the soldiers' midst and felled three troopers. He was finally killed by a bullet in the head, but his example inspired a Cheyenne warrior to gallop into Elliott's command. The Cheyenne succeeded in striking down two more soldiers before a bullet broke his leg and toppled him to the ground. The Arapaho and the Cheyenne had turned the tide, however; there was a general rush by the warriors, and within moments the soldiers were overwhelmed and slain to a man.

During the Battle of the Rosebud in 1876, the Cheyenne chief Comes-in-Sight galloped from the midst of his warriors toward General Crook's flank in a courageous display. His horse was killed, however, and the chief was stranded just in front of the infantry position. Before the soldiers could zero in, another hard-riding figure emerged from the Cheyenne ranks and galloped toward him. Comes-in-Sight vaulted up behind the rider, and the two thundered back toward admirers. The rescuer was the chief's sister, Buffalo-Calf-Road-Woman, who had come to the scene of the fighting to help with the horse herd. Native Americans would refer to this skirmish as the Battle Where the Girl Saved Her Brother. Eight days later, Walking-Blanket-Woman rode into battle at the Little Bighorn to avenge the death of her brother, who had died at the Rosebud, since no other fighting men were left in her family.

The most outstanding warrior on the historic Little Bighorn battlefield was White Bull, chief of the Miniconjou Sioux. During the fight with Custer, he counted seven coups, six of which were firsts. He also killed two soldiers, captured two guns and a dozen horses, and took a bullet in the ankle. Covered in glory, White Bull presented two pairs of confiscated soldier breeches to his father, Makes Room, who proudly composed a song in honor of his son.

In 1860, George W. Baylor, along with his brother and four other men, fought six warriors near Weatherford, Texas. The braves stood their ground, but five of them soon were gunned down. The surviving warrior, filled with battle lust, repeatedly attacked the six white men until he, too, was shot to death. Baylor later remarked, "I don't think during the entire war between the states or in all my frontier experience that I ever saw such cool, desperate valor displayed as this young Indian showed."

Kiowa were driven to suicidal desperation by the prospect of imprisonment. When the old warrior Satank was arrested, he was determined to die fighting. While being transported with several other captive Kiowa to Ft. Richardson, he indicated a tree down the road and announced in Kiowa, "I shall never go beyond that tree." Beneath his blanket, he tore his hands free of their shackles, badly ripping his flesh to do so; then he gripped a knife he had concealed in his breechcloth. As the wagon approached the tree, Satank shouted and stabbed the nearest guard. The other guard leaped off the wagon as Satank seized his rifle. The venerable brave was fumbling with the unfamiliar mechanism when he was killed by a mounted sergeant.

MOST INNOVATIVE
ENTERPRISES

Westerners were optimists, confident that the problems posed by a vast and untamed land could be overcome with resourcefulness and imagination. During the California gold rush, for example, mail delivery from coast to coast took weeks. So a system of relay riders was devised—courageous young frontiersmen who galloped alone across a hostile West. These brave riders, members of the Pony Express, became national heroes. Despite a mere year and a half of operation, the Pony Express earned a permanent place in the lore of the Wild West.

Following the Civil War, a hungry market for beef developed in the urbanized Northeast, and millions of longhorns roamed the ranges of Texas. For the next two decades, long-distance cattle drives were conducted, capturing the nation's imagination and elevating the cowboy to folk hero status. During that same period, city dwellers of the East began to enjoy inexpensive goods that were mass-produced by America's industrial revolution. This shopping cornucopia was unavailable to isolated westerners—until Montgomery Ward and Sears, Roebuck brought the department store to farmers through mail-order catalogs. Other innovative enterprises included wagon trains, Harvey Houses, cattlemen's associations, and Wild West shows.

The Pony Express hired mostly slender teenage boys, who rode mustangs at a furious pace.

THE PONY EXPRESS

During the 1850s, the fastest mail delivery to California was along the Butterfield stagecoach route. Business messages could be telegraphed from the East Coast to Missouri, then placed on stagecoaches that angled southwest through Texas, plodded through southern New Mexico and Arizona, then turned north into California. One-way travel took about 21 days, and return messages required another 21 days. Perhaps this pace was tolerable for personal correspondence, but business mail needed speedier delivery.

The enterprising freight firm of Russell, Majors & Waddell devised a system of relay riders who could traverse a more direct northerly route and provide delivery in mere days. The Pony Express stretched from St. Joseph, Missouri, to Sacramento, California. Relay stations were placed every five to 20 miles; there were 157 stations along the 1,840-mile route. Most of the 400 horses were mustangs, while most of the 80 riders were slender teenagers. Other employees included station keepers, stock tenders, route superintendents, and teamsters who shuttled supply wagons to the stations. Isolated station employees and solitary riders faced mortal danger from war parties who lusted after the company's horses.

Each rider was assigned a 75-mile route, which he would ride back and forth, east and west. Saddles were lightweight, and the mail was carried in a leather mochila slung over the saddle. There were four locked pockets, two on each side of the mochila, which could carry about 250 letters written on tissue paper. The cost was $5 per half-ounce.

On April 3, 1860, crowds in St. Joseph and Sacramento cheered as Pony Express riders galloped toward each other from separate ends of the frontier. The youthful "pony riders" became national heroes as they galloped alone through hostile country. Pony Bob Haslam accepted a bonus to carry the mail continuously when Paiutes were on the warpath; he rode 190 miles eastbound in only 18 hours. After he rested a few hours, the westbound mail arrived, whereupon Pony Bob mounted up for another 190 miles.

In a similar situation, 15-year-old Billy Cody supposedly rode 322 miles. Another future frontier celebrity, James Butler Hickok, shot Dave McCanles and two other men while working at the Rock Creek Station. Line superintendent Jack Slade killed Jules Reni at the Julesburg Station.

The Pony Express came to an abrupt end after only a year and a half of operation. The first coast-to-coast telegraph was completed in October 1861, and a suddenly obsolete Pony Express delivered its last mochila on October 24. The unprofitable enterprise had cost Russell, Majors & Waddell at least $200,000, but it left a colorful legacy of bravery and adventure.

In 1860, Russell, Majors & Waddell hired 80 Pony Express riders. These brave young men captured the imagination of the American public.

Above: A Pony Express station in Nebraska. There were 157 stations, placed from five to 20 miles apart along the 1,840-mile route. The Pony Express kept 400 horses, mostly mustangs. Below: The Pony Express operated for only a year and a half, until the first coast-to-coast telegraph was completed.

CATTLE DRIVES

By the end of the Civil War, there were as many as five million longhorn cattle roaming the open grasslands of South and West Texas. Most of these wild beasts belonged to no one, and many Texans recognized the profit potential of delivering herds of cattle to northern and eastern markets. This business development produced one of the most colorful and enduring chapters of frontier history. For the next two decades, cowboys drove herds of tough longhorns north to raucous Kansas railheads.

The Chisholm Trail was blazed by Jesse Chisholm through central Texas, where there were no forests, and into Indian Territory, where there were no mountains or farmers. North of the Red River, the route passed through a sea of grass all the way to Abilene and Ellsworth. These ramshackle Kansas cow towns provided saloons and brothels for the entertainment of cowboys, and hotels and stock pens for the convenience of cattle buyers. As tracks were extended south toward Texas, first Newton, then Wichita, and finally Caldwell, each enjoyed a rowdy heyday as railheads. During the 1870s and 1880s, Dodge City, terminus of the Western Trail out of Texas, became the most famous of the Kansas cattle towns. The Goodnight-Loving Trail, founded by legendary cattleman Charles Goodnight and partner Oliver Loving, went west from Texas to the Pecos River, which herds followed north to Colorado.

No western activity captivated the public imagination more completely than cattle drives. The era of the famous "long drives" on the open range lasted from the end of the Civil War until the mid-1880s.

For two decades, a stream of herds moved up these major trails. Even after railroads began to penetrate ranch country, most cattlemen preferred trail drives to more costly train transportation. If a herd proceeded at a leisurely pace that allowed good grazing, cattle might actually weigh more at the end of a long drive. The best herd size was between 1,500 and 2,000 head of cattle. On the trail, drovers contended with stampedes, storms, dangerous river crossings, and many other difficulties. At the end of perhaps three months on the trail, cowboys were paid $100 or more, which sometimes was spent in just three or four days of cow-town celebration.

By the mid-1880s, the West was crisscrossed with railroads and wire fences, ending the colorful era of the long drive.

COWBOY CURES

Asthma: Catch a frog. Pry open the frog's mouth and blow your breath into it. This must be done before daylight. The frog will die before sundown, but the asthma will go into the frog and never bother you again.

Colds: *Vaqueros* take red chili peppers, swallowed whole.

Cuts: These will heal if you let your pet dog lick them.

Dog Bite: Apply hair from the dog—or else he'll bite you again!

Earache: Melt the grub of a dirt dauber into a spoon and pour it into the ear.

Fever Blister: Put your little finger into your ear and get a little ear wax, then rub it on the blister.

DIMMITT'S COUGH BALSAM,

Dimmitt's cough balsam was probably a far more reliable medicine than other "cowboy cures" of the day.

Hiccoughs: Have somebody pull out your tongue until it bleeds a little.

Hives: Make a tea of sheep manure; drink when warm.

Indigestion: Eat the dried lining of a chicken gizzard.

Labor Pains: Hold the sharpened edge of an axe against the woman's stomach. This "cuts" her pain.

Measles: Roast a mouse and eat it.

Pink Eye: Wash sore eyes with cowboy urine.

Pulling Baby Teeth: Don't just throw away the tooth, because if a dog steps on it, a dog's fang will come in where the tooth had been pulled.

Rheumatism: Mix half a bottle of vinegar with one handful of red ants and drink.

Sty: Say these magic words, "Sty, sty, pray leave my eye, and catch the first person that passes by."

Tapeworm: Feed patient ground glass; it will cut up the tapeworm.

Bladder Trouble in a Horse: Insert a match into the horse; relief will be sudden, although the patient may stampede.

Lockjaw in a Horse: Drive a nail into the horse's skull. This is a sure cure—unless the nail kills the horse.

NICKNAMES FOR LIQUOR

Stagger Soup
Gut Warmer
Wild Mare's Milk
Coffin Varnish
Tarantula Juice
Tonsil Paint
Tanglefoot
Lamp Oil
Scorpion Bible

THE MAIL-ORDER
CATALOG

The flood of cheap manufactured goods produced by American industry was made available to eastern customers through urban department stores. But rural Westerners were largely excluded from this inexpensive and useful variety of products—until Montgomery Ward brought the department store to the country through catalog buying.

After the Civil War, farmers began to organize for cooperative buying and selling, as well as for united political action. The first farmers organization was the Patrons of Husbandry, popularly known as the Grange. Recognizing the possibilities of direct selling to vast numbers of newly organized farmers, Montgomery Ward and Company opened its doors in 1872 specifically to "meet the wants of the Patrons of Husbandry." The primary device for selling to isolated farm families was the catalog, an illustrated list of goods detailing prices, sizes, colors, and other tempting information.

Aaron Montgomery Ward was a dry-goods salesman who had worked across the West. Hearing complaints about high prices in general stores, Ward bought $1,600 worth

A Sears, Roebuck wishbook. Although Sears, Roebuck is indelibly identified with catalog buying, the business was pioneered by Montgomery Ward.

of goods, and from a 12×14-foot room in Chicago, published a sheet listing 167 items. By 1875, his catalog had grown to 72 pages with nearly 2,000 articles, and within two decades, the 624-page catalog offered 75,000 items. The only significant problem was shipping rates, but in 1896 Congress enacted Rural Free Delivery.

Rural residents of remote homesteads and ranches eagerly welcomed the "wishbooks" from Ward's company. On little parlor tables, a Ward wishbook would be placed beside the King James Bible. Little girls would gaze with wonder at dolls, boys would examine pocketknives, mothers did their window-shopping through the pages, and fathers priced tools, boots, and saddles. Last year's wishbooks went to the outhouse for perusing and for tearing out pages to use as toilet paper (instead of the customary—if somewhat rough—pile of corncobs). Cowboys in lonely line shacks first viewed all manner of items in wishbooks before ever seeing the real thing, and many certainly lingered wistfully over the pages picturing women's personal apparel.

VOICES OF THE WEST

Deadwood, South Dakota

"Anyone who has been here for a space of a week and has witnessed the shootings, robbings, and brawls that enliven our nights and interrupt our days must realize that it is high time that some form of recognized law be established in Deadwood City."

Deadwood's Black Hills *Pioneer, 1876*

"Grandest of God's terrestrial cities."

Naturalist John Muir, on the Grand Canyon

"At this writing, Hell is now in session in Abilene."

Topeka Commonwealth, 1868

"The smoke of battle almost never clears away completely in Bodie [California]."

Mark Twain

"In the dim light I could see the great post of Fort Lincoln. Our quarters were lighted, and as we approached, the regimental band played 'Home, Sweet Home,' followed by the general's favorite 'Garryowen.'"

Libbie Custer, upon arrival at Fort Abraham Lincoln, 1873

"Fast men and fast women are around by the score, seeking whom they may devour, hunting for a soft snap, taking him in for cash. . . ."

Dodge City tourist, 1877

"Out thar in the Yellowstone, thar's a river that flows so fast it gets hot on the bottom."

Jim Bridger

Piper's Opera House, Virginia City, Nevada

"Money was plenty as dust; every individual considered himself wealthy, and a melancholy countenance was nowhere to be seen."

Mark Twain, on Virginia City, Nevada, 1863

"He is said to have been a bad man, and though it is perhaps inhuman to rejoice over the death of anyone, it was a fortunate occurrence for him, as his untimely death was a certainty, sooner or later."

Belmont, Nevada, Courier *on the death of one of its citizens, 1874*

". . . a foul cesspool."

Temperance crusader Carrie Nation, on Caldwell, Kansas

"Every tombstone needs its epitaph."

John Clum, explaining how his newspaper, The Tombstone Epitaph, *got its name*

". . . it was nip and tuck between a temperance orator in one room and a gambler in the next to determine which could yell the loudest and attract the biggest crowd."

Local newspaper, on Leadville's opposing residents

"There's no bravery in carrying revolvers in a civilized community. Such a practice is well enough and perhaps necessary when among Indians or other barbarians, but among white people it ought to be discountenanced."

The "Civilized" Editor of the Abilene Chronicle, *1871*

INVENTIONS
THAT TAMED
THE WEST

In order to survive, the men and women who ventured to western frontiers were compelled to be innovative, inventive, and adaptable. Taming these frontiers and transforming wildernesses into settled, productive regions required imagination and ingenuity.

Unlike eastern warriors, Native Americans of the West were mounted and had repeating weapons—bows and arrows—which could be fired from horseback. Pedestrian pioneers with single-shot muzzleloaders could not successfully fight horse Indians—until hard-riding Texas Rangers adapted Samuel Colt's revolving pistol to a mode of warfare that would be utilized across the West.

Generations of pioneers had built log cabins and rail fences—until they reached the treeless plains of the West. But sod houses and dugouts quickly were devised, and the invention of barbed wire soon solved the fencing problem. When the light, inexpensive iron plows of the East failed to penetrate the thick root network of western grasslands, a heavier, steel plow was developed. Other dilemmas were solved by such creative devices as windmills, blue jeans, telegraphs, and chuck wagons.

Throughout the 1860s, stagecoaches were the best means to transport passengers and mail across the West.

REVOLVERS

Sam Colt (1814–1862), inventor of the revolving pistol, a repeating weapon that western riders could use while in the saddle

Repeating arms of various designs had been produced as early as the sixteenth century, but none of them proved to be practical or effective. In the early 1800s, percussion caps began to replace the centuries-old flint as the means of ignition in firearms, finally giving gunsmiths such as Sam Colt the technology they needed to produce multishot revolving-chamber weapons. When Colt patented his initial design for the revolver in the 1830s, he took the first step toward a technology that would shape the history of the West and forever symbolize the violent and self-sufficient character of frontier life.

While a settler's single-shot flintlock was a powerful, long-range weapon, a bow and arrow held one distinct advantage over it: A skilled bowman riding at a full gallop could easily unleash a dozen arrows or more in the time it took to reload the rifle. Colt's first revolving pistol, a light five-shooter, changed all that. The Texas Rangers used it to great effect against Comanche and Kiowa horseback warriors in the 1840s. The mounted Texans could now fire repeatedly while on the move, and they developed tactics to take advantage of this. During mounted fights, Rangers tried to stay on the right side of an adversary, who usually was right-handed and found it difficult to return fire with his bow and arrows.

Following suggestions from the Rangers, Colt redesigned the weapon into a six-shooter of larger caliber and greater balance. With the improved gun, Texans distinguished themselves in combat during the Mexican War and taught the U.S. Army the potential of revolvers. During the 1850s, the Army organized two cavalry regiments to fight horse Indians, and the revolver continued to be the key to battling western warriors.

By the 1850s, young men flocking to the California gold camps commonly carried revolvers to ensure their personal safety. In these lawless communities, miners drank and gambled as their primary recreation, and large fortunes were found, won, lost, and coveted. This volatile atmosphere bred violent confrontations, and more often than not, determined adversaries went for their guns to settle things. Texans, inhabitants of a violent region who were already accustomed to revolvers, blazed away at one another over drinks, cards, or family feuds. After the Civil War, they turned their revolvers against Reconstruction officials, rustlers, and personal enemies. As mining districts and cattle operations spread across the West, the prospect of fortune and freedom brought more violent men into more lawless areas—and the revolver was inevitably there as the final arbiter of whatever disputes arose.

Even in territories and states with relatively effective legal organization, shoot-outs between individuals rarely resulted in problems with the authorities. When there was a fatal fight, a coroner's jury was quickly assembled, and if the dead man was armed, the usual ruling was self-defense. When a killing did go to

trial, western juries often did not convict for any but the most blatant or heinous murders.

The 1870s saw cap-and-ball ammunition replaced by the more reliable cartridge, leading to the development of the classic western six-shooter, the Colt Peacemaker. Soon there were "self-cockers," double-action revolvers that required only the pull of a trigger. With ever-improving weapons, gunplay continued as a means of settling personal quarrels into the 1890s and, in some cases, into the early years of the twentieth century.

Across the West, Colt's invention put fame, fortune, and personal destiny into the hands of anyone who had the nerve to wield it. His revolver and the many imitations produced by Colt's competitors contributed materially to the western tradition of violence and to the popular image of the tamers of the last frontier.

The Paterson Colt, patented in 1836, carried five balls in the chamber and had a recessed trigger that appeared only after the hammer was cocked. The shape of the handle was awkward, and Texas Rangers would suggest important improvements.

STEEL
PLOWS

For more than two centuries, American farmers made use of a light, inexpensive iron plow. But when pioneers reached the Great Plains, they found that this plow could no more break the sod than a fingernail could scratch open a tin can. The thick plains grass had a tangled root system several inches deep, and cowboys who revered this natural grazing land pointed out to encroaching farmers that "the best side is already up."

In 1837, John Deere fashioned a plow from a saw blade. He continued to work on improving plows and eventually produced a heavy steel model. In 1868, James Oliver de-veloped a chilled-iron plow with a smooth-surface moldboard that slipped through dense prairie soils without clogging. Equipped with heavier plows made of stronger metals, prairie sodbusters quickly discovered the magnificent fertility of the plains soil.

Another improvement moved the farmer from behind the plow into a seat above the machine, greatly speeding up the process of plowing. As early as 1844, patents for a sulky plow were registered, but not until farmers reached the Great Plains was the need great enough to inspire improvements and mass manufacturing. One significant improvement provided the sulkies with additional plowshares, per-mitting a farmer to turn over two or three furrows at once.

On semi-arid western home-steads, dry-farming methods were used, such as plowing furrows 12 to 14 inches deep to loosen the soil and allow water to move upward. After rainfall, farmers harrowed their fields to create a dust mulch that would deter evaporation. In 1880, western farmers began to use the lister, a double-moldboard plow that dug a deep furrow and cast earth up on either side, si-multaneously planting corn at the bottom and covering the seed.

The light iron plows used by generations of farmers in the eastern half of the United States could not penetrate the thick root system of prairie grass. A heavy steel plow was devel-oped for western sod-busters.

CATTLE BRANDS

A brand was read top to bottom, left to right, and outside in. By the time ranch children started school, they already knew the alphabet.

BQ Top to bottom, left to right, the Bar-B-Que brand spelled out one of the Southwest's favorite foods.

JA The JA brand was designed by legendary cattleman Charles Goodnight to refer to John Adair, the English moneyman behind their Palo Duro Canyon ranch.

⊞ Teddy Roosevelt's Maltese Cross brand. Dakota cowboys, assuming that "Maltese" was the plural of something, usually called the ranch the "Maltee."

6666 It was rumored (incorrectly) that

Spanish herdsmen brought branding irons to the New World, and Mexican *vaqueros* taught the practice to Anglo ranchers.

the Four Sixes brand of Texas cattle baron Burk Burnett represented the poker hand that won his vast ranch.

XIT It was rumored (incorrectly) that the XIT brand signified that the three-million-acre Texas ranch covered all or part of ten counties (which it did).

Ψ The Pitchfork Ranch was in West Texas.

ᚴ The British-owned Rocking Chair Ranche Company also was in West Texas.

⅃5 A ranch that was defended with a Colt .45.

♥ The Broken Heart brand represented the typical lonely cowboy.

FOOL Texas rancher T. J. Walker philosophized that "a man's a fool to raise cattle."

2HOT It was often Too Hot in ranch country.

2FAT Western cattle rarely were Too Fat.

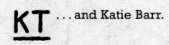

YY Texas rancher J. J. Barwise devised a brand, Bar Ys, that would make it clear who owned the beef. . . .

BR . . . as did Jack Barber . . .

KT . . . and Katie Barr.

IC Brand of a Texas rancher who suffered thefts by a nearby rancher.

ICU The rustler's altered version of the original brand.

ICU2 After ordering his cowhands to steal the cattle back, the first rancher added another registered brand.

BLUE
JEANS

Levi Strauss was 18 in 1847 when he immigrated to the United States from Bavaria to work as a merchant in New York. In 1853, he decided to join a brother-in-law, David Stern, in the dry-goods business in San Francisco.

Embarking with a supply of cloth, Strauss sold almost all of it en route, arriving in California with a single bolt of canvas tent cloth. As he stepped ashore in San Francisco, he met a miner for whom he promptly designed a pair of heavy canvas pants. Recognizing opportunity, Strauss bought large quantities of canvas sailcloth from ships that stood empty in San Francisco Bay, deserted by sailors bound for the gold fields. Rapidly producing durable canvas pants for miners, within a year Strauss and Stern had become California's largest pantmakers.

In 1872, a tailor and customer, Jacob Davis of Reno, Nevada, sent a letter to Strauss suggesting the manufacturing of stout work clothes with pockets and seams reinforced by copper rivets. Davis already had used this design with local success. Strauss agreed to acquire a patent, and

Levi's were manufactured in California by Levi Strauss & Company. Strauss produced the most popular trousers among Westerners and enjoyed the most famous first name in the West.

Davis joined him as production manager.

The tough pants with copper rivets quickly became known as blue jeans or Levi's, and they were immensely popular among western workingmen. Levi Strauss & Company was incorporated in 1890, and the San Francisco plant employed 500 workers to meet the demand. Strauss, who now could claim the most famous first name in the West, grossed a million dollars annually. He died in 1902, but four nephews continued to produce Levi's.

At first, cowhands resisted the sturdy denim pants, looking on them as the uniforms of farmers, miners, and other sedentary toilers that the cowboys so disdained. In time, though, Levi's became regulation wear for cowboys. Turned-up cuffs, used to hold horseshoe nails while shoeing horses, became fashionable, and by the early 1900s Levi's often were worn with shirts sporting snap buttons. Rodeo cowboys, who sometimes were caught on saddle horns by unyielding shirt fronts after being bucked off, requested snap buttons so they could quickly free themselves from a wild bronc.

TALLEST TALES

This cutting horse was so good he could cut the baking powder out of a biscuit without breaking the crust.

This same horse was riderless on the prairie, prancing through all manner of intricate maneuvers. When his rider walked over, he saw that the horse was atop an ant bed, cutting the bull ants out of the herd and separating them from the others.

Cowboys were so tough that a Native American chief once asked General Phil Sheridan for a cannon. "What!" exclaimed Sheridan. "Do you want to kill my soldiers with it?" "No," replied the chief, "I want it to kill cowboys. I can kill soldiers with a club."

A grizzled southwestern rancher opined: "One thing I'll say for the West is that in this country there is more cows and less butter, more rivers and less water, and you can look further and see less than in any other place in the world!"

How to gauge wind on the Great Plains: "Hang a log chain on a post. If the wind raises the chain straight out from the post, it's a calm day. But when the end links start snapping off, expect rough weather."

A prairie farmer was plowing his fields when the sun got so hot that the corn popped on the stalk. Thinking the popped corn to be snow, his mules froze to death.

At a fashionable Tucson saloon, Bob Leatherwood bet a man that he could not recite the Lord's Prayer. "Hell, yes, I can!" the man replied indignantly. "Now I lay me down to sleep, I pray the Lord my soul to keep—"

"You win, you win!" Bob broke in, shoving the money across the table.

When Sam Clemens went west, he did not neglect to bring a firearm: "I was armed to the teeth with a pitiful little Smith & Wesson's seven-shooter, which carried a ball like a homeopathic pill, and it took the whole seven to make a dose for an adult. But I thought it was grand. It appeared to me to be a dangerous weapon. It only had one fault—you could not hit anything with it."

Legendary cattleman Charles Goodnight joined the church shortly before his death at 93. When asked what denomination it was, Goodnight answered: "I don't know, but it's a damned good one."

Winters were so cold on one Texas panhandle ranch that the few threadbare blankets did not provide much warmth. "If I owned a ranch," proclaimed cowboy Peter Wright, "I would buy these blankets and use them as a refrigerator in the summer."

Charles Goodnight and his bride checked into the Drover's Hotel in Pueblo, Colorado, on the same night that two outlaws were lynched outside. The next morning, Molly Goodnight exclaimed that two men were hanging from the telegraph pole. "Well," stammered Goodnight, who had played a role in the summary justice, "I don't think it hurt the telegraph pole."

CHUCK
WAGONS

In 1866, pioneer cattleman Charles Goodnight made preparations to drive 1,000 cattle west from Texas, then north along the Pecos River to the Colorado mining region. To prepare for the drive, Goodnight bought a surplus army wagon and took it to a woodworker in Parker County. He had the vehicle rebuilt with *bois d'arc*, the toughest wood available, and the customary wood axles were replaced with iron axles. On one side of the wagon bed was a big toolbox, and on the other sat a water barrel large enough to hold a two-day supply of drinking water. The wagon bed also had wooden bows to accommodate a canvas cover.

At the back end, Goodnight installed an item of his own design that would make the wagon a staple of the cattle industry—the chuck box. Filled with drawers and shelves and covered with a hinged lid that dropped down on a swinging leg to form a cook's worktable, it was the defining feature of the chuck wagon. The drawers and shelves were packed with whiskey, castor oil, bandages, vinegar, tobacco, matches, plates, cups, cutlery, sugar, dried fruit, pinto beans, coffee, a coffee pot, salt, lard, baking soda, molasses, and sourdough. The boot, or lower part of the chuck box, contained skillets and dutch ovens.

Along with flour sacks and other provisions, the wagon bed hauled the bedrolls of the crew, slickers, an extra wagon wheel, rope, guns and ammunition, and a lantern and kerosene supply. During the day's travel, firewood was gathered and stored beneath the wagon for the evening fire. The toolbox held such articles as horseshoeing equipment, hobbles, an ax, and a shovel.

Though conceived for use on the trail, the chuck wagon also earned a place on the range. It was used during roundups, and the chuck box sometimes was detached and nailed to the wall of a line shack as a self-contained kitchen and dining table. Goodnight's arrangement was so efficient that his design was copied by outfits all over the West. Eventually, the Studebaker Company and other wagon makers manufactured chuck wagons to this popular pattern. During the 1920s, Goodnight proudly remarked to his biographer that the chuck wagon "has been altered little to this day."

A range crew gathers around a chuck wagon. Legendary cattleman Charles Goodnight devised a supply wagon equipped with a chuck box, with a hinged lid for the cook's worktable. Bachelor ranchers sometimes nailed a chuck box to a kitchen wall for their pantry and table.

THE TELEGRAPH

During the 1850s, the development of the California gold fields, half a continent from the line of western settlement, created a desperate need for rapid communication. The Butterfield Stagecoach Line delivered mail in 21 days, and the short-lived but colorful Pony Express cut that to ten days, but the real promise of faster communication lay in the electromagnetic telegraph, developed by Samuel F. B. Morse in 1844.

The capital required to build a telegraph line was comparatively modest, and the California State Telegraph Company was formed in 1853. Lines were extended from San Francisco to numerous communities, and a connection was established with Los Angeles in 1860. That same year Congress passed the Telegraph Act of 1860, providing $40,000 annually for ten years to any company that would build a line from Missouri to San Francisco.

Jeptha H. Wade organized California's telegraph industry into the Overland Telegraph Company. With $1,250,000 in capital, Superintendent James Gamble set out to construct a line eastward to Salt Lake City. A telegraph line already extended from the East to Omaha, and the Western Union Telegraph Company organized the Pacific Telegraph Company to construct a line westward toward Salt Lake City. Superintendent Edward Creighton spent the summer of 1860 surveying the route.

Samuel F. B. Morse (1791–1872), with his hand on a telegraph key. Morse developed the electromagnetic telegraph by 1844, and his invention provided instant communication across the vast expanse of the West.

Overland Telegraph construction crews could obtain the needed glass insulators and wire only by sea around South America. The acquisition and delivery of poles to crews on the treeless Great Plains involved incredible difficulties. Warriors sometimes raided construction workers or cut lines. But Gamble and Creighton overcame these and other difficulties with admirable resourcefulness. The lines were joined on October 24, 1861, far earlier than had been expected. President Lincoln received a telegram that the East and the West were connected by telegraph and that California would remain loyal during the war that had erupted between the North and the South.

BEST WESTERN ARTISTS

When famed motion picture director John Ford filmed cavalry movies, he ordered his cinematographer to study the paintings of Frederic Remington. Indeed, these excellent John Ford cavalry films, starring John Wayne, look like Remington paintings come to life. Remington himself would have treasured this compliment, because he trained carefully to be able to reproduce horses and the men of the West with accuracy and style.

Although Charles Russell lacked formal training, he had natural gifts that brought him renown as the "Cowboy Artist." Like many other youngsters of his time, Russell left home to become a cowboy. He cowboyed for years in Montana, but as his talent developed he became a full-time artist, immortalizing the life he loved with brilliant colors. Other artists who memorably depicted the West included George Catlin, Albert Bierstadt, Alfred Jacob Miller, Thomas Moran, and Alfred E. Mathews. This section not only profiles these talented and fascinating individuals but also showcases their legendary artwork.

Frederic Remington, the most famous western artist, excelled as both a sculptor (*left*) and painter (*above*).

ALBERT
BIERSTADT

1830—1902

Artist Albert Bierstadt was overwhelmed by the magnificent vistas of the West, and he depicted that grandeur in enormous, dramatic paintings worthy of the expansive spirit of the frontier. One gigantic landscape, *The Rocky Mountains*, was painted on 60 square feet of canvas. Through his art, Bierstadt transmitted powerful visual impressions of the Last West.

Bierstadt was born in Germany in 1830, but the next year, his family immigrated to New Bedford, Massachusetts. In his early 20s, he returned to Germany to study painting at the noted academy at Düsseldorf, with periodic sketching trips to the Alps and the Apennines. His work was imbued with the romanticism characteristic of the Victorian era. Bierstadt came back to New Bedford in 1858, but he yearned to see the fabled Rocky Mountains of the frontier.

At his own expense, he accompanied a military expedition commanded by General Frederick W. Lander, who was directed to survey a wagon road from Fort Laramie to California. Throughout the summer, Bierstadt gaped "with unqualified delight" at the majestic mountains and sweeping prairies. He sketched incessantly and took the time to snap primitive photographs.

In the fall, Bierstadt returned to his New York studio with his sketches and photographs. Undaunted by the size and majesty of western landscapes, he rendered what he had seen on great canvases appropriate to the overwhelming dimensions of the West. For Bierstadt, nature was a starting point, and he romanticized the western landscape as an Eden, with shimmering lakes, golden shafts of light, and towering peaks. Smaller oil studies offered a more accurate interpretation.

Bierstadt began exhibiting his Rocky Mountain works in 1860. The response of Easterners to his panoramic paintings was immediate and enthusiastic. He returned to the West in 1863, venturing all the way to California. As his work grew grander in scale, he became America's most popular painter. Wealthy patrons of the Gilded Age offered vast sums for his mammoth canvases. Bierstadt's 1863 painting *Lander's Peak, Rocky Mountains* brought $25,000, reportedly a record price for an American landscape at that time. He gained such renown for his massive mountain landscapes that one of the Rockies, with a 14,045-foot peak, was named Mount Bierstadt.

Financial success allowed Bierstadt to build a large studio on the Hudson River at Irvington. When this palatial facility burned in 1882, he opened a studio in New York City. Although the popularity of his exaggerated landscapes was declining by this time, Bierstadt began to paint the wild animals of North America, following in the footsteps of James J. Audubon and others.

During the 1850s, Bierstadt excitedly sketched the majestic Rocky Mountains, sketches that soon were transformed into enormous canvases.

A handsome man of polished manners and distinguished bearing, Bierstadt did not marry until middle age. In 1893, his first wife died after seven years of marriage, but the next year, he wed a wealthy widow. Although his work was out of favor with popular tastes when he died in 1902, Bierstadt had painted dramatic landscapes on a scale to match the great Rocky Mountains. Within his lifetime, he witnessed the beginning of the great migration to the West, the Indian Wars, and then the disappearance of the geographic frontier. Perhaps sensing the ramifications of western migration, he painted the beginning and end of the Indian's decline—the landing of Columbus and the last of the buffalo.

Bierstadt, a native of Germany, completed *Among the Sierra Nevada Mountains* in 1868. It is one of Bierstadt's numerous romantic landscapes that captured public appeal.

FREDERIC
REMINGTON

1861—1909

"I knew the wild riders and the vacant land were about to vanish forever—and the more I considered the subject, the bigger the forever loomed," recalled Frederic Remington. "Without knowing exactly how to do it, I began to try to record some facts around me, and the more I looked, the more the panorama unfolded."

Born in 1861 in Canton, New York, Frederic Remington was the son of a prosperous newspaper publisher who had served as a lieutenant colonel of cavalry during the Civil War. Sent to a military school as a child, young Frederic then enrolled in Yale as an art student at age 16. During two years of instruction, Remington received sound techni-cal training, but his work was uninspired, and he acquired a lasting distaste for academic art.

After his father died in 1880, his mother persuaded him to seek more conventional employment. For several months, he tried to satisfy his mother, but he yearned to pursue art. During this time, he met Eva Caten, whose father disliked Remington and halted their budding courtship.

Remington's problems over his sweetheart, his mother, and his profession were forgotten after he treated himself to a trip to Montana. Remington found the West exhilarating and its inhabitants fascinating. Already a fine horseman, Remington learned the arts of handling a six-gun and a lariat.

One evening, a veteran teamster shared his campsite with young Remington and talked to him of the Old West. The old-timer convincingly pointed out that the coming of the railroad would tame the last frontier. At that moment, Remington decided to record this vanishing way of life.

Remington began to sketch western characters and scenes. His sketchbooks bulged with cowboys, horses, cattle, roundups, prospectors, warriors, and Indian camps, all portrayed with accurate detail. In February 1882, a sketch of cowboys, redrawn by another artist, appeared in *Harper's Weekly*, which encouraged him to pursue a future as a magazine illustrator.

Remington, at work on *The Indian Trapper* in 1889. Remington equipped his studio with weapons, clothing, and other frontier artifacts.

He traveled widely, prospecting, cowboying, and riding with military expeditions. There were failed attempts at ranching and saloonkeeping. He sent regular submissions to eastern magazines, but only one was accepted—again by *Harper's Weekly*. When his partners cheated him out of his saloon investment, his young wife, Eva Caten, had to return home to her family.

Remington made a desperate attempt at prospecting in the Southwest but failed. Yet, once again, he was swept away by the magic of the last frontier. The final military campaign against Geronimo was in progress, and Remington was captivated by troopers, scouts, and cavalry horses. He sketched them ceaselessly. Much later, during the Golden Age of Hollywood, the gifted movie director John Ford filmed a cavalry trilogy, and he studied Remington's cavalry drawings for his camera compositions.

Young Remington turned up in New York City late in 1885 with only three dollars in his pocket—but with a rich collection of sketchbooks and portfolios brimming with western drawings. Eva rejoined him in a small Brooklyn boarding house, and he doggedly walked from one publishing house to another, trying to peddle his illustrations. Finally, *Harper's Weekly* used one of his pieces for a cover illustration in January 1886—a bit of luck that proved to be his breakthrough.

Suddenly, Remington's work was in demand, and he eventually became one of the most highly paid illustrators in the world. He illustrated *Theodore Roosevelt's Ranch Life*

and the *Hunting Trail*, and he began writing western short stories and articles, illustrated with his own drawings. In 1895, despite a lack of technical instruction, Remington started producing bronzes, beginning with *The Bronco Buster*. Then, at the height of his success, he eagerly served as a correspondent during the Spanish-American War.

In 1909, at the age of 48, Remington died from complications of appendicitis, but not before publishing illustrations in 140 books and 40 magazines and producing more than 2,700 paintings and drawings. Like Charles Russell, Remington was aware of the fading of the frontier, but his attitude toward that realization was different. Early on, his paintings of heroic military units tended to champion the winning of the West. Toward the end of his life, however, he wanted to be recognized as a fine artist, not as an illustrator, and his later work reveals a more painterly style, with dark shadows and nocturnal scenes.

The cavalry was a favorite subject of Remington. This scene depicts mounts being led to the rear; when troopers dismounted to fight as skirmishers, every fourth man served as a horse holder.

ALFRED JACOB MILLER

1810—1874

In 1837, painter Alfred Jacob Miller experienced the opportunity of a lifetime. Born in Baltimore in 1810, Miller had demonstrated unusual drawing ability as a child. He was given art lessons locally, and in 1833 he journeyed to Paris for a year of study, venturing also to Rome and Florence.

Returning to Baltimore in 1834, Miller tried to paint portraits and landscapes, but he experienced scant success at home. He moved to New Orleans, setting up a studio in a dry-goods store. Again his sales were modest.

In the spring of 1837, Sir William Drummond Stewart entered Miller's little studio, apparently by random choice. A Scottish nobleman and adventurer, Stewart had served as an officer under Wellington at Waterloo and was the master of Murthly Castle in Scotland. In 1833, he had begun to travel to the American West for hunting expeditions.

Stewart genuinely admired and liked mountain men, and they returned his friendship, especially because he freely shared his fine cigars and liquor with them. Stewart reveled in the wild excitement of the annual Rendezvous, and when he planned another expedition for 1837, he was determined to engage a painter to produce an artistic record of his western adventures.

In New Orleans, Stewart chanced upon Miller, and the artist readily accepted the offer to paint in the West. Stewart led Miller

Pawnee Running Buffalo by Miller. A single journey to the West, which included the 1837 fur traders' Rendezvous, provided Miller with material for more than 400 works depicting the early frontier.

and a small party to St. Louis, where they linked up with the American Fur Company trade caravan. There were 20 horse-drawn carts loaded with trade goods and provisions for the 100-man company. Stewart added two mule-drawn wagons laden with hunting and camping equipment, a few luxuries he liked to bring into the wilderness, and Miller's art supplies.

The 1837 Rendezvous was located at Green River, in what is today western Wyoming, a journey of nearly 1,000 miles from St. Louis. The caravan ventured along the Oregon Trail, and Miller became the first American artist to see and to paint such landmarks as Fort Laramie, Chimney Rock, Scott's Bluff, and Independence Rock.

Passing through the Rocky Mountains, the caravan reached the Rendezvous site and

A Sioux camp scene by Miller. Much of Miller's work on the West was produced at the castle of his Scottish benefactor, Sir William Drummond Stewart.

settled in for a month of trading and carousing. In addition to the mountain men, including such celebrated frontiersmen as Kit Carson and Jim Bridger, there were 3,000 Native Americans who gathered for the colorful celebration and bargaining. Miller sketched out scenes depicting horse racing, wrestling, trading between white men and Native Americans, a Native American parade, trappers at work, and various other activities from the colorful pageantry of the Rendezvous. Afterward, Stewart led his little party into the magnificent Wind River country, his favorite region of the West, before returning to the Green River and subsequently St. Louis.

Miller went back to his New Orleans studio to begin transforming his sketches into finished paintings. His first exhibition was in Baltimore in 1838, and in 1840, Stewart brought him to Scotland, where he lived at Murthly Castle for more than a year while painting large landscapes for the palace walls. During his stay in Scotland, Miller finished over 400 works based on his sketches.

Miller lived until 1874 but never returned to the West. Critics of his work complain about its stilted quality, and of its less-than-accurate depictions of Native Americans as children of nature, frolicking in the wilderness. Although Miller's work is not completely satisfying to critics, he had the unique opportunity of documenting a Rendezvous and mountain men in their native element, only a short time before this colorful chapter of frontier history ended.

THOMAS MORAN

1837–1926

In about 1840, Edward Moran, the eldest of 16 children of a working-class English family, immigrated to the United States via steerage passage and with his belongings tied up in a bandanna. Settling in Philadelphia, he worked to establish himself as an artist, and he enjoyed enough sales to bring his family to America within the next few years. The last contingent arrived in 1844 and included Edward's seven-year-old brother, Thomas.

Edward Moran founded one of the most important family dynasties in the history of American art. No fewer than 16 men and women of the Moran clan became noted artists. Thomas became a distinguished western artist, while his wife, Mary, and their son, Paul Nimmo Moran, were also accomplished artists.

Moran became known as "Yellowstone" Moran and, before he died at age 90 in 1926, the "Dean of American Painters."

Thomas Moran trained in Philadelphia and later studied in England, France, and Italy. By 1871, this 34-year-old father of three was living in Newark, New Jersey, and earning most of his livelihood as an illustrator for *Scribner's Monthly*. *Scribner's* editor Richard W. Gilder assigned Moran to improve some crude first-hand pencil drawings to illustrate an article entitled "The Wonders of Yellowstone." As he worked, Moran became fascinated by the spouting geysers. Consumed with an urge to see and record Yellowstone, Moran borrowed the money to accompany geologist Ferdinand Vandiveer Hayden into the relatively unexplored regions that later became Yellowstone National Park. On that journey, he met photographer William Henry Jackson, and the two became lifelong friends.

Slight of physique, Moran was not a horseman, and he detested the fried foods that were the staple fare around campfires. But the wiry artist took to western travel with ready aptitude and endurance. Moran proved fearless in traversing mountain trails. He learned to handle a horse, and he supplemented his diet by adroitly fishing for trout.

Moran was awestruck by the wonders of Yellowstone, which he sketched at a furious pace for 38 days. When he returned to Newark, he worked rapidly on an ambitious canvas measuring 7×12 feet. A gifted colorist, Moran captured the magnificent panorama of *The Grand Canyon of the Yellowstone*. "Watching the canvas grow," remarked Gilder, "was like keeping one's eyes open during the successive stages of world creation."

Moran produced a series of Yellowstone illustrations for *Scribner's*, as well as a large number of watercolors. His friends called him "Yellowstone" Moran. Hayden lobbied Congress for legislation to create Yellowstone National Park, and his use of Moran's art was instrumental in passage of the bill. *The Grand Canyon of the Yellowstone* was displayed in several cities, then was acquired by

Moran's *Miracle of Nature.* Moran eagerly traveled into rugged country to obtain material for his art, and his daughter recalled, "He was always starting for or coming from strange, beautiful places."

Congress for $10,000 and hung in the U.S. Capitol. Moran's great painting was the first landscape ever purchased by Congress.

In 1873, Moran accompanied Major John Wesley Powell on an expedition through the Grand Canyon of the Colorado. Upon his return, he created another 7×12-foot panorama, *The Chasm of the Colorado*, which Congress bought for $10,000.

"He was always starting for or coming from strange, beautiful places," reminisced his daughter Ruth. Moran became an inveterate traveler, venturing often into the West, but he also journeyed from Maine to Florida, with an occasional trip to Europe. The public was particularly drawn to his mountain landscapes, and one of the Tetons was officially named Mount Moran. Moran held a different view of landscape painting than other artists. Neither a strict realist nor an academy-style painter, Moran approved of investing subjective impressions into one's work.

Late in life, he moved closer to his western subject matter, setting up a studio in Santa Barbara, California. At 87, he traveled for the last time into Yellowstone, then produced another large and successful canvas. He went on a sketching trip to Arizona's Grand Canyon at the age of 88. When he died at age 90, he was regarded as the "Dean of American Painters."

ALFRED E. MATHEWS

1831–1874

Like many early westerners, illustrator Alfred E. Mathews was consumed with wanderlust. For years he traversed the Rocky Mountains, taken with "the numerous grand and awe-inspiring views that are scattered so profusely throughout the entire length of this vast belt of mountains...." Mathews avidly sketched these scenic wonders, but many other artists proved more gifted at producing western landscapes. Mathews, however, was a lithographer who recorded in great detail many pioneer communities, thereby providing an important pictorial history of post-Civil War mining towns.

Mathews was born in England in 1831. When he was two years old, his father brought the family to Ohio. His father was a book publisher, and the family was artistically and musically inclined. During his teens, Alfred was trained as a typesetter, but entrepreneurial interests and a nomadic impulse put him on the roads of New England as a traveling bookseller. Simultaneously, he painted and sold landscape drawings: "I fill up odd times with such work and find it profitable."

When the Civil War began, he enlisted in the Union Army and engaged in numerous campaigns. His skill as a draftsman was utilized in drawing topographical maps of battlefields. Mathews also produced numerous lithographic views of battle scenes, prompting General Ulysses S. Grant to pronounce them "among the most accurate and true to life I have ever seen."

After the war, Mathews resumed his travels, gravitating to the West. In 1865, he produced detailed lithographs of Nebraska City, Nebraska, then proceeded on to Denver. He solicited subscribers for street scenes and a bird's-eye view of Denver, then provided the same service for nearby mining towns such as Blackhawk and Central City. Details of these frontier communities were faithfully recorded, along with such human interest items as dog fights, everyday means of transportation, and mining equipment. Mathews compiled *Pencil Sketches of Colorado* and peddled copies for $30 apiece.

He worked in Colorado through 1866, returned east for the winter of 1866–67, then returned to Colorado for more work. Mathews proceeded into Montana, sketching at Virginia City, Helena, and other towns, as well as at numerous scenic attractions. He spent the winter of 1867–68 in New York City, turning *Pencil Sketches of Montana* into a set of lithographs. In 1868, ever the entrepreneur, Mathews exhibited his work in Colorado and Montana. "Receipts were from $58 to $117 per night," he recalled happily, "and sometimes we had to close the doors and refuse to admit more."

Mathews's sketching trips covered "about 6,000 miles" during a three-year period. He

Mathews produced a rich pictorial record of several important mining towns in the Rockies.

recalled, "These expeditions were performed, excepting during one summer, entirely alone, and principally with ponies; but on two or three occasions on snow-shoes and in a small boat. One pony was used for riding—the other carried a small, light tent, bedding and provisions." Equipped in this way, the artist was prepared to camp wherever and whenever so inclined—the tent being a security against wild animals at night.

Mathews produced another lithographic volume, *Gems of Rocky Mountain Scenery*, in 1869. For the next few years, he promoted the Colorado settlement of Canon City, although he sketched in southern California during the winter of 1872–73. He died in 1874 at the age of 43, apparently from appendicitis, but he left a rich pictorial legacy of Rocky Mountain mining towns.

Above: During a three-year period, Mathews traveled "about 6,000 miles" through the West, usually riding one horse and leading another that carried his tent, bedding, and supplies. **Below:** Mathews arrived in Denver in 1865, faithfully depicting street scenes for his *Pencil Sketches of Colorado*.

VOICES OF THE WEST

"There is but one way to gamble successfully and that is to get *Tools to work with and have the best of every Game you get into.*"
E. N. Grandine, manufacturer of advantage tools for gamblers

Bat Masterson

"Gambling was not only the principal and best-paying industry of the town at the time, but it was also reckoned among its most respectable."
Bat Masterson

"I always like to set a lot of silver on the table in front of me all the time. That's the main reason my table always got the biggest play. It was like flies after molasses syrup."
John Dunn, frontier gambler

"I am conducting a fair, legitimate business. My mission is to trim suckers."
Charles "Doc" Baggs, frontier gambler

"On the plains
The wind draws the water
And cows chop the firewood."
Great Plains homily about windmills and cow chips

"No hay to pitch,
No tits to pull.
Just punch a hole
In the son of a bitch!"
Cowboy tune honoring Borden's canned milk

"They say that heaven is a free range land,
Goodbye, goodbye, O fare you well;
But it's barbed wire for the devil's hat band;
And barbed wire blankets down in hell."
Cowboy tune about barbwire

"Sometimes the water would drip on the stove while I was cooking, and I would have to keep tight lids on the skillets to prevent mud from falling into the food. With my dress pinned up, and rubbers on my feet, I waded around until the clouds rolled by. Life is too short to be spent under a sod roof."
Pioneer, commenting on her sod house

"Be not afraid of any man, No matter what his size;
When in danger call on me,
And I will equalize!"
About the Colt .45 Equalizer

"You can shoot a Henry all week and not reload until Sunday."
About the Henry long-barreled repeating rifle

"I've never seen anyone grow humpbacked carrying away the money they won from me."
Poker Alice Ivers, frontier gambler

Poker Alice Ivers

"There are truly many men who can do anything with a rope except throw it straight up and climb it."
Ramon Adams, cowboy expert

"Why wasn't some Kipling saving the sagebrush for American literature. . . ? What was fiction doing, fiction the only thing that has always outlived fact?"
Owen Wister

"Their jagged summits, covered with snow and mingling with the clouds, present a scene which every lover of landscape would gaze upon with unqualified delight."
Artist Albert Bierstadt, when he first viewed the Rocky Mountains

"I have wandered over a good bit of the Territories and have seen much of the varied scenery of the Far West, but that of the Yellowstone retains its hold upon my imagination with a vividness as of yesterday."
Thomas Moran

"As the sun was going down, we saw the first specimen of an animal known familiarly over two thousand miles of mountain and desert—from Kansas clear to the Pacific Ocean—as the 'jackass rabbit.' He is well named . . . [with] the most preposterous ears that ever were mounted on any creature but a jackass."
Mark Twain

"This is the West. When the legend becomes fact, print the legend!"
From the screenplay of John Ford's The Man Who Shot Liberty Valance

"Genius is sustained attention."
Zane Grey

"If it had not been for my years in North Dakota, I never would have become President of the United States."
Theodore Roosevelt

"Go West, young man, and grow up with the country!"
Horace Greely, in an editorial in the New York Tribune

"These steers are walking fifty-dollar bills."
Oklahoma rancher Clem Rogers, father of Will Rogers

"When you can see the cow chips floating, then we've had a rain."
King Ranch livestock manager

"Hasten forward quickly there!"
Harvard-educated rancher Theodore Roosevelt, shouting a command that convulsed his cowboys with laughter

"Sometimes I say that any cowman of open range days who claimed never to have put his brand on somebody else's animal was either a liar or a poor roper."
Texas rancher Ike Pryor

"He was so tall, he had to shorten his stirrups to keep his feet from draggin'."
Cowboy slang

Almost every chuck wagon meal on a trail drive featured "Pecos strawberries" (beans) and "overland trout" (bacon).

"Sometimes we have the seasons in their regular order, and then again we have winter all the summer and summer all winter [in Nevada]. It is mighty regular about not raining, though. . . . But as a general thing . . . the climate is good, what there is of it."
Mark Twain

"A warrior I have been; now it is all over. A hard time I have."
Sitting Bull

"Shooting at a man who is returning the compliment means going into action with the greatest speed of which a man's muscles are capable, but mentally unflustered by an urge to hurry. . . ."
Wyatt Earp

"If we ever owned the land, we own it still, for we never sold it."
Chief Joseph

"I didn't want to send a man to hell on an empty stomach."
Clay Allison, after killing a man whom he had taken to dinner

"They tell you I murdered Custer. It is a lie! I am not a War Chief. I was not in the battle that day. His eyes were blinded, so he could not see. He was a fool and rode to his death. He made the fight, not I."
Sitting Bull

"Hanging is my favorite way of dying."
Bill Longley, killer of 32 people